Mob Adjacent
A Family Memoir

Jeffrey Gentile and Michael Gentile, Jr.

ISBN-13: 978-1979639316
ISBN-10: 1979639310

DEDICATION

To Mike and Mary Ann Gentile.
Their hard work made everything possible.

CONTENTS

PART ONE: JEFFREY

.

PROLOGUE

Normal is what happens every day. When you're a kid, the lack of perspective fosters automatic acceptance: This is where I live; this is where I sleep; these are the people I know. The realization that something exists beneath the surface comes slowly. Born in 1955 and 1956, my older brother Michael and I went about the business of being Eisenhower-era kids. If we had thought about it (which we did not), or if someone had asked (which they did not), we would have said our lives were perfectly ordinary. Michael liked sports; I liked television. We had a home in the suburbs of Chicago, a stay-at-home mom, and attended private school. All perfectly ordinary, just like I saw on television. Eventually the light bulbs lit, and we realized our family wasn't like other families. Before long, the entire marquee blazed, and we watched with astonishment as criminals, convicts, and crime lords filtered in and out of our home as casually as the milkman and the mailman. I will always remember the first time I glimpsed what lay hidden behind the façade of our lives.

In Italian households like ours there is a social ritual known as "Coffee And." When people visit, any decent hostess serves coffee and cake, or coffee and cookies, or coffee and cannoli, but always coffee and something. Coffee And. My father's family were among our most frequent visitors. His sisters, "the Aunts," (Jeanette, Rachel, and Marie), along with Uncle Joe

(Marie's husband) and Uncle Larry (Rachel's) gathered to enjoy a casual mid-week Coffee And around the turquoise Formica table in our upstairs kitchen. (Every Italian family with a basement had a second kitchen for heavy-duty cooking, sometimes with fatal results. See Giancana, Sam).

On this particular evening, Aunt Jeanette spoke gravely about someone going away "to college." She said this person received a considerable "scholarship."

Dad asked, "How long will he be in school?"

"Oh, a long time," Aunt Jeanette said heavily.

A moment of silence hung heavily over the table.

It didn't add up, and I said, "You make it sound like he's going to jail."

My family looked at each other uncomfortably.

Dad barked, "Go watch television."

I scurried off, but after that I started listening more closely. I was ten-years old.

For Michael, his moment came one afternoon when he was about eleven. Dad's mob connected and mob adjacent pals were regulars at our house in Bellwood. There would be lots of eating, drinking, smoking, and swearing. To us, they were part of the extended family, each an honorary uncle. It always meant fun whenever they visited. We could be certain to hear words we weren't allowed to use and jokes with punch lines we didn't always understand. But we loved it. They spoke in code, too. They talked about "that guy over there" doing "that thing" and whispered about "his pal in that guy's office."

But the thing that usually made their visits fun was coat duty. Michael and I jockeyed over who got to take their overcoats into the bedroom. Dad's friends tipped us like hat-check girls in the old movies, so we fought for the job. Always stronger and more aggressive, Michael muscled past me with outstretched arms and was promptly buried under a mountain of wool, cashmere, and fur collars. Half blinded by the tower of outerwear, he staggered toward our parents' bedroom. Suddenly, a pistol fell out and landed on the linoleum floor. It wasn't that we lived in a world that typically rained weaponry, but since no one seemed concerned, Michael took his cue from the grown-ups. He wasn't alarmed to see a handgun skate past his feet, just confused. One gun. Many coats. Whose gun, which coat? Crap! The weapon's owner, Uncle Tony, promptly called out for Michael to pick up the gun – by the barrel – and put it back in his coat.

At the same time, Mom was preparing Coffee And. She asked over her shoulder for the cake knife, and my two-year old sister Lisa reached for it. It was sweet the way she wanted to help Mommy. Just then, Mommy looked over her shoulder, horrified to find her baby armed with a flat, eight-inch blade and shouted, "Stop her!"

Dad snatched the knife mid-air like a pro. Crisis averted.

Michael continued on his mission. On the way to the bedroom, it occurred to him that if a two-year old handles a knife, everybody goes on red alert. But if an eleven-year old holds a handgun, no one is concerned. Good to know. Then he wondered why Uncle Tony carried a gun. Curious, he frisked the mound of coats and found another gun in another pocket. Who were these people?

Once Michael and I started paying attention, the veneer that wrapped around our family fiction cracked, and there was no putting it back together. One day you're a kid learning to read; the next you're reading the newspaper, and there's an article about the man who came to dinner last week. Pictures, too. Yup, that's him. The newspaper said he'd been indicted for running a suburban gambling ring and looking at five years in prison. Last Sunday that same man brought a box of Italian pastries – sfogliatella and pasticiotto – from Albano's Bakery in Elmwood Park. Mom loves a good pasticiotto.

Though we didn't realize it at the time, Michael and I grew up at the intersection of Hoodlum and Gangster, not <u>in</u> the world of organized crime, but <u>near</u> it – mob adjacent. Born in Chicago's Little Italy, we were steeped from infancy in an environment where crime and criminals existed invisibly alongside our everyday lives. For us, *The Wonder Years* collided with *The Sopranos*. We grew up surrounded by mobsters, gangsters, hoodlums, bone-breakers, safe crackers, and second-story guys. We heard stories about vendettas and vengeance and idolized the awe-inspiring power of their protection. But we were always one step removed from the action. By deliberate design.

At Dad's wake in 1995, Aunt Jeanette said, "Your father was never a gangster. He just knew people."

It was true. Dad's family had lived near the intersection of Aberdeen Street and Grand Avenue for more than fifty years. That "old neighborhood," known locally as the Patch, became the fertile field and proving ground for the next generation of post-Capone criminals. The boys from the Patch – guys like Sam Giancana, Joseph Lombardo, John DiFronzo, and Jackie, Frank, and Jimmy Cerone – would grow up and hold rap sheets containing charges for murder, assault, robbery, extortion, bookmaking, loan-sharking, and so forth. But to Dad, those men weren't criminals; they were the kids he grew up with, the friends he kept until the last days of his life. To Michael and me, they were the guys who stopped by for Coffee And, came to Sunday dinner, and brought fat envelopes to weddings, graduations, and funerals.

We make no attempt to paint over the damage organized crime caused to people and communities – the violence, intimidation, and terror. It's not because we consciously choose to ignore it, but because the darker aspects of organized crime never came near our tidy little Camelot world. Sure, men brought guns into our house – but no one used them, at least not in our house. Here's the thing: After those men finished doing whatever they did, or were alleged to have done, they went home to families and friends and lived ordinary lives. Legendary crime boss Sam Giancana didn't die in a fiery gun battle with the Feds. No, he was assassinated at close range by a trusted friend while he fried up a late-night snack in his basement kitchen.

I once asked Dad if he ever met Sam Giancana. He laughed and said, "YOU met Sam Giancana!"

Many of the people in these stories are gone, and their footprints grow fainter with each generation. But their presence dominated our lives for decades, and we wanted to capture the time, place, and people whose actions changed us – and the world, in some cases.

When Michael and I started this project, it seemed respectful to seek out some of the surviving mob guys, the Old Lions. Since we planned to tell tales and name names, we wanted permission – or at least assurance – that no one objected. Michael has cordial relations with guys from Dad's day, so he made an appointment with one of the Old Lions. (We're not divulging his name because he's entitled to his privacy, and it's none of your fucking business.) Michael brought a box of persimmons because the Old Lion likes persimmons. (and what kind of animal shows up empty-handed when he goes to visit somebody?) He explained our intent, and the Old Lion said, "Do whatever you want. If anybody's got a problem, tell them I said to go fuck themselves." Then he mentioned the name of another criminal associate and suggested we talk to him, too. That's how I started exchanging letters and emails with an international jewel thief, presently enjoying the hospitality of a federal correctional institution.

Through a combination of geography and happenstance, for the last half of the Twentieth Century my family has had front row seats to as much real-life mob drama as you'll find in a Martin Scorsese/Francis Ford Coppola movie marathon. For us, growing up mob adjacent yielded dividends and taught lessons. But perhaps most importantly, being mob adjacent meant we got the best seats in the house. It also meant we got to go home after the show.

1 CRASH ADJACENT

The beginning of a story is never really the beginning. What happened here is because of what happened there. It's the Butterfly Effect: If Giovani Gentile had flapped his wings farther north and immigrated from Sicily to Ontario instead of Chicago, his family's history would have been different. But this story started before Giovani flipped a coin and chose Chicago over Ontario because Chicago was much farther south, and he thought it would be warmer.

Following the Potato Famine in Ireland, millions of starving Irish immigrants began arriving in Chicago around 1850. They were wholly unwelcome. Landlords posted signs expressing the prevailing sentiment: "No dogs or Irish." The Irish then endured decades as Chicago's designated underclass before rising to social dominance. By the end of the 19th century, the new Irish ruling class proved as unwelcoming and hostile toward the new wave of Italian immigrants as the European Protestants had been to them fifty years earlier.

In 1896, Giovani Gentile and his wife, Vincenza, emigrated from Palermo, Sicily, with their three children – six-year old Mamie, two-year old Matteo (called Mickey on his immigration papers), and baby Charlie, arriving first in Ontario, Canada. Giovani and his family were part of the great wave of Italian immigrants that began flocking to America twenty years earlier. Most found tenements and turmoil instead of gold and opportunity. Photos of Giovani show a dour, bald, hollow-cheeked, toothless man, with broad-shoulders and a barrel-chest. Vincenza had warm eyes, apple cheeks, and a gentle smile. Long salt-and-pepper braids wrapped around the top of her head like a crown. Together, they would make a new life in the new world, far from Sicily's feudal poverty and the rumbling of fascism and revolution.

Giovani's family eventually settled in Chicago's Little Italy. He was lucky – he came to America with some money. Giovani bought a horse and wagon and started peddling fruits and vegetables on the neighborhood streets. Eventually he bought a house, and the Gentile family prospered in a hostile environment, surrounded by the detestable Irish who resented their presence and denigrated their culture. Over the next decade or so, Giovani and Vincenza's family expanded to include Mary (born in 1897), Antonina (born in 1899), Katherine (born in 1902) and Rose (born in 1908). Vincenza had her last baby at the astounding age of forty-two. At the time, girls married around age sixteen; by thirty they were typically finished bearing children. For Vincenza to have her seventh baby at age forty-two seemed almost indecent.

Mickey married Angeline Filetti in 1909. He was sixteen; she was fifteen. She was shapeless and sour; he was small and stern. Like many in that era, the marriage was arranged by their families, with little input from the marital participants. Angeline was American-born, which made her a highly desirable bride. Off-the-boat Italians looked with envy at their American-born counterparts. American-born meant better-born. Despite the advantage of her birth, the Filetti family had trouble finding a husband for Angeline. She proved exceptionally headstrong, shockingly opinionated, and more than a little bigoted. To close the deal, the Filetti family provided a dowry sufficient to purchase a two-story, white clapboard house on Aberdeen Street. Angeline's older sister, Simonetta, lived down the block in her dowry house.

The relationship between Mickey and Angeline proved volatile from the start. It probably wasn't helped by Angeline's prejudice against foreign-born Italians (she called them "greaseballs"). Neither appeared to have much inclination toward marriage, which may explain why it took five years for their first child to appear. After John was born in 1915, Mickey and Angeline added to their family with Jeanette (in 1917), Rachel (in 1922), and Marie (in 1925).

Mickey followed Giovani into the produce business and bought a horse and wagon. The horse, a brown mare named Biscotti, lived in a barn behind the house. Decades later, Jeanette described her heartbreak at coming home to find Biscotti gone, replaced by a used truck that smelled worse than the horse. Biscotti had been the only truly beautiful thing she'd ever seen – the way she tossed her mane, stamped her feet, and let her lips linger on Jeanette's palm even after the treat was gone, as if kissing her hand. So what if Biscotti couldn't carry as much as a truck? Jeanette said she cried for days. But Mickey didn't care about his daughter's tears. The truck was their future.

According to his children, Mickey had a fearsome temper. On more than one occasion he swept the dinner table with his arm and sent plates flying. In the classical European tradition, he felt entitled to mistresses, known euphemistically within the family as his *braciolas*.

[For non-Italians and non-cooks, *braciola (brah-zhōl)* is a side dish made of rolled, stuffed meat, trussed with string, and soaked in wine. The image practically paints itself.]

In Mickey's culture, as long as he kept a roof over his family, food on the table, and coal in the stove, he could do as he pleased the rest of the time. And no one had the right to question him about it or have an opinion about it.

People had more important things to worry about than broken dishes and extramarital affairs by 1929. A short-sighted decision to legislate morality led to the double whammy of the Eighteenth Amendment and the Volstead Act. By certifying these genius pieces of legislation into law on January 29, 1919, Prohibition – and organized crime – came to America, thanks to Andrew Volstead and all those blue-nosed moralists. The bootlegger became a common fixture in American life. And thanks to the truly organized efforts of organized crime, they delivered alcohol as easily as milk.

Over the next decade, Prohibition brought the kind of opportunities that led people to believe the hooey about the streets in America being paved with gold. Prohibition made people rich beyond the dreams of Midas practically overnight. As the government took pointless steps to criminalize prostitution, alcohol, and gambling, members of organized crime grew wealthy and powerful by providing prostitution, alcohol, and gambling to those who wanted prostitution, alcohol and gambling. Cause and effect. Organized crime became the natural by-product of organized government. And in a city ruled by a corrupt political machine, only a criminal organization had the power to fight City Hall. And it did.

This was the world our father, Michael John Gentile, was born into on Tuesday, October 29, 1929. The stock market crashed that day, too, ushering in the Great Depression. But at 460 North Aberdeen Street on the West Side of Chicago, people worried about more immediate concerns. Angeline struggled with the birth of a fifth child at what was considered late in life (she was thirty-six). The one-two punch of Prohibition and the Depression meant Mike was born into a boom town for organized crime, thanks to the efforts of the most determined imbeciles in the history of American government.

Chicago's criminals operated with impunity because so many cops, judges, and prosecutors were on their payroll. The modern equivalent exists in the hallowed halls of Congress, where corporate "people" buy Representatives and Senators by the dozen to use as hand puppets. That's what the Outfit did with members of law enforcement. By the end of the 1920s, crime kingpins Al Capone and Johnny Torrio were earning $100,000 per week (the equivalent of $1,277,418 per week in 2017), and their beer and liquor trucks rumbled unmolested down city streets. They got crime organized and established kick-back levels for protection from City Hall. Crap games – sixty percent; horse races and pool – fifty percent; roulette – forty percent. Chicago knew how to make crime work.

Over the months that followed the worst financial collapse in the history of the world, President Herbert Hoover believed offering help to struggling Americans would make people dependent on government hand-outs and destroy decent Christian values like individuality and self-reliance. Marie Antoinette "let them eat cake." President Hoover let them eat nothing. Homeless encampments became known as Hoovervilles while the President and his wife dined formally at the White House each night, serenaded by a full military band. Fortunately, the global Depression didn't have much influence on Mickey Gentile's finances. Rich or poor, people needed to eat. Mickey got another truck for sixteen-year old John and increased the family's income with a second route. The Gentiles lived comfortably while bankers jumped out of windows.

Baby Mike became known as Junior, even though he wasn't named after his father. The reason was perfectly simple. While John resembled Angeline, Mike was his father's doppelganger in appearance, personality, and temperament. Little Mike was a junior-sized version of Mickey. So, like so many childhood nicknames, Junior stuck. But outside the family and neighborhood, he was Mike. As he grew into boyhood in the Patch during the 1930s, Mike was the family prince. The women in his family fussed and fawned over Junior, his every whim instantly indulged. For him, life was a fairy tale.

Life in Chicago's ethnic neighborhoods was hard, regardless of national origin. Back in Italy, secret societies began around the twelfth century to give common people a voice against corrupt government. The *Camorra* protected southern Italy; '*Ndraghetta* in the north; and the *Mafia* in Sicily. In the New World, Black Hand extortionists ruled the city and spread terror and mayhem throughout the immigrant community. Their modus operandi was simple: a black-bordered note demanded cash payment on threat of unnamed "consequences." A few high-profile consequences like bombing a business or murdering a family member generally kept people fearful, quiet, and compliant. Getting rid of the freelancers became a priority as Chicago began coalescing around a boss-dominated structure in the 1920s and early 1930s under the city's first Boss of Bosses, James "Big Jim" Colosimo.

For the Italian immigrants, the hated Sicilian Black Hand offered a measure of safety and protection the lawful authorities were disinclined to provide, but their safety and protection brought inevitable shakedowns. Vincent Benevento, known locally as Don Vincenzo, was the Black Hand boss in Little Italy. He owned an imported food shop on Grand Avenue, and the local media called him the Cheese King of Chicago. By coincidence, his family lived across the street from the Gentiles.

Every Friday the Don made his rounds and collected an illegal street tax from each business. The police didn't care; neither did the newspapers. Someone's shaking down the greaseballs. Big deal. Mickey paid like everybody else. As a Sicilian, however, protocol should have exempted him from the street tax. But the Don exempted no one. This practice ignited a simmering resentment that slowly came to a boil. While the tax created a financial burden for the poor Italians, it provided insurance against the roving bands of "Irish pricks" that caused trouble. Even more trouble could be guaranteed by not paying the Don his weekly tithe.

Mickey maintained a nodding acquaintance with Don Vincenzo beyond the weekly collection. Their wives went to church at Santa Maria Addolorata together; their boys played together. Mickey was also a member of the Unione Siciliana, where the Don served as local president. Ostensibly a social club, the Unione Siciliana's ties to organized crime and its deep political influence stretched back to the early 1920s. Local president was a highly coveted role, and several past presidents had been assassinated.

"Big Jim" Colosimo, had been content running his restaurant, gambling dens, and brothels, while doting on the much-younger mistress who became his second wife. A cultured, opera-loving man, Big Jim created the classic gangster style with his preference for flashy white suits, diamond rings, and other jewelry. At his peak, Colosimo had nearly 200 brothels in the seedy area of Chicago known as the Levee. When Black Hand extortionists tried to put the muscle on him, Colosimo brought his nephew from New York to solve the problem. Johnny Torrio took care of the Black Handers for his uncle by bringing his trusted pal Al Capone from New York. Chicago would never be the same.

Capone turned the Black Hand's tactics on them and used murder, intimidation, and assorted acts of violence to rid the city of its freelancers. Torrio and Capone started *organizing* crime. But when Big Jim expressed indifference to bootlegging, Torrio decided it was time for his uncle and mentor to retire. In 1920, Colosimo was gunned down in his beloved Colosimo's Café at 2126 South Wabash. The murder was never solved, and his vast fortune disappeared. It's long been assumed Al Capone was the shooter. Under Johnny Torrio, Chicago moved toward a centralized, top-down corporate structure. The organization Torrio eventually created was not the Mafia. The Mafia comes from Sicily and limits its membership to Sicilians. It became known as the Outfit in Chicago. Unlike the Mafia, the Outfit was open to all Italians and even non-Italians. Their alliance with the New York families was the Commission. Together, New York and Chicago divided North America.

Between the effects of the Depression and Prohibition, Chicago looked to its gangsters for relief from the gray every day. Guys like Al Capone and Frank Nitti provided jobs when no one else did. Throughout the 1930s, Americans eagerly followed the exploits of hometown Chicago hoodlums like a sports team, guys like Jackie "Machine Gun" McGurn, George "Bugs" Moran, Lester "Baby Face" Nelson, and the infamous John Dillinger. Across the nation, newsreels fed America a steady diet of Charles "Lucky" Luciano, Ma Barker's Boys, and Bonnie and Clyde. When government fails, Robin Hood becomes a hero. "Slick" Willie Sutton robbed banks because that's where the money was, and people loved him for it. Hollywood picked up where gangsters left off, and gave desperate audiences Judy and Mickey, Fred and Ginger, and little Shirley Temple to distract a nervous nation. At the same time, Hollywood gangster movies with George Raft, Edward G. Robinson, Humphrey Bogart, and James Cagney created a hoodlum archetype that endures to this day. "I made it, Ma. Top of the world!"

Speaking of Hollywood, Post-Prohibition, the Outfit looked toward labor unions as the next golden goose. Hollywood labor unions presented a particularly rich prize. Not to dip too deeply into history, a former Chicago pimp and whore-beater-turned-labor-leader named Willie Bioff briefly ran a $2.5 million extortion operation against the Hollywood film studios on the

Outfit's behalf. Bioff threatened strikes and other acts of malice unless the studios paid. They paid. A grateful United States government placed Willie Bioff in a witness protection program after he squealed. God forgives; the Outfit does not. On November 4, 1955, Bioff got behind the wheel of his truck and pressed his foot on the starter. That's all it took to activate the dynamite charge. Parts of Willie and his truck scattered across the front yard of the Phoenix home where he lived for the better part of a decade. Wags renamed his apartment building "The Bioff Arms (and Legs)." He wouldn't be the last rat to meet a messy end in Arizona.

Things got crazy after Prohibition ended in 1933. Everything changed. But there's an old mob saying: When God closes a vault, He opens a bank bag. The infrastructure of American organized crime was firmly in place and shifted operations away from bootlegging into new markets. When Al Capone went to prison in 1932 for failing to report the profits earned by his crimes to the Internal Revenue Service, Frank Nitti took over. The first thing Nitti did was to re-introduce the street tax, which gave power back to people like Vincent Benevento. Nitti's reign as Number One didn't last. Facing indictment over the Bioff scandal, Nitti chose suicide in 1943.

After Nitti's death, Paul "the Waiter" Ricca should have assumed leadership. But Ricca picked up ten- years in the fall-out of the Bioff scandal and cooled his heels in prison until Outfit legal mastermind Murray Humphreys figured out how to spring him. The torch passed instead to Anthony Accardo, known to friends and associates as "Joe," a short version of his nickname "Joe Batters," which referred to his skill using a baseball bat for things other than America's favorite pastime.

Joe Accardo began his administration by reining in the independent vice peddlers, taking over the local wire services, and managing a vast army of bookmakers. Under his leadership starting around 1944, the Outfit operated virtually undisturbed by the authorities for more than a decade. By the late 1950s, Accardo was the most powerful mob boss in the country. Eventually, on Paul Ricca's advice, Accardo moved to a less visible consiglieri role and let Sam Giancana stand in the spotlight. For the next nine years, Giancana led with a flash not seen since the white suit days of Colosimo and Capone.

Every once and a while, the local government made noise about organized crime. A few people got arrested, and the newspapers convinced a willingly gullible public that all was well. The truth was more complicated. America has loved its gangsters since Bonnie and Clyde helped make the Depression less depressing. Chicago in particular loved its hometown hoods. They were as much a part of the city as the Cubs, the Bears, and Italian beef sandwiches.

Chicago's long-ruling Mayor Richard J. Daley ran the city from 1955 through his sudden death in 1976. Daley purportedly didn't care about organized crime as long as His City maintained its national reputation as "The city that works." As a result, the city worked just fine for the Outfit. You couldn't tell the good guys from the bad guys. Chicago Sheriff and future Illinois Governor Richard B. Ogilvie unwittingly hired a Made member of the Outfit named Richard Cain as one of his most trusted subordinates. When Ogilvie ran for Sheriff in 1962, he had at least thirty-six employees with Outfit records. It nearly ruined him. As a member of the Chicago Police Department, Cain was responsible for making graft payments to mob-friendly members of the police force, among his other criminal activities. Later, Cain worked for the FBI. So did Jack Ruby and Lee Harvey Oswald. Sam Giancana and Richard Cain both briefly worked for the CIA, too. Who were the criminals, and who were the lawmen?

FBI Director J. Edgar Hoover insisted for decades that mob crimes were one-off events and not the work of a coordinated criminal network. Why? It's been said that Hoover refused to acknowledge the existence of organized crime because of photos certain mob members possessed showing the FBI Director in women's apparel. Truth or scurrilous gossip? No one knows. The fact remains that the Outfit prospered nationally for decades and made billions through government indifference, corruption, and incompetence.

If you lived in Little Italy in the 1930s and 1940s, you or someone in your family knew someone in the Accardo, Giancana, Aiuppa, Caifano, Cerone, DiFronzo, Ferriola, Lombardo or other mob-connected families. In a small, closed society like Little Italy, people recognized them as businessmen, customers, neighbors, and parishioners. Mike went to grammar school and high school with future mob bosses John DiFronzo and Joe Lombardo. Lombardo is presently serving a cruel and unusual life sentence in solitary confinement, courtesy of the "good guys" in law enforcement.

Mike kept his friends from the old neighborhood, and the boys grew into men who could fix a trial, rig an election, and accept contract hits on Fidel Castro or the President of the United States. Their criminal enterprise eventually grew powerful enough to change the course of world events. What happened was this: A bunch a street kids got tired of being victimized and rebelled against the entrenched ruling class and the vicious Black Hand. Shakespeare wrote plays with lesser themes.

Ever since Johnny Torrio, there's been one guy at the top of the Outfit.

The Sicilians dominated New York, where five constantly feuding families ran an inefficient criminal enterprise. In Chicago, it took one guy. And it was always one guy. I'm not criticizing New York; I'm just saying Chicago put the "organized" in organized crime. Colosimo defined the modern crime family; Torrio refined it; Capone made it into a brand as recognizable as Coca-Cola; and since then the Outfit's power has flowed through Joe Accardo, Sam Giancana, Joe Aiuppa, Joe Ferriola, John DiFronzo, and Joe Lombardo. But before they were crime bosses, capos, enforcers, foot soldiers, and whatnot on the Outfit's organization chart, they were boys on the streets of Little Italy. And those boys made friendships that lasted a lifetime, even if those lifetimes were sometimes shorter than expected. Eventually, the Outfit radiated power that rivalled the United States government.

Like most criminal enterprises, the Outfit had its roots in poverty. Between 1850 and 1860, thousands of poor immigrants arrived in Chicago and built a rickety shantytown known locally as Mrs. Conley's Patch. History books refer to the "decrepitude" of the homes and the "depravity and dark crimes" of its residents. Legend said the neighborhood – a tinderbox of wooden structures – was home to Mrs. Katherine (or Catherine, depending on the source) O'Leary and her famous cow (named Daisy, Madeline, or Gwendolyn in various accounts) that caused the Great Chicago Fire on October 10, 1871. History says the cow kicked over a lantern in the O'Leary's barn at Jefferson and DeKoven. The subsequent fire destroyed some 17,000 buildings and left 100,000 people homeless. It also claimed about 250 lives. While the story was never proved, at a time when Irish immigrants were particularly reviled, the Irish Mrs. O'Leary made a handy scapegoat for the city's rage. Mayor Roswell Mason called the fire an "appalling public calamity."

As the city rebuilt, Italians claimed the Patch. By the time Giovanni Gentile and his family settled in the Patch, the area teemed with Sicilian immigrants. Chicago's Little Italy was a hodge-podge of poor, white neighborhoods (though some considered Italians not quite white). For our family, the world was defined by Grand Avenue at the north end of Aberdeen Street. If people asked where we came from, we said Grand and Ogden (the nearest main artery to the west). Wooden houses and brick apartment buildings dotted the neighborhoods, and Italian families dominated the area for the next fifty-plus years. The police seldom ventured into Little Italy – they didn't care what happened to the Italians. The unrelenting poverty, filth, and disease made life a misery for the people who fell between society's cracks. Mike talked about the smell of shit, garlic, and garbage in the summer.

Farther south, the Levee blazed with red light districts. In the first of many curious coincidences that kept our family mob adjacent for decades, future Outfit leader Sam Giancana grew up down the street. While our family lived in a nice residential neighborhood at Grand and Aberdeen, the Giancana family lived in squalor at Aberdeen and Dearborn in an area lined with speakeasies, flop-houses, and whore-houses. Pimps and white-slavers used professional rapists to "break-in" the new girls. Peep shows offered boys their first glimpse of sex. Drug stores sold dope and hypodermic needles to drug addicts, and the junkies gave each other injections of morphine and cocaine in plain view.

Ostensibly under the control of famously corrupt First Ward Alderman Michael "Hinky Dink" Kenna and "Bathhouse" John Coughlin, competing street gangs freely roamed the streets beginning after the first World War. Future Outfit Chairman of the Board Anthony "Joe" Accardo belonged to the Circus Café Gang. The 42 Gang operated under the leadership of Joey Colaro, described as a "smooth-talking tough guy." Colaro, Sam Giancana, Leonard Caifano, and their gang of "Smartheads" or "Youngbloods" robbed houses and businesses. Ever the planner, Colaro took ten dollars each month from gang members to cover any arrests. Chuck Giancana (Sam's younger brother) described them as "a Mad Hatter's assortment of screwed-up kids and sociopaths."

Beaten, abused, and briefly locked away in a reformatory after being labeled a hopeless delinquent, fourteen-year old Salvatore "Mooney" Giancana found his natural place with the 42 Gang. He initially distinguished himself as a first-class wheelman, whipping corners for fast getaways. His skill behind the wheel would lead to a future job as driver and bodyguard to Paul Ricca and destiny. Murder was the next step up the ladder, and Giancana took to it without hesitation.

The police – mostly Irish – happily took payoffs from the Black Hand and ignored pleas for justice from the harassed Italians. To the Italians facing the violence and extortion of the Black Hand, the street gangs represented hope. They were heroes, not criminals. This decision to see the lesser of the bad guys as the good guys formed the foundation of Chicago's love affair with its hometown hoods.

Decades later, Mike's brother John talked about how Colaro invited him into the 42 Gang in the early 1930s. The pitch was simple: "This is your chance to make some money. Doesn't your family need money?" Sure, the Gentiles needed money. They had another mouth to feed with Junior. But John didn't want to hurt anybody, so he declined the offer, mostly because he thought Sam Giancana was crazy and wanted nothing to do with him. But the next invitation John got, he accepted.

By 1930, Frank Nitti was in charge of Al Capone's liquor distribution operation and doing very well. Nitti's success came from hiding crime in plain sight. Under his plan, every fruit truck, coal truck, milk truck, and diaper truck carried liquor across the city – some by the case, some by the bottle. John started borrowing his father's truck at night. Mickey never asked why. His son always brought the truck back with a full tank, even if it wasn't full when he borrowed it.

Angeline suspected John was doing something illegal. Talking to Mickey didn't help. He was proud of his son. The first time John mentioned going out to meet some of Frank Nitti's friends, Mickey knew it meant bootlegging. Sometimes the air in Little Italy reeked from the smell of hundreds of makeshift stills cooking illegal alky in basements, barns, and bathtubs. The public's insatiable appetite made alcohol the liquid gold that lifted families out of poverty. Mickey earned a decent living and felt proud that he never joined the army of alky cookers. But he wasn't immune to the appeal of extra money, especially with seven mouths to feed.

John's daughter, Tammy Gentile, repeated a story that haunted her father for half a century. In the summer of 1931, John and a pal were delivering liquor to a speakeasy. He hopped out of the truck and unloaded a couple of cases. Suddenly an argument started. The speakeasy owner pulled out a pistol and shot John's pal in the face. It happened in an instant. One minute the guys were swearing. Then bam! A produce man to the end, John compared the guy's face to an exploding tomato. A bloody stump connected to a blood-stained yellow shirt.

The police quickly appeared and arrested everybody. John rode in the back of the police wagon covered in flesh, bone, and blood. He followed instructions and called Frank Nitti, and Nitti sent someone to bail him out. John asked for a clean shirt, too. He couldn't go home with blood all over him. What would he tell his mother? After that, he wanted nothing to do with bootlegging and bootleggers. When Prohibition ended in 1933, John's involvement with hoodlums happily ended. But for his baby brother, things were just getting started.

2 NEIGHBOR ADJACENT

Morning battled the remnants of night as Mickey Gentile left his house and started another work day in the spring of 1943. Twenty-eight-year-old John and fourteen-year old Junior had left the house half an hour earlier. Mickey would meet his boys at the South Water Market a couple of miles east of their home. There they would stock up at the wholesale produce houses, bargaining for the best goods at the lowest prices. Then father and sons would work the neighborhood streets selling fruits and vegetables to earn a day's pay. But that was several hours in the future.

Mickey walked north on Aberdeen Street to Grand Avenue, then turned east toward the garage where he paid the owner a few dollars a month to park their two trucks at night. With the war raging in Europe and the Pacific, used trucks were hard to find. Mickey had been lucky – he always seemed to have an element of luck. He bought a used 1929 Ford truck just before America entered the war. The crank engine fired up every morning, regardless of the weather. Mickey considered the truck a fine purchase, a step up from the horse and wagon that preceded it. Replacement parts were beyond his financial reach. That's why Mickey carried the hand crank. He had one stolen from the truck once before when he left it on the front seat overnight. Mickey didn't want to face that trouble and expense again. The other reason for carrying the crank was equally pragmatic. The Irish pricks enjoyed finding an Italian walking alone – especially a little one like Mickey – and beating the shit out of him, just for kicks. The hard, steel, hand crank evened the odds.

Many of the people living in the north/south residential streets owned or worked at the businesses on east/west Grand Avenue, and Mickey sometimes passed neighbors on their way to work at SanFillipo's Grocery (later Cozzo's Grocery), D'Amato's Bakery, or Benevento's Imported Foods. In the days before supermarkets, women went to different stores for different things – bread and baked goods at D'Amato's, canned goods at SanFillipo's. The best cheese came from Vincent Benevento's store at 1057 West Grand.

As Mickey walked toward the Don's darkened shop, he heard fists against flesh and looked around. A moment later, he heard grunts and groans, and more fists against flesh. He followed the sound behind Benevento's store. In the alley, Mickey saw Vincent Benevento getting the shit kicked out of him by two Youngbloods. The Don fought back, but the odds were against him. So, Mickey did what seemed right – he helped his neighbor. He lifted his right arm and brought the engine crank down hard on the head of the nearest goon. The man's hands went to his head and he turned to face Mickey with murder in his eyes. A second later, the goon's eyes fluttered back, and he fell to the ground.

In the split-second of confusion, Benevento came from behind and wrapped his forearm around the neck of the second attacker and squeezed. Mickey watched the man struggle and gasp, his eyes growing wide and desperate. Suddenly, there was a crunch and resistance stopped. Don Vincenzo released his arm. The goon – whether dead or unconscious, Mickey didn't know and wouldn't ask – slipped to the ground, near the other dead or unconscious heap. The Don glared at the garbage and spit twice – once on each filthy lump.

Mickey silently tipped his hat and went on his way. The boys would wonder why he was late. Mickey wouldn't tell them, or anyone, ever. Mike only learned what happened because Frankie Benevento told him later that day. Frankie described waking up to his mother's hysterical wails and his father's voice trying to calm her. He listened from halfway down the stairs as his father told how a couple of guys jumped him.

The Don said to his wife Jennie, "Lucky for me, Mickey Gentile came out of nowhere swinging a lead pipe and put one of those sons-of-bitches down like a sack of potatoes. Then I got my arm around the other one. Took care of him. Nicky's cleaning up."

"Nicky" was Nick De John, Vincent's nephew, a chubby, small-time climber always eager to do favors for someone with power. De John ran a gambling operation. In two years, after De John brought too much heat down on the Black Hand bosses, San Francisco authorities would find his strangled corpse in the trunk of a car after his sleazy role in an abortion mill extortion scheme came to light.

In one year, Jennie Benevento would watch from their home in Lake Zurich, Illinois, as her husband is pulled out of bed and assassinated by two masked men. Frankie and Mike will remain friends for the rest of their lives. Frankie will become a doctor – a podiatrist. Fifty years later, when my brother has a foot problem, Mike will call Frankie's office. And Frankie will offer to stay late and wait for Mike's boy. Because that's what old friends do.

In the moment, the Don promised Jennie to do right by Mickey. And he did.

Not many would thank Mickey for saving the Don's life. Against tradition, Benevento took a cut of every business on his turf. The Youngbloods confronted the Don at a Unione Siciliana meeting. Most of the neighborhood men were members. A public protest carried weight. They said Italians don't prey on each other; that's what the *"Medigani"* were for! But the Don insisted in his thick, Italian accent, "You don't tell me what to do!" The Youngbloods didn't tell him again. First, they beat him. A few months later, he would be shot five times – and survive. Then a year later, the young thugs had the last word in Lake Zurich.

After the incident behind the cheese shop, the Don stopped collecting the street tax from Mickey. He never said anything directly. He simply omitted Mickey from his Friday collection rounds. Passed him over. Once a week thereafter, Mickey sent Junior to deliver a large box of fruits and vegetables to the Don's back door to show his respect and appreciation.

Mickey worked without complaint six days a week and passed that work ethic to his sons. But on Sundays during the summer, he took his boys to the Cubs' home games. They sat in the bleachers roasting in the sun, and Mike described those days as some of the happiest of his life. Mike didn't give a shit about baseball, but he idolized his father and loved spending time with him. From Mickey's perspective, every day you put on armor for battle, just like his precious Cubs put on their uniforms. It was a for-or-against world, and you fought for whichever side was right. Mickey loved going to the games. It was the only time the men spent together when they weren't working or surrounded by their women. The games were a special extravagance, but Mickey always managed to find enough so the boys could go to the ball game, and the girls could go to the picture shows.

The Don's formal display of gratitude came inside an envelope: season tickets for the Sunday Cubs' home games at Wrigley Field. The seats from the Don were in the stands, the best in the park. Over one small act, a man of great power felt indebted to a man of little consequence. Mickey Gentile was one of millions of scrappers looking to feed his family another day. But once Don Vincenzo "blessed" the Gentile family, they stayed blessed.

Despite the new-found alliance with the Don, Mickey feared the Black Hand boss and worried Junior might get too close. He put limits on his son's friendship with Frankie Benevento. The boys could play stickball on Aberdeen and hang around after school, but Mickey wouldn't allow Junior to go to the Benevento's house on Lake Zurich. He reminded his young son to exercise caution: "The Black Hand slaps with both sides." Junior resented Mickey's hard-ass decision.

Resented or not, Mickey wanted to keep his son safe. "I may not always be right, but I'm always the boss," he said. (Mike later adopted this exact phrase when his sons pushed back against *his* hard-ass decisions.)

Mike made two other lifelong friends in the neighborhood – Johnny DiModica and Sammy Cicero. Both would serve as groomsmen when Mike married, and each would serve as godfather to one of his sons. But back in the day, Mike was skinny and wore his dark hair slicked back. In general style, he resembled a young Frank Sinatra. If he was Sinatra in their Aberdeen Street Rat Pack, Johnny was Dean Martin. Tall and reed-thin, Johnny was always ready for a good time or a good nap. Sammy was their Joey Bishop, the affable third-banana who always carried his own weight. He had the classic Italian traits – warm olive complexion and dark, wavy hair. Frankie was their Peter Lawford, the smooth-talking, good-looking, smart-guy. Mike was the glue that held their Rat Pack together through sheer force of personality. He was the guy who thought things through and didn't act impulsively.

Another World War broke out around the same time. Mike was twelve when the "Japs" invaded Pearl Harbor. He also lost his virginity around that time. He said it was with an "older" woman, but we never found out how much older. One thing proved true in the years that followed: Mike Gentile had a way with the ladies.

There was no rationing during World War II at 460 North Aberdeen Street, and no one did without. Jennie Benevento passed extra ration coupons to Angeline. Where Jennie got them, Angeline never asked. Who asks questions about extra coffee, sugar, butter, and flour? Christmas 1943 opened the house on Aberdeen Street to the neighborhood. Angeline and her daughters baked for weeks and fed the neighbors with the bounty that came from extra ration coupons. Mickey's "friendship" with Don Vincenzo not only made him a big deal at the local Sicilian American club (as the Unione Siciliana was renamed), it also made Angeline a big deal around the neighborhood. She got the best cuts of meat and the best service at all the shops. But every holiday, Angeline brought a platter of baked goods across the street to Jennie Benevento.

With Don Vincenzo gone and a generation of Youngbloods itching for their turn at the top, Angeline recognized the job in front of her. Keeping Junior away from the "bad elements" became her life's work. During Prohibition, she watched with horror as the sons of other mothers got swept up by the opportunities crime presented. Angeline attended their funerals and comforted their grieving mothers. She knew other families with sons heading down the wrong path. Mike and Carmela Lombardo were having nothing but trouble with Joseph, born the same year as Junior. Angeline knew Carmela from church. Their boys went to school together. Poor immigrants like the Lombardos were objects of pity, shame, and charity, the Italian version of white trash. Angeline felt sorry for them, but she didn't want Junior anywhere near Joe or that other troublemaker, John DiFronzo. (Decades later, both Lombardo and DiFronzo would reach the highest level of Outfit leadership.)

Angeline didn't object when Junior left school after the tenth grade. Mickey needed the extra hands, and it kept Junior busy at a time when boys his age were getting into trouble. By the time Mickey, John, and Junior came home from work, cleaned up, and ate supper, they were too exhausted to go anywhere. When he wasn't working or sleeping, Angeline found chores to keep Junior busy. Shameless in her use of guilt, Angeline made sure Junior never got too close to anything that would cause her to lose sleep or say extra rosaries. He lost track of how many rooms he painted for how many relatives, or how many pieces of furniture he moved from one room to another. If her machinations kept Junior busy at night and off the street, the end easily justified Angeline's means.

Her over-protectiveness became an issue with Mickey. "You can't raise a boy like a hot house flower," he insisted.

She held her ground: "And I'm not taking flowers to his funeral because I let him run with hoodlums." By objective measures, Angeline succeeded in raising a good boy. Junior got good marks in school (with an aptitude for arithmetic); he'd never been in trouble with the authorities; he treated his sisters like ladies; and never disobeyed his father. He deferred to his older brother and treated his mother like a deity. Girls liked him; that might become a problem later. But otherwise, he was hard-working, uncomplaining, and diligent. She intended to make damned sure everything stayed that way.

As the war raged overseas, Mike and his crew started hanging around bars and nightclubs when they were fifteen. Nobody "carded." If the bartender thought you looked old enough to drink, he poured one for you. Plus, Italian men always looked older than their age. With the man shortage, any teenager with facial hair could get lucky three times over the weekend if he put his wood to it. Angeline thought modern girls were a disgrace. But she would rather have Junior chasing skirts than dodging bullets.

Why did Mike choose working on a truck over hijacking trucks? Chicago offered wide open career paths after the war. Everybody's business was booming, and the Westside neighborhoods were thick with friends and family members connected to Outfit guys. When he was about seventeen, Mike had an opportunity to do "some work," as he called it. "A guy knew a guy who knew a guy." That's as much detail as he ever offered. He wasn't one to talk about someone else's business. It's one of the reasons he kept such powerful friends. Most likely the "work" involved "boosting" something – stealing or transporting stolen merchandise. Could have been anything. Mob 101: There's always something to steal. It was easy money; Mike was clear on that. Several friends were participating. But something didn't feel right. When opportunity knocked, he declined. The job went off without a hitch, and his pals made a nice piece of change, but Mike didn't feel left out. It didn't feel right *for him.*

He used to say, "You've got to know who you are." Mike could toss hundred-pound sacks of potatoes off the back of the truck all day, but he couldn't run to the end of the block because he had bad lungs. He knew what he could do – and what he couldn't do. And Mike knew he wasn't the guy to boost a truckload of eggs and cheese. But he could make a hell of a cheese omelet for you.

Mike also saw what happened when friends got involved in "work." The lucky ones only ended up in courtrooms and jail cells; the unlucky ones ended up dead. When that happened – and it did – Angeline dragged him to their funerals; she wanted Junior to see what happened when boys didn't listen to their mothers. But he didn't need to see dead bodies to make his choice. Mike's path in life came down to one simple fact: He always wanted to be his own boss. A man who earned his living with his own hands depended on nobody. Mike said, "As long as you work for someone else, you're just a monkey dancing on the organ grinder's chain." And Mike Gentile never liked dancing.

3 WAR ADJACENT

As the boys from the neighborhood became men, some gravitated toward the world of organized crime. Mike went out on his own after he turned eighteen. While Mickey and John worked Little Italy, Mike got the bright idea to move north into the Jewish neighborhood. Mickey resisted. He distrusted outsiders. But Junior followed his hunch, and the decision proved a knock-out. He couldn't keep merchandise on the truck. Decades later Mike described how the delighted housewives came running outside waving money. "You'd swear to Christ they never saw an onion before.

Around the same time he started working the North Side route, Mike met members of the Cerone family at a neighborhood restaurant – there was John Cerone (called Jack) and his cousins Frank (known as Skip) and Frank's younger brother Jimmy (known as Tar Baby). Meeting those men would permanently alter the trajectory of our family and keep us connected to the highest levels of Outfit leaderships for the next half century. Patsy's Restaurant on Grand and Ogden was owned by Pasquale "Patsy" Spilotro. The place was popular with locals and known for some of the best Italian food outside your mother's kitchen. Patsy's son Tony became one of the Outfit's most legendary and vicious killers. (A fictionalized version of Tony Spilotro is played by Joe Pesci as "Nicky Santoro" in *Casino.*)

The extended Cerone family lived around Elizabeth Avenue and Grand, less than a quarter mile from Aberdeen Street. John Phillip Cerone, Sr. was a regular customer at Patsy's. Called "Jackie the Lackie" by those smug pricks who wrote for the newspapers, he served as chauffeur to Boss of Bosses, Joe Accardo, in the early-1940s. Accardo called Jackie a "pilot fish," the guy who always knew how to get where he needed to go. The ability to navigate would serve Jackie well over the coming decades. When Joe Accardo took over as Chairman of the Board after his predecessor, Paul "The Waiter" Ricca, went to prison, Jackie got a promotion. Under the new structure, he reported directly to Outfit CEO Sam Giancana.

For many years, no one held more sway over our family's fortunes than Jackie Cerone. Once Jackie put his arm around Mike, he was protected, even from the police in some instances. Jackie didn't ask for anything in return, only loyalty – a rare commodity in his world. On Jackie's say-so, the corruption and bureaucracy of City Hall stepped aside. On Jackie's say-so, you advanced or lagged. In some cases, you lived or died on Jackie's say-so. His business was primarily gambling; not personally gambling as in putting a C-note on this team or that race. No, he facilitated the gambling activities of others. And he became very rich. If gambling had been a Dow Jones industry, Jackie would have been CEO of a Fortune 500 company.

Jackie Cerone was a man of contradictions – a devoted family man who doted on his vivacious wife, Clara, and ruthless in business. He was a small, plump, bald man – about 5' 6" and 200 pounds. Despite his lack of height, Jackie was a tough motherfucker when he needed to be – and sometimes he needed to be. It's said he was among the crew responsible for the gruesome 1961 torture and murder of Outfit enforcer and juice collector William "Action" Jackson. The three-day orgy of violence included baseball bats, guns, knives, cattle prods, ice picks, and a blow torch.

To people around the neighborhood, Jackie was a kind and friendly man. Others didn't have such a rosy view. Frank "Lefty" Rosenthal is quoted in Nicholas Pileggi's book, *Casino* saying, "There's nobody as obnoxious as Jackie Cerone when he's drunk... a real, real ignorant man." Jerry Gladden, chief investigator of the Chicago Crime Commission said of Cerone, "He was a little more...cordial than other hoodlums but just as bloodthirsty." It's been said Sam Giancana detested the spotlight-craving Cerone, and Joe Aiuppa wanted Cerone dead.

In his book, *Captive City*, Ovid Demaris refers to Jackie, as "an expensive dresser in the old tradition of flashy gangsterism...a feared gunman and Syndicate executioner." When they first met, Mike knew him as the man who ran a tavern. Rocky's Lounge on North Avenue in Melrose Park was Cerone's venture with Joe Lombardo's brother, Rocky. Before coming under Jackie's protection and sponsorship, Mike became friends with Jackie's cousins, Skip and Jimmy. Those two men served as Mike's principle conduits into the Outfit. Skip is described by Demaris as "active in narcotics and gambling" and "considered a hit man." Demaris' portraits of Jackie and Skip reduce each man to a shadow of himself. Jimmy isn't mentioned at all, despite his deep involvement and convictions in connection with Outfit operations. Apparently, even hoodlums have a celebrity hierarchy.

Eventually Mike met other members of the Cerone family, some mob adjacent, some not. Skip and Mike became good friends. He respected hard-working people who kept their mouths shut. It gave Skip pleasure to help his friends, and he considered Mike Gentile one of his friends. So, when Skip heard about a mob-friendly piece of property on Harlem Avenue on the South Side of Chicago, he asked if Mike would like to open a store.

Mike liked the idea very much. First, he presented the idea to Mickey. Peddling in the streets was the old way. Women didn't stay home listening for the fruit peddler's bell. They went shopping – and while they were out, they stopped to pick up lettuce, carrots, and oranges. With trucks, you could go blocks and not make a sale. You missed customers or customers missed you. Let people come to you. "Pile 'em high, watch 'em buy," Mike would say. Mickey reminded his eager son how he'd supported a continually growing family through a pair of World Wars and the Great Depression by treading the streets of Little Italy with horse-drawn wagons and later with trucks. Who needed the expense and headache of a store?

Mike had precedent working in his favor. He'd been right about the North Side route and felt certain he was right about a store. But there was more to it than making money. By 1948, Mickey was fifty-four-years old, and after decades of back-breaking manual labor, the work had taken a physical toll. His smoking habit didn't help. Mickey joked that he started smoking on the boat from Italy when he was two-years old. Working at a store would be easier. A store could be more profitable, too – and wouldn't cost much more than the expense of fueling and maintaining three used trucks. Big brother John deferred as always to his father. In the end, Mickey preferred to stick with what he knew. But he gave his blessing and encouraged his young son to try.

The deal was made, and at eighteen Mike owned a produce market, thanks to Skip Cerone. He was his own boss, a structure Mike preferred for the rest of his life. Days began the same. At 4:00 AM Monday through Saturday, he drove to the South Water Market and loaded up for the day. From there, Mickey and John drove up and down the streets of Little Italy, and Mike went to the South Side. The store was an immediate success. He lured people in by painting the top portion of the big windows with black chalkboard paint and listing the day's specials in big letters. The end of the war meant a lot more people back home. That meant more mouths to feed. The stream of customers never ended. Every week he gave money to his father and slipped some into his mother's apron pocket. Sometimes he bought her pieces of jewelry, brooches mostly.

Many decades later, Aunt Jeanette let a truth slip. She said Junior bought jewelry for their mother when he needed to be forgiven. Judging from the number of brooches in Grandma Gentile's dresser drawer at the time of her death, Mike needed a great deal of forgiveness. The brooches have passed among our family ever since.

In 1948, Mike was riding a wave. Two years after leaving Wells High School to help support the family, business was booming. He had money in his pockets and game in his talk. He met a girl named Ruby Privo and fell hard. Details on his romance with Miss Privo came courtesy of Mary Ann Dinardi, who went to St. Patrick's High School with Ruby. Mary Ann said Ruby was flashy and easy, the kind of girl who came to school looking like she'd been out all night. The nuns often sent Ruby to the bathroom to wash off her mask of makeup. (Mary Ann's assessment of Ruby's character and moral fiber may not be trustworthy for reasons that will become apparent in a few years.) Successful and in love, the future looked bright for Mike, and he was ready to close the deal. But Ruby made it clear their relationship had limits. Being successful wasn't enough; she wanted a rich husband. It turned out Ruby had been doing double duty, dating both Mike and a rich man. When the rich man proposed, she dropped Mike like a rotten potato.

As the situation in Korea degenerated from a Police Action to an Undeclared War, Mike sensed trouble and considered his options. One option included buying a draft deferment from one of his connections. The Universal Military Training and Service Act of 1951 (otherwise known as the Selective Service Act) screwed up Mike's plans. Fact: If a guy enlisted in the Army, he had some say about what he did and where he went. But if you waited until you got drafted, you went wherever Uncle Sam sent you and did as you were told. Mike enlisted to stay ahead of the draft. His mother cried for days. Sammy Cicero enlisted, too. What Mike did, Sammy did. What Mike chose, Sammy chose. With barely 30 days to get his life in order before leaving for basic training, Mike put his brother John in charge of the produce market and kissed his mother goodbye.

Unlike the other branches of the armed forces, the Army offered something unique – military occupational specialty (MOS) jobs. This was a guaranteed job offer in a guaranteed location the moment you enlisted. No other branch of the military offered such a sweet deal. The enlisted man decided how he would serve his country. If his preferred MOS wasn't available, he could pick another, or not enlist. Of course, not enlisting left him open to the crap-shoot of the draft, which brought a series of unpleasant non-choices. Luckily for Mike, his preferred job was available. He chose Culinary Service – Cook. For reasons that have baffled us ever since, Mike (who hated the cold) chose to go to Alaska. Sammy (who hated the heat) picked South Carolina.

Private Gentile wasn't used to being ordered around, except maybe by his mother – and even when she bossed him around, her voice dripped with honey and devotion. The structure of a military base – with its "Sir, yes, sir" hierarchy – felt foreign. But as the saying goes, "You're in the army now," like it or not. There wasn't much to like: sharing a drafty room with a bunch of farting men, lousy food, not enough sleep, nothing to do at night, and endless physical activity during the day. It was ten weeks of bullshit. In cold weather, physical activity was particularly challenging as Private Gentile had a medical issue. Had he thought to disclose it when he enlisted, the army might have rejected him as 4F – not acceptable for service due to medical reasons. A bout of pleurisy brought on by a viral infection when he was about eight or nine left him with weakened lung capacity for the rest of his life.

[A short medical lesson: Think of the *pleurae* as sacks holding your lungs. Their job is to keep the lungs lubricated. When a viral infection brings on a fever, the pleurae become inflamed. This inflammation tightens the sacks, impairs their lubricating function, and causes painful breathing. There is no cure for this condition. End of medical lesson.]

The cigarette habit he picked up at age twelve didn't help. Mike was plagued by colds and lung infections. But he still smoked. No one should smoke cigarettes; medical science is clear about that nowadays. And there are some people who really shouldn't smoke – like children, pregnant women, asthmatics, and people with other lung conditions. But everybody smoked in the 1940s and 1950s. Hell, doctors in advertisements said smoking was good for you! The entire film noir genre owed its hazy atmosphere to people smoking like chimneys.

[Mike smoked for another thirty-five-years, until one day he decided he didn't want to smoke anymore. He crushed a half-smoked pack of L&M's and never smoked another cigarette. Some people struggle to quit smoking; Mike simply decided. Because that's the kind of man he was.]

He also could have avoided military service by buying a draft deferment. Though Skip and Jimmy completed their prison sentences for selling fake deferments in the early 1940s, Skip still had the ability to make someone disappear from the Draft Board's radar. Mike never considered it. The price was too high in every sense. That was among his earliest lessons in mob adjacency: just because one of your mob pals can make something happen, that doesn't mean you should go along with the plan. A man had to choose what kind of man he wanted to be. Mike didn't want to be the guy who cheated his country out of military service so he could do something else.

After completing ten weeks of basic, Private Gentile took another nine weeks of training in culinary arts and sciences. He was never sure if making shit-on-a-shingle constituted an art or a science. Regardless, he left basic training as PFC Gentile, Food Service Specialist, assigned to the 59th Engineering Construction Company and shipped to Anchorage, Alaska, destination Elmendorf Air Force Base. He stopped in Chicago on the way. His mother cried happy tears for the first day before switching to sad tears for the last two days of his stay.

Mike spent the next two years serving the 59th Engineering Construction Company breakfast, lunch, and dinner. Before long, he was in charge of the kitchen. Far removed from the danger of war, sometimes Mike forgot he was in the Army. The "Sir, yes, sir" bullshit remained in effect, but absent the danger of the battlefield, men on a military base slip into an ordinary life – eat, work, shit, sleep, repeat. Since one of the primal drives in every animal is the need to eat, the cook becomes a very important man on a military base.

Private Gentile was a get-along kind of guy. He came into the game with his eyes open and the scoreboard in front of him. He wasn't looking to be a hero and wasn't looking to make trouble. No. He had a very specific goal: Do what the Army tells him for the next two years, and go home. Somewhere between peeling potatoes, scrambling eggs, and frying chicken, Mike sensed an opportunity. But first he had to make dinner. He kept the cookbook *Army Technical Manual TM-10-412, Recipes* after the war – in case he needed to feed a battalion, or a family of Italians. And he would. And in case you ever need to make dinner for 100, here are some recipes courtesy of the U.S. Army.

No. M-16. Country Style Chicken Southern Fried
Yield: 100 servings, 12- to 14-ounces each

Chicken, 80 pounds (New York dressed), or Chicken, ready-to-cook (eviscerated), 60 pounds
Flour or Breadcrumbs, 3 pounds
Salt, 6 ounces (12 tablespoons)

Pepper, 3/4 ounce (3 tablespoons)
Chicken fat for frying

1. Clean chicken; cut in halves or quarters according to size desired.
2. Mix flour or breadcrumbs, salt, and pepper together; roll chicken in flour or breadcrumbs.
3. Heat enough fat in roasting pan or skillet to partially cover chicken.
4. Place chicken in hot fat, largest pieces first, do not crowd; fry until brown, turning occasionally
5. Carefully add enough boiling water to cover bottom of the pan.
6. Cover pan tightly and continue to cook, turning occasionally, allowing the chicken to steam for about 30 minutes.
7. If crisp skin is not desired, continue cooking chicken covered for an additional 10-minute period. If crisp skin is desired, remove cover for a like period.
8. Use drippings to make cream gravy.

No. S-35. Yellow Cake
Yield: 100 Servings, 1 piece each, 2-1/2" x 3"

Sugar, granulated, 7 pounds, 4 ounces (3-1/4 quarts)
Lard, 2 pounds (1 quart)
Flour, sifted, 5-1/2 pounds (5-1/2 quarts)
Salt, 2 ounces (4 tablespoons)
Baking powder, 4 ounces (11 tablespoons)
Milk, evaporated, 3/4 quart
Water (for milk), 3/4 quart
Milk, powdered, 6 ounces (1 quart)
Eggs, dehydrated, 10 ounces (3/4 quart)
Water (for eggs), 3/4 quart
Water, 1 quart
Vanilla, to taste

1. Cream sugar and shortening until light and fluffy.
2. Reconstitute eggs and fold in above mix.
3. Add evaporated milk and water or reconstituted whole milk and mix thoroughly.
4. Add water and vanilla to above.
5. Combine flour, salt, and baking powder and fold into above.
6. Turn into greased pans and bake at 350-degrees F for 45 min.

Ask a grunt on an isolated military base what the worst part is, and he'll say it's the boredom. Hour after hour of nothing to do – eat, work, shit, sleep, repeat. And a guy can only jerk off so many times a day before he starts shooting steam. It's even worse on a military base in Alaska where the days and nights were each six-months long, and there's nothing around but more and more nothing. One thing is one hundred percent guaranteed: Guys want to have a good time, and they're willing to pay for it. The "oldest profession" is the world's oldest precisely because men have always been willing to pay for a good time. Broads? Hard to find. Booze? Available but costly. But gambling? Gambling was easy. And it passed the time.

Military Command, with its focus on order and discipline, certainly didn't allow organized gambling on a United States military base. But consider the latent hypocrisy: You're not supposed to gamble, but isn't war just a gamble on who gets killed first? Approved or not, gambling was everywhere – two guys playing gin rummy on their bunks, a couple more shooting craps behind the garage, and a few betting on a football game on the radio. You could always find something to bet on. There's a saying among gamblers: Shoot a nun, and she can fall either way. With nowhere to go and nothing to do, Private Gentile fell back on the hospitable nature of his Italian heritage.

Truth: The army depends on its cooks more than its generals. And they value the cooks more than the generals, too. You want to eat? Don't piss off the cook. You may have to say "Sir, yes, sir" outside the mess hall; but inside, it's 'Sir, thank you, sir." Or you'll be eating the sole of your boot for the next six weeks. Even the highest of the high command wants a decent dinner at the end of the day. And they know a happy cook is more likely to know about a certain porterhouse steak in the back of the refrigerator.

Truth: An Army cook has access to virtually unlimited supplies -- if he knows how to make 2+2=5. On *TM-10-412*, page 1, section 2, C, it says: "The number of men who will be present for each meal must be determined before supplies are ordered." That number is decided by the cook. Now, an army cook isn't a food service specialist; he might easily make a mistake and order too much food. If the cook had access to extra food, and an empty mess hall with tables and chairs, he could make the extra food and the empty space available to his friends. There's a radio in the kitchen. You can have music or listen to the Army-Navy game – all for a fee that includes sandwiches and beer. When the war is over, the cook might have enough money to buy a brand new red Buick and a bar on Clybourn Avenue. But let's not get ahead of ourselves.

Private Gentile enlisted (pardon the expression) a captain as his partner. The captain, an Italian from New York, looked the other way in exchange for a piece of the action. The captain's other contribution included pinching beer and booze from the Officer's Club to serve the grunts. The partners split the proceeds fifty-fifty. Serving as a one-man casino, the enterprising private funded a series of games – mainly craps and poker – on Monday, Wednesday and Friday. Weekends were dedicated to that great American pastime – betting on professional sports. The two World Series played during Mike's stint in the army were huge successes, and the men bet heavily on the games. Everybody gambled against the house, and the house always won. All things considered, one man's army offered peaceful comfort and a chance to build a post-service stake.

One member of the Gentile family suffered terribly during the Korean War – Angeline Gentile. Frightened and bereft by Junior's absence, his sisters wrote long, sad letters documenting their mother's anguish – the crying, the sleepless nights, the endless rosaries. With the holidays approaching it grew worse. And then Rachel mentioned Ruby Privo in a letter. She was back at her mother's house, and Ruby's marriage was over before it started. The sting of her rejection was long past, and Mike felt sorry for Ruby. He had loved her, but she was used goods now. No one would want another man's cast-off. Mike would have married her – wanted to marry her – before she chose wrong. They would have had children – in fact, it was a lucky break they didn't have children already, all things considered. That gave him an idea.

The next day, Mike wrote a letter to Johnny DiModica, still back in Chicago. Johnny had decided to take his chances on the draft and enjoy the extra women until his number came up, dice in one hand, and a blond in the other. In case of censors, Mike made his request clear without asking Johnny to do anything. It went: "They tell me Ruby's pregnant, and I have to marry her immediately. Tell me truly. Mike." The arrival of the letter was enough to awaken John's senses. Mike didn't write letters. But Johnny got the drift – his pal was angling for a leave over Christmas. Johnny promptly wrote a letter to Mike saying Ruby was pregnant, and he needed to marry her immediately. He put in a few extra flourishes to make it all sound legit. Then he licked a stamp and laughed his ass off.

Private Gentile subsequently shared a deeply personal letter with his Commanding Officer. His girl was pregnant, he said with shame, and he needed to marry her right away – so the baby would have A Name. His C.O. reminded Private Gentile that it was highly unusual to grant holiday leave to a subordinate when his superior officers were duty-bound to serve their country, Santa Claus or no Santa Claus. But the Irish Catholic commander saw the bigger picture. Back then, the birth certificate of a child born out of wedlock was marked "Illegitimate," and the child carried that filthy stigma for life. His C.O. said Christian decency mandated an immediate marriage, for the sake of the child. The fornicators would have to answer to God, but the baby was an innocent. The necessary forms were signed, and Private Gentile packed his kit for Christmas in Chicago. Wouldn't Ma be surprised!

Black-and-white snapshots from Christmas 1950 show a stick-thin soldier in a neatly pressed uniform. Mike didn't tell his mother how he managed to get home because he knew she wouldn't approve. Instead, he posed happily for photos in the living room. The boughs of the Christmas tree are barely visible in one of the pictures. Junior's home! Who gives a shit about Christmas?

Mike gave Mickey two-thousand dollars to hold – profits from his casino operation. Then he drove to his market and was dismayed by what he found – rotted goods on display, garbage on filthy floors, stinking trash cans, and a general air of decay and failure. The store had customers, but no one was buying. They came in, looked around, and left. When he opened the books, the story got worse. The thriving business he left in his brother's hands less than a year ago was slipping into the red. It came down to different philosophies. To lower costs and increase profits, John started buying cheaper produce, things that "showed a little trouble." But Mike's customers were accustomed to higher quality goods; they didn't want melons that showed "trouble" or potatoes that smelled.

John believed offering the lowest prices would bring in the most customers. His logic: You're going to cut up a cantaloupe anyway. If you cut off the bad spot while you're cutting the rest of the melon, and you can get the melon for 75-percent off, who doesn't want to buy that melon? The idea that someone might not want to buy rotten fruits and vegetables didn't occur to him. It was a dismal meeting. But there was nothing Mike could do but urge his brother to aim higher and hope the market survived until Uncle Sam discharged him from the Army.

Then he called Johnny DiModica to go get drunk. Johnny was already half in the bag. He was at his mother's house. Frankie Benevento was there, too, back home from school. They were drinking scotch, and Johnny's mother was feeding them. She yelled toward the phone for Junior to come over. He no sooner hung up when the phone rang again. Angeline complained with a delighted smile that the phone hadn't rung that much since Junior left. It was Sammy Cicero calling. By a happy holiday coincidence, he was also home for Christmas. Sammy was down the block at Jimmy Annerino's bar, and Jimmy swore he saw Mike going into his mother's house. Sammy called to check, and Mike hurried to the bar at the corner of Hubbard and Aberdeen.

After a lot of back-slapping and well-what-do-you-know, Mike got down to business. He told Sammy about his operation in Alaska. "What about the C.O.," Sammy asked? Mike's answer was simple: "Make the captain your partner!" Cutting the captain in on the action was the equivalent of buying an insurance policy. The captain would look the other way, and he'd deflect attention from the base commanders if necessary. Mike suspected his Commanding Officer knew what was going on, but he never did anything to stop the operation.

Mike thought his C.O. probably saw the merits in keeping off-duty men occupied. It was better than fights breaking out between bored soldiers with too much unused testosterone. More to the point, Mike said, the C.O. was probably afraid if he squashed the operation, he'd never get another decent meal. If you don't gamble, a guy could make $500 a month (that's about $4,000 per month in 2017 dollars). Over a two-year tour, that turned into a nice piece of change. He leaned close and told Sammy he gave Mickey two-grand already. Sammy whistled long and slow and decided to try the scheme when he returned to South Carolina.

Then they went to meet Johnny and Frankie. The foursome proceeded to finish a bottle of scotch, two loaves of bread, and a pan of lasagna while Johnny's mother filled cannoli shells. Johnny pretended to wipe a proud tear when Mike told the gang about scamming Uncle Sam with Johnny's help to make it home for Christmas. Everybody laughed. Then Mama DiModica slapped her son and Mike on the backs of their heads. Both at once. Two hands, no waiting. Then everybody laughed even harder. Mike didn't remember much about the rest of the night. He woke up at his mother's house, tucked in warmly with an extra blanket, and stinking of B.O., booze, cigarettes, and – he sniffed his sleeve – cheap perfume. He felt an urgent need to buy a brooch.

Private Gentile returned to Elmendorf after New Years' with a sad tale about a miscarriage, a shattered romance, and a cancelled marriage. Then he got back to business. He later said his stint in the Army passed completely without significant events or incidents. Aside from the major victories of war – not being shot, wounded, captured, or killed – Private Gentile came out of the Army with some handy new skills. He learned how to prepare vast quantities of food, entertain people, and empty their wallets. Those skills would come in handy because he had an idea about what he wanted to do next.

The market was gone. Mickey didn't know exactly what happened, and John's story never made sense. Either the store failed and John sold it, or it failed and someone else took over. End result: The store was gone. Fortunately, Mickey still had the money Mike gave him. Mickey thought about giving some to John as he watched the market slip underwater, but he sensed it was good money after bad by that point and didn't want Junior coming home to nothing. John was back on the trucks where he was happiest, working with Mickey. Mike joined them on the route while he figured out his next move. He had the kind of cash stake that let a man decide his future.

Sammy got out of the Army not long after Mike. True to his word, he had set up a casino operation at Fort Jackson. His results were equally impressive. Mike got the bright idea to go to the Buick dealer and buy two identical new cars, figuring they would get the best price if they bought in bulk. And they did. A magnificent pair of 1952 red Buicks. Sammy put a down payment on a house with the rest of his money. Mike found a bar on Clybourn Avenue.

It wasn't anything fancy. The place didn't even have a name, just a red neon sign in one of the two windows facing Clybourn. It said BAR. The sign came with the lease. But there was one problem: The landlord couldn't sell to someone without a liquor license. Given the bureaucracy and graft at City Hall and the veritable zoo of asses that needed to be kissed and palms that needed to be greased, Mike might be able to get a liquor license in four to six months. By then, of course, the bar would be long gone. That's the kind of government bullshit that attracts people to organized crime.

A person should be able to go down to City Hall, apply for a liquor license, show proper identification, present the relevant qualifications, and acquire the necessary license. But that's not how it worked in Chicago. Even a veteran fresh from the tundra couldn't get a break at City Hall. He'd have to grease those palms, kiss the aforementioned asses, and have the patience of Job, for which he might be rewarded with a liquor license when they got around to it. And fuck you, go to the back of the line if you don't like it. You can't run a business – or a city – that way.

Here's where being mob adjacent comes in handy: Because Mike knew a guy like Jackie Cerone with heavy pull at City Hall, it took one call to one guy to get a liquor license within 24-hours – for the actual $40 cost, without the grease, ass-kissing, or bullshit. Done. With license in hand, Mike Gentile closed the deal and kicked off the next phase of his life.

The North Side of Chicago belonged to Ross Prio, a slight, doughy, owl-faced man with dark hair and round glasses. He looked more like a college professor than the executioner he was claimed to be. In addition to other responsibilities as a top Outfit enforcer and loan shark, Prio controlled every bar, tavern, and strip joint north of the river. Called "the sweetest plum in Chicago," the North Side had once been the kingdom of George "Bugs" Moran (until a certain St. Valentine's Day party put an end to his reign) and mob florist Dion O'Banion (who died amongst their broken blossoms).

When Mike wanted to buy the bar a Clybourn, Jackie greased the wheels with Ross Prio, too. In exchange for letting Mike operate in Prio's territory, Mike observed Outfit protocol – he bought inventory from mob-controlled vendors and hired labor from mob-controlled unions. The bosses profited on the back-end by taking bets and making loans, plus the money from the juke box, cigarette machine, Kotex machine, rubber machine, and their cut of the food and liquor. Everybody won. Mike knew the score. He'd been playing the game since his North Side produce route. Back then, if Jackie or one of the other bosses gave him a package for another boss, Mike made the delivery. He never looked inside and never took money for the deliveries. He said, if you took money, best you were an employee, worst you were an accessory. But if he did a favor, he's a friend. Over the long-term, friends are more valuable than a few bucks today. The monkey always collects the change. But when you do a favor, nobody's yanking the chain.

Technically, the guy who delivered betting slips was the "runner." One of the main sources of Outfit profits in the 1950s came from a source that had been long scorned. The "policy racket" also known as "the numbers game" was considered a nickel/dime operation for the poor blacks; similar "bolita games" fleeced the poor Hispanics. The name "policy" came from its similarity to cheap insurance – the bet might pay off. Sam Giancana learned about the hidden treasure while in prison with Edward Jones, king of the South Side numbers racket, a game played by eighty-percent of the blacks in South Side ghettos. Nickels and dimes added-up to dollars. Giancana got out of prison and promptly stole the business. In the policy racket, the mark attempted to pick three digits to match numbers that will be randomly drawn the following day. Like the wheel in bingo games or modern state lotteries, a policy wheel revolved to pick three numbers. The runner carried the money and betting slips between locations.

Working as a runner often served as the entry point for guys looking to make their bone in the Outfit, the equivalent of starting in the mail room. Mike wasn't looking for a way in; he was steadfast about staying out. But he wasn't opposed to doing a favor for a friend. And when the time came, Jackie Cerone wasn't opposed to doing a favor for a friend when City Hall started dicking Mike around about a lousy $40 liquor license.

As the 1950s began, Mike had a solid relationship with the extended Cerone family on business and personal levels. As Jackie, Skip, and Jimmy went about their Outfit business and Mike went about his, they remained connected by the old neighborhood. Mike was the guy who went to the same places and knew the same people. His brother knew your sister; his father knew your father; his aunt went to school with your cousin, or their barn backed up to your garage; or their mothers dipped their fingers in the same holy water at Santa Maria Addolorata or one of the dozen other Catholic churches in Little Italy. Mike was almost like family – family adjacent – and in Italian culture, almost was good enough.

4 BAR ADJACENT

One small window faced Clybourn Avenue. Suspended from a rusty chain, a sign made of red neon tubing read BAR. Mike juggled the key in one hand and looked at his purchase. John and Mickey thought he was crazy. What did junior know about running a bar? He was going to lose all that money he made in Alaska; they were both sure of it. But Junior's eyes danced with excitement. On one point everyone agreed: It wasn't much. Junior took stock of his empire: Cigarette machine in the vestibule to the left – fifteen-cents a pack. A row of wooden pegs for hats and coats straight ahead. Twelve scuffed stools in front of a scuffed wooden bar running nearly the length of the far wall. Ten scuffed tables, each with a collection of battered chairs. A Wurlitzer jukebox divided the room. Two toilets in the back across from a store room/mop room. Back door leading to the alley.

Mike flipped a switch and a bank of overhead lights came on in sequence. At the same time, Angeline, Jeanette, Rachel, and Marie came in the front door carrying buckets, mops, and boxes of cleaning supplies, with their hair tied up in kerchiefs. Larry and Joe followed with tools and two-by-fours. It only took one day to knock down the walls of the storeroom/mop room and build a kitchen in the expanded space. The city didn't make noise about health code regulations, building codes, and permits, especially at a "declared" place. Mike operated under the protection of North Side boss Ross Prio. That meant the police stayed out, unless they wanted to buy a drink. Then their money was as good as anyone's.

While the men worked on the walls, the women scrubbed and polished every surface, dusted every half-filled liquor bottle and scoured the ice bin with bleach. The next day, Junior and John loaded up a truck on Aberdeen Street with Aunt Simonetta's old kitchen appliances. She gave everything to Junior when she moved in with her daughter – the stove, refrigerator, and the kitchen set. They took the pots, pans and dishes, too. Junior had a plan. With four burners, a griddle, and a double oven, John could crank out feasts while he kept the drinks flowing.

Despite its modest appearance, the bar on Clybourn did great business from the start. Korean War veterans flooded the city, and a lot of them were looking for a night on the town. Jackie kept a discreet bookie on the premises. A loan shark wasn't usually far behind. Mike didn't care. If people wanted to piss away their paychecks on booze and gambling, who was he to judge? He was running a bar, not a church. As long as everybody behaved, paid their tab, tipped the waitress, and didn't piss on the floor, Mike didn't get involved in the private conversations of his customers.

Some businesses specialize in one product, while others sell everything from apples to zippers. Similarly, the Outfit offered a complete line of bookmaking, loan sharking, prostitution, fraud, extortion, and blackmail. Each division had designated leaders and workers. It's important to understand how the machine worked, because at its core the Outfit was a finely-tuned, integrated, multidisciplinary organization. Where one stood on the org chart mattered.

Mike stood completely in the social sphere, removed from the business of being a hoodlum. He got to know people in a social context, when they were most at ease. The guy at the gas station, or the guy at the bakery or sandwich joint, you saw for a few minutes and went on your way. Not so with a bartender. A guy could spend hours with his barkeep – more hours than he spent at home or work. Women had their hairdresser; men had their bartender. Mike knew those guys at the deepest level. He knew who was cheap; who was a loud-mouth, who couldn't hold his liquor; who chased skirts; who chased cock; and who ate like a pig? The barkeep knows. And like priests and lawyers, he kept it to himself. For the Outfit guys, Mike's presence was a positive trigger – the sign of a good time to come. Decades later, when the guys saw Mike, they remembered the good times, and a cloud of goodwill swirled around the barkeep long after he turned in his bar towel.

With the kitchen up and running on Clybourn, sometimes Mike sent a tray of hot appetizers around the room. Often, a little hot food reminded people it was time for another cold drink. And with the markup on liquor significantly greater than the markup on food, giving away food actually made money. More importantly, it built goodwill with the customers, all for the price of something on a fucking cracker or a slice of bread.

In the early days, it called for ingenuity. Five pounds of ground round became ten pounds of meatballs, meatloaf and hamburgers. All in Aunt Sim's magic pans. When the place started to fill up, Mike yelled from behind the bar. "John, fry some sausage!" He left the bartender hired from the mob-controlled union behind the counter and went into the kitchen.

Mike grabbed a long, thin loaf of crusty bread and started making short slices for two-bite sandwiches. John cranked the heat under Aunt Sim's cast iron pan and splashed in some olive oil. Then he swirled the oil and lowered a coil of sausage into the smoking pan. A crackling hiss and a cloud of fennel-scented smoke filled the room while an inverted box fan sucked the smoke out of a small window.

"And fry some peppers."

John went to the refrigerator and grabbed a glass bowl filled with sliced green peppers. By the time the sausage was ready to be turned, the second cast iron skillet was ready to go, oil and garlic, simmering. John poured in the bowl of peppers and gave everything a quick toss.

Mike laid the bread on a big platter. When the sausage was cooked, he sliced it thin, put a piece on each piece of bread, laid a pepper sautéed in garlic across the top, sprinkled a blast of parmesan cheese and called it an appetizer. He spent $2 making a snack and sold $20 worth of drinks. Host 101, courtesy of Mike Gentile. Whenever the sound of the cash register singing started slowing, he'd shout, "John, fry some sausage."

Mike knew there was more to running a bar than food and drinks. Running a business in Chicago meant negotiating with a cluster-fuck of unions. Taking control of the unions had been among the Outfit's top priorities after Prohibition ended. Union pension funds were the greatest thing since mother's milk, both of which were generated with little effort. By the 1950s, if you wanted to do anything in the city of Chicago that involved goods or labor, it meant negotiating with the Outfit. The bosses owned the unions and the businesses they unionized. They made money coming and going, considering they also controlled the liquor, produce, meat, dry cleaning, vending machines, garbage collection, juke boxes, and just about everything needed to run a bar, restaurant, or hotel. You name it, there was a union for it, sometimes more than one, with redundancies that can only come from fine union minds. You had:

The Bartenders and Beverage Dispensers Union, Local 278

The Hotel and Restaurant Employees and Bartenders International Union, Local 593

The Drugstore, Fountain, and Luncheonettes Union, Local 658

The United Industrial Workers of America, Local 286

The Bakery Wagon Driver's Union, Local 734

The list went on and on – like a career criminal's rap sheet. Making a profit despite the union bullshit took someone with a good head for business. A bar could be very profitable. But in order to profit, someone needed to keep an eye on things. The mark-up on liquor was astronomical, hence the profitability. But the opportunities for liquor to pour out without payment was also great, as was the possibility that payment for drinks didn't end up in the cash register.

In the summer of 1953, Mike Gentile was twenty-four-years old – a young man in his prime. While he liked the bar business, working every night until three in the morning didn't allow much of a social life. And then Ruby Privo turned up one night. Everybody knew her story, so she didn't bother bringing it up. Ruby focused on the here and now. Right here, right now, Mike Gentile looked awfully good – a man with a brand-new car and his own business. If she had tried to spark flames any harder, the liquor would have combusted. Used goods or not, Ruby kept her looks. And she was amenable to his crazy hours, so he started going around with her. But he could never be serious about Ruby again.

Mike was a product of his time. Rigid piles of bullshit held up 1950s society. Everybody tried to pretend everything was hunky-dory and happy days, that there wasn't the Bomb and the Cold War, and growing problems with the Negroes. Men saw the horrors of the battlefield and still pretended a girl needed to be a virgin to be marriage material, even as they burned through "rubbers" and "johnnies" deflowering as many girls as possible. For Italians with their inflated sense of masculine honor, the bullshit piled even higher. Ruby was not the kind of girl Mike could ever take home to his mother. But he could do other things with her. He probably didn't want to go to a birthday party for one of Ruby's high school gal pals, but it was the end of the evening that really mattered, not the bullshit in the middle.

Mary Ann Dinardi knew about love from the movies. She drank heavily from its well of fantasy and believed wholly in Grand Romance. To prepare her daughter for what "romance" entailed, Mary Ann's dutiful immigrant mother, Virginia, gave a detailed talk about s-e-x. It went exactly like this: "Don't lift your skirt for anybody; don't let anybody touch you." End of sex talk. Armed with that knowledge, Mary Ann faced the world as a young adult woman. She'd had a few incidental boyfriends in high school – dates for homecomings, proms, and formals. No one of consequence. After high school, she worked first as a cashier in a movie theater and later for the telephone company, where she quickly rose to supervisor and waited for the man who would give her life meaning. She loved her job – getting up in the morning with a sense of purpose, putting on a pretty outfit, taking the bus across town, mixing with people, and being in the thick of things – but she knew its shelf-life ended with the words "I do."

While she waited, there was always something to do. Every year from Thanksgiving to New Year's was one long celebration. Midway through the holiday season – December 16, 1953 – Mary Ann accepted an invitation to a birthday party for her girlfriend, Toni. She wore her new navy-blue suit from Marshall Field's and felt every bit the young sophisticate. Halfway through the evening, Ruby Privo arrived with a wonderfully attractive man. Mary Ann didn't think much of girls like Ruby, the kind who lifted their skirts. The man caught Mary Ann staring at him and smiled. She felt her face flush and wondered if it showed. He was tall and thin, in that Frank Sinatra way she adored, with a sly smile and deep-set eyes. His hair was dark, slicked back, and smooth. His shirt was crisp and white, suit impeccably tailored. He looked like a movie star.

Toni arranged an introduction. "Mike Gentile, this is my girlfriend Mary Ann. Mary Ann Dinardi."

Mary Ann thought: "Bless you, Toni, and happy, happy birthday."

She would later say Mike Gentile was very sweet, very polite, and very proper. She spent the rest of the evening answering his questions: What did she like to do? Where did she like to go? Where had she gone to school? She answered each question in eager anticipation of the next. Later that evening Toni's mother took Mary Ann aside and casually informed her that Mike Gentile would be her husband one day. Mary Ann stared incredulously. Then she thought about it. He was tall, handsome, charming, and attentive – a girl could do worse.

Throughout the evening, Mary Ann turned around and there he was, smiling and asking another question. At the end of the night he asked if he might drive her home. She thought the idea strange since he'd come with Ruby. Mike quickly side-stepped her hesitation and said Ruby would be coming along. Ruby didn't look happy. But Mary Ann wasn't ready for the night to end and said yes anyway. He talked to her the whole way while Ruby fumed over the knowledge that she'd just lost Mike Gentile to that little virgin in the back seat.

To Virginia Dinardi's horror, flowers arrived for Mary Ann the next morning. She hadn't understood why her daughter had been so chipper. Then the damning evidence arrived, and she suspected something improper happened. She hoped there wouldn't be consequences and demanded to know what kind of man sent flowers to a girl he just met.

"A gentleman, Ma," Mary Ann replied.

Her gentleman called several times before she agreed to go out with him. He scared her. He was too mature, too worldly. And then she accepted. After their first real date, as they stood under the porchlight he leaned over and kissed her forehead. She was hooked. Mike showed her the nicest places in Chicago, the best restaurants, the swankiest nightclubs. There were little gifts of perfume, flowers, and candy. A few months later, they went to her friend's wedding. Mary Ann was a bridesmaid.

Mike looked up between bites of chicken and asked, "What would you say if I asked you to marry me?"

A piece of chicken lodged in Mary Ann's throat. She managed to swallow and said, "I don't know. Ask me."

"I just did." Mike looked into her eyes and said, "I happen to love you very much."

She started to cry. They became formally engaged on her birthday, May 1, 1954. With the ring on her finger, Mike wanted to know when they could get married. She'd always dreamt about a June wedding. Since it was already May, June was out of the question. Even if it could be pulled together, what would people say about an engagement and marriage taking place in less than a month? She suggested a year from June.

Mike didn't understand. "How long does it take to plan a wedding?"

At the very least, she figured it would take six months.

"Then we'll get married in November."

She didn't argue the point. In fact, she said it made her love him even more. He wanted to marry her NOW, not a year from now. If it took six months to plan the wedding she wanted, that was all right. But no longer.

Throughout the wedding plans, he focused on making money. Mike had every reason for optimism. Business was thriving. Then a month or so before the wedding, Ruby Privo showed up and made one last try with Mike. They were meant to be together, she said. If only she hadn't made that one wrong decision – dumping him, marrying another man, moving to another state before the quick collapse of her hasty marriage, followed by a mortal sin divorce, and a ruined reputation. One wrong decision? No sale.

Mike sent her away. And rather than risk Ruby going to Mary Ann to make trouble, he told his fiancé about Ruby's visit. Some girls got jealous about those kinds of things. But Mary Ann didn't feel jealous or angry. Feeling smug and victorious felt too satisfying.

As a child, I sometimes amused myself sorting through a box of old photographs. One day I found a photo of a woman. She looked beautiful, fragile, and hard all at the same time. The lady wore a tailored suit, and a flat felt hat, with dark curls framing her face and a beauty mark under her lip. I waved the photo and asked, "Who's this?"

Mom looked over, scowled, and snatched the picture. "That's Ruby Privo." Then she tore it to shreds and let the bits flutter into the trash.

5 MARRIAGE ADJACENT

Conflict arose almost immediately regarding where Mike and Mary Ann would live after their marriage. Angeline carried on believing Junior and his bride would naturally move into her house and live in what had been his childhood bedroom. After all, that's where Junior lived. She considered painting the room, but the color reminded her of when he was a boy, and she couldn't bear to change it.

Mike floated the balloon about living at his parents' house after another comment from Angeline about "after Mary Ann moves in." He inserted the subject as carefully as possible and asked his fiancé about living on Aberdeen Street for a few years "to save for a house." Was he joking? He had to be joking. Prince Charming wanted his bride to move in with his mother – and his three sisters? Didn't he know there was a fairy tale about that basic scenario? It didn't go well for the girl.

"So, what do you think?" Mike asked expectantly.

Time stopped for Mary Ann, and she considered her answer in the frozen silence. A pragmatist to the core, she sensed an opportunity. Previously, Mike had been unwilling to consider that she might keep her job after they married. He'd been immovable on the subject. Whether she wanted to work, needed to work, preferred to work, or longed to worked made no difference. No man wanted to look as if he couldn't support his wife. What would it say about him? No one gave a thought to what it said about her – going from gainful employment to a life strapped to a house, gagged with a dust rag, and chained to a vacuum, until the babies started. Why couldn't a woman have a family and a job?

What was Lucille Ball except America's foremost working mother? She was the star of the most popular television show on the planet, co-owner of a television production studio, and a mother of two. What did it say about Desi Arnaz that his wife worked? It said he was one lucky son of a bitch to have such a wife. Lots of mothers had jobs. Marlene Dietrich, Elizabeth Taylor, Bette Davis, Joan Crawford, Judy Garland. Marjorie Merriweather Post ran a food empire from her boudoir in Palm Beach. Mothers all.

Mary Ann met the wives of Mike's friends "from the old neighborhood," as she called the hoodlums and gangsters that appeared in their lives and at their restaurant tables. She couldn't imagine any of those women with jobs. Being *his* wife was *her* job. The idea made Mary Ann throw up in her mouth. Among the unmarried women she knew, their goal was to get married and quit her job at the department store, beauty shop, typing pool, switchboard, or wherever. She'd get her hair done on Friday afternoons and go out on Friday night. Her life would be perfect. Just like the movies.

Mary Ann suspected a fool's errand but decided it was worth one more charge up that hill and made her pitch: Yes, they could stay at his parents' house for a year. She'd keep working and bank her salary, and they would have enough for a substantial down payment on a house.

Mike hadn't expected a counter-offer. The women in his life – his mother and sisters – typically did whatever he said, so he wasn't used to negotiations. He found himself at the first of many marital crossroads. Mike wanted to stay in his parent's house to make his mother happy and because it was easiest. Best case, Mary Ann wouldn't object, and he'd get to please both women with no personal inconvenience. "Why do you want to get up every day and go to work?"

"Because I like contributing."

"You contribute by running the house."

Mary Ann wanted to put a pin in that point, since she didn't know the first thing about running a home. She'd been making $2.54 an hour, $101.60 per week – fifty-cents an hour more than the girls she supervised, plus benefits that included vacation plans, insurance plans, savings plans, sick leave, and stock options. By every objective measure, Mary Ann had the better job. And he wanted her to quit. Because that's what wives did. And she said no.

Mike looked aghast and insulted. "I own the bar. You only work for Ma

Bell. Ma Bell tells you how much money you can make. But I can always figure out how to make more money."

She wasn't going down without a fight. Mary Ann said the extra $20 per week she earned would pay a girl to clean the house and do the shopping and laundry. They'd still be $4,200 ahead in a year. There was no denying the math. *If* the goal was to save money.

"I don't want my wife working." There it was. It wasn't about money. It wasn't even about pleasing his mother. It was about his pride. The man who fought in the war for freedom wanted to suppress freedom at home because he didn't like how it made him look. Men pretended to be so strong, but they were fragile little boys. If she had to give up something she loved, he should have to feel some pain, too. If *homemaker* and *career girl* stood on opposite sides of a line in the sand for Mike, so did *wife* and *boarder* for Mary Ann. She didn't know what her future would bring, but it would not be delivered to Angeline Gentile's address.

Mary Ann put her foot down firmly. She told Mike if he wanted to live with his mother, he shouldn't get married. They would start married life on their own – or not at all. The solution lay at the end of Aberdeen Street. When Angeline's elder sister Simonetta got married, their father provided a dowry in the form of a red brick, two-flat, apartment building at the end of the block, next to Annerino's bar. Aunt Sim lived in the top unit with her husband. When he died, she went to live with her daughter – and gave her kitchen things to Junior for his bar. Spacious and clean, with two bedrooms, one bath, and an eat-in kitchen, Mary Ann liked it immediately.

Mike liked that she liked it. And he liked that his brother lived on the ground floor with his wife Doris. Happily, Mary Ann and Doris became fast friends, and everybody won. Most importantly, Angeline had her son exactly five houses away, and her apron strings could comfortably reach that far. She would still see her precious Junior every day. They could come for dinner, because that girl didn't know how to cook. Angeline felt certain of it.

[Angeline was right. Mary Ann Dinardi couldn't even make coffee.]

A week later, Mike and Mary Ann stood in the empty apartment as she pointed out where she planned to put things. Mike didn't care about furniture arrangements. He was glad her working situation and their living situation were both resolved without too much pain – for him. A truck rumbled to a stop outside and a horn tooted. Mike looked out the window and waved.

"Who's that?" Mary Ann asked.

Mike smiled and said, "A delivery." Their doorbell rang, and he opened the front door.

To Mary Ann's surprise, two men carried in a cocoa-brown, brocade, sectional sofa. Two other men brought in another matching segment, while two more carried end tables, then a coffee table, and several lamps.

The man leading the first sofa section asked, "Where do you want it, lady?"

Mary Ann stammered and whirled in a circle. "There," she decided. "Yes, there."

Once both pieces were set in an L and the various tables arranged, the men went out the door.

"Oh, Mike, it's beautiful."

"They're not done." He took Mary Ann by the shoulder and moved her out of the way. The men carried in a bedroom set next – double bed, headboard, footboard, two nightstands, a long dresser, framed mirror, and a tall bureau. "Show them where you want everything, Mare."

Mary Ann dashed into the bedroom, barely containing her excitement.

Mike looked outside again. Two men were taking a dining table and then chairs off the truck. He hadn't expected any of this, certainly hadn't asked for it. But when he told Skip Cerone he was getting married and mentioned their new apartment, Skip asked for their address and said he wanted to send something over "for the happy couple." That's what he said. "something for the happy couple." And what did he send? Three rooms of new furniture. Last week, Mike and Mary Ann went down to Montgomery Ward's and splurged on an RCA console television. They thought it was a big purchase.

Mary Ann and the crew exited the bedroom as the dining table and chairs started coming through the door. She gasped and looked at Mike with wonder and delight. He lifted his shoulder and turned his palms upward. After the last piece of furniture was in place, the men left. The apartment that had been empty in the morning looked like a home in the afternoon. All they had to do was fill the cabinets, closets, and drawers. It wasn't until later that something bothered Mary Ann when she went home and told her mother about the surprise delivery.

After describing each piece, it occurred to Mary Ann that while everything was very nice, it would have been nicer to pick out their own furniture in a store – to test different mattresses and imagine watching *I Love Lucy* from this chair or that sofa. What if she didn't like a brown sofa or a turquoise kitchen table? The fact that she liked both seemed beside the point. The furniture represented more decisions Mary Ann didn't get to make for herself. The entire male world aligned itself to make it easy for her to become a wife.

As a single young woman living at home (as was the custom of the day), Mary Ann had had a good life. She earned a comfortable living at Bell Telephone and had an active social life with her large extended family and many friends. Every week she gave money to her parents for room and board (though they never asked) and saved something for her future. She treated herself occasionally, but Mary Ann was always smart about money. Had she chosen a different path, Mary Ann could have supported herself financially without the benefit of a husband. But in her day, a good wife (especially an Italian wife) didn't work outside the home; she cooked, baked, cleaned, washed, ironed, and nursed. Mary Ann took to those tasks like a fish to mountain climbing. But that's all ahead.

November 7, 1954 turned out to be a beautiful, warm, cloudless, Indian summer day in Chicago, with golden leaves and warm breezes. Mary Ann floated down the aisle swaddled in satin, lace and seed pearls and into the arms of her only love. She also carried a small secret. November 7 was six months and one week to the day since she had agreed to marry Mike. That pushed Mary Ann's dream wedding into mid-autumn, with its chance of cold and rain. She fretted terribly about the weather in the days before the wedding, checking the forecasts almost hourly. Her mother finally ordered her to sit down and stop looking out the window every five minutes. Checking wouldn't change anything. Mary Ann's heightened state triggered the unthinkable – she got her period. On her wedding day. She didn't know how to tell Mike. He'd made it absolutely clear he intended to get to the business of being man and wife as soon as the priest signed their "permission slip." In the moment, each had one line – "I do." The rest would keep until later.

Dad's friends from the old neighborhood attended the celebration and brought fat envelopes to the reception at the Edgewater Beach Hotel. Jackie, Jimmy, Skip and some of his other Outfit pals sat with their impeccably dressed wives at a corner table at the back of the ballroom. Early in the evening, Mike took the photographer aside and pointed to their table. Don't take pictures of those people, he said. Any of them. Not even in the background. Then he slipped the guy a twenty to make sure he remembered. Decades later, he would repeat this exact procedure at the wedding receptions of his son and daughter.

Mickey hadn't looked well all day. Rather early in the reception, Angeline told her son they were leaving. She explained it away as "tired." But Mickey had been "tired" for the past few years, and everyone worried about it. Junior kissed his mother, hugged his father, and promised to call when they got to Miami, where the newlyweds planned to honeymoon for two blissful weeks at The Fontainebleau Hotel. Skip called a guy and set up everything. It was another little gift in addition to the fat envelope he stuffed into Mary Ann's bulging satin bag. Oh yeah, and all that furniture.

The bride danced so enthusiastically that she tore the lace under both arms of her dress – and she didn't care. She never got it fixed or cleaned. The dress – as is – represented her wedding day. Toward the end of the reception, someone got word to Mike that his mother was on the phone. Mickey collapsed. The doctor was on his way. A moment later, so were Mike and Mary Ann.

In the car, he didn't consult with her and didn't ask her opinion. He simply announced they weren't going to Florida. How could he at a time like this, he asked? Mary Ann sat stunned and disappointed. She told herself she understood: How could Mike go on his honeymoon knowing his father was ill? But what could he do in Chicago other than worry? Why shouldn't they go on the trip as planned? She didn't ask because she felt petty and guilty for thinking it in the first place.

On Aberdeen Street, everyone gathered around the kitchen table. The doctor came out of the bedroom and confirmed the incurable lung cancer Mickey had been keeping secret. It wasn't advanced, not yet, but there wasn't much medical science could do. The best estimate gave Mickey a couple of years. Mary Ann loved her own father very much, and couldn't imagine how she would cope with losing him. Her heart went out to Mike, and she stood in her torn wedding dress behind her husband's chair and rubbed his shoulders. What terrible, terrible news. And she still hadn't told him about getting her period! As they drove to the hotel near dawn, Mike put his hand on his bride's leg. Out of habit, Mary Ann moved it. A good girl didn't let a man put his hands on her.

Mike laughed and said, "Hey, I married you!"

She laughed, too. They both needed it. The night had taken a terrible turn. After a day that went on far longer than either hoped, they finally stood alone in the honeymoon suite of the Pick Congress Hotel. The hotel was popular with Chicago's criminal element. The newlywed's honeymoon suite was a gift from Jackie Cerone. He knew the owner. And, yes, he stuffed a fat envelope into Mary Ann's satin bag, too. Mike closed the door, and Mary Ann giggled.

"I've never been alone in a hotel room with a man," she said.

Mike puffed air and laughed. "I sure as hell hope not!"

His mortified wife then explained her menstrual predicament. She looked so pretty in her pale blue nightgown, and Mike loved her so much that he managed to laugh and said he could wait a few more days.

Mary Ann never realized how easy it was to get pregnant. About six weeks after getting married, she broke the news to her scandalized mother. "So soon?" Virginia asked, with a hint of accusation. Then she remembered her daughter's period on her wedding day and felt relieved. Mary Ann was equally stunned. Yes, they planned to have a family, expected to have one, naturally, and looked forward to one. Someday. But not before they finished writing thank you notes for the wedding presents! Some women bloom during pregnancy and radiate maternal energy. Mary Ann was not one of those women. Sick from the start, the cruelly named "morning sickness" lasted all day and throughout the duration of a miserable pregnancy.

She first thought about leaving her husband when she was five months pregnant. He was gone all night, slept all day, snapped at her about cooking and housekeeping, and she felt miserable and abandoned. One night she packed a bag and called her sister Louise to come pick her up. Louise hurried over and listened while her baby sister cried and listed grievances. When Mary Ann finally stopped crying, Louise asked the one question that ended the discussion: "What are you going to tell Ma?"

What indeed would Mary Ann tell her mother? That she changed her mind about a promise made in church before God? That she was bored, lonely and had an upset stomach, so she was leaving her husband with the intention of getting a divorce? As she unpacked the suitcase, Mary Ann took stock of her husband's crimes: He worked a lot and left her home alone. He had high expectations about housekeeping and frequently voiced displeasure at the state of their home and the quality of their meals. He doted on his family, and they were constantly under foot. Constantly. Dating Mike Gentile had been exciting. They went to nice restaurants, shows, and nightclubs. He wooed and won her. And now that he'd won her, he wanted to know what she planned to cook for dinner and when she planned to dust the living room. But he never raised his hand. He provided a generous allowance. And he was a patient, respectful, and extraordinary lover. She felt more embarrassed with each garment she removed from the suitcase.

Finally, she came to the blue silk and white lace nightgown she'd worn on her wedding night. It was very pretty but not very practical for nightly wear. Of the many nightgowns in the dresser drawer, why had she packed something that didn't even fit at the moment? And then she knew why. Because the first night she spent with Mike Gentile – even though she had the amazing bad luck to get her period – was the most memorable night of her life. She could walk away from the marriage and the wedding and even the elaborate, ruined wedding dress boxed in the closet. But she couldn't walk away from the memories of the night she felt a naked man pressed against her for the first time. As she had hastily packed to leave him, Mary Ann came upon the blue nightgown and couldn't leave it. And she couldn't leave him. It wouldn't be easy for two people more stubborn than wise. Mary Ann put the nightgown back in her drawer and made Coffee And for Louise.

That nightgown stayed in her dresser drawer, wrapped in the same tissue paper from 1954, for the rest of her life.

6 COURTHOUSE ADJACENT

On July 29, 1955, Mike and Mary Ann became Dad and Mom when Michael John Gentile, Jr. joined his new family on Aberdeen Street. And wouldn't you know it, six months later, on New Year's Eve 1955, Mike knocked up his wife again. Mom later said she owed the second pregnancy to that second champagne cocktail. The first pregnancy hadn't been a happy time; the second fared no better. At the same time, Mike's business kept growing, and things never looked better financially. He didn't want her to be unhappy. But she didn't always seem to understand that he worked the long hours for their benefit. She watched too many movies. That's what he said. They gave her screwy ideas.

But Dad knew she was right about the hours. They were fine for a young, unmarried man. But he had a wife, a child, and another on the way. He needed to be *part* of a family if he wanted to *have* a family. As mob adjacent luck would have it, his Outfit friends knew about an opportunity. A tavern called the Bridge offered something that made it perfect: By a zoning peculiarity, because of the Bridge's location on Dearborn Street and its proximity to the nearby courthouse, it could be open for business no later than 5:00 PM. Dad could be home for supper every night. He sold the bar and bought the Bridge.

Mom was delighted to have him home at night, and in some respects their marriage started from scratch. She worked harder at learning to cook the foods he liked and tried her best to make a good home. Mike threw himself into fatherhood, and our family photo albums showed numerous pictures of father and son gazing adoringly at each other.

The Bridge was a success from the start. Bigger, brighter, with a better kitchen and more seating, Dad saw nothing but opportunity. He started by giving it the Mike treatment: First you clean a place really good to see what you've got; then you make things appealing; you treat everybody right; and you go home with money every night. While Dad ran the bar, Uncle John worked the bigger kitchen with a bigger menu.

Like its predecessor on Clybourn, the Bridge drew a mob crowd. Fact: Drawing a mob-connected crowd increased the allure of a joint. People liked a little danger with their martini. They either came to watch and drink, or they came to drink and bet, or they came to bet and stayed to drink, and then the loan sharks swept in to dine on the desperate. There was nothing Mike could do, not that he was inclined to do anything. Jackie, Skip, and Jimmy were regulars, and their friends and associates followed. The mob bosses brought the underbosses, and the underbosses brought the foot soldiers, and soon the place was crawling with somebody connected to somebody about something. That brought the looky-loos and the climbers. They all bought drinks, and a lot of them ate.

The Bridge became an exercise in Great American Democracy. Cops, lawyers, criminals, and judges elbowed each other as equals at the bar for drinks, food – and discreet gambling. You could put $5 on the daily double, order a hot lunch, and get a drink – all in less than an hour. It was the United Nations of mob joints. Various crews from various parts of the city used the Bridge as a clubhouse and met to hash out grievances and settle disputes. Prosecutors met with lawyers to negotiate plea deals before court dates. Lawyers met with their nervous clients. Judges met with their bookies. Mike never asked questions. He poured drinks and put money in the drawer. The joint was never empty, from the time he opened at 11:00 AM until the time he closed on the dot at 5:00 PM. The cash register made as much noise as the jukebox.

Late one night the following summer, in her last trimester during a brutal summer heatwave, Mom lay in front of a fan praying for September 30. Though that was her official due date, she hoped the baby would come a day early. Dad was born October 29 and Michael Junior on July 29. She liked the idea of "Mark" or "Cynthia" being born on September 29. She would get half her wish in a little over a month. Her baby would end up being born on September 29 – another boy, but for reasons he never made clear, Dad detested the name Mark. He told her to pick anything else. Mom liked the alliteration of Jeffrey Gerard Gentile.

While she wished for a swift conclusion to a miserable pregnancy, Dad went next door to Annerino's Bar for a drink. Michael was asleep in his crib, and she was dozing in front of the television when a commotion woke her. Mom hoisted herself off the sofa and lumbered to the window, where she heard her husband threatening to bust somebody's "fucking head open."

Dad had been having a quiet drink with Jimmy Annerino. His place drew a neighborhood crowd, mostly Italians. Occasionally he'd get one of the Irish alkies who got kicked out of their own joints. A drunk started getting loud. Jimmy told the guy to shut up, and there was a short burst of swearing back and forth. But the drunk wouldn't let it go. Dad put himself between the drunk and the bar while Jimmy reached for a pistol. The drunk was big, and Dad was maybe 140-pounds with a 10-pound brick in each hand. But Dad doesn't give a shit. He gave the drunk a smack upside the head that probably made his ear ring for a month. Then he shoved him down on the floor and dared the drunk to get up "and I'll split your fucking head open with a fucking bottle."

Which were the exact words Mom heard coming through the open windows. She moved as quickly as possible, checking on baby Michael – still asleep – and then pulled herself down the stairs and pounded on John and Doris' apartment door. She was panting, and Doris maneuvered her to a chair. Mom said Mike was having a "headache" next door, so John put on shoes and rushed over.

For his efforts, John got hit in the side of the head with a bar stool almost immediately upon entering the bar and went down hard. What happened was this: The drunk – apparently learning nothing about pissing off a skinny Italian guy holding a bottle – got up. On his way up, he grabbed the leg of a bar stool, lifted it as he rose, and swung just as John came in the door. Bam! Jimmy ran around the bar with a pistol and beat the guy senseless all the way to the door.

The battered drunk staggered blindly. He wanted out as much as Jimmy wanted him out. Finally, Jimmy stopped swinging and opened the door. He lifted his foot and kicked the drunk in the stomach. That's when Dad grabbed the gun. Infuriated, he fired several warning shots – "above that drunken Irish prick's head," he later swore – and the guy ran off, never to be seen at Annerino's Bar again.

Nothing clears out a bar faster than gunfire. Customers scattered, and some busybody called the police. Jimmy took the gun, and Dad helped his brother up off the floor. He knew exactly what to do next. It didn't matter that it was after midnight on a weeknight. Dad walked behind the bar and placed a call to a house around the corner, to the home of Skip Cerone. Around the time he hung up the phone, he heard the police sirens in the distance. Jimmy Annerino yelled at Dad and called him a hot-head.

"The drunken Irish prick hit my brother with a bar stool. He's lucky I didn't kill him."

At that time, Skip Cerone was a man of undeniable power. There wasn't a cop in the city who didn't know his face, either as a patron or a suspect. He came running around the corner wearing a bathrobe, pajama bottoms and bedroom slippers. Skip arrived at the same time the cop car pulled in front of the bar. People started coming out of their houses and it became a neighborhood scene. Jimmy glared at Dad. Hot-head. Mom stood on the sidewalk with Doris. Dad held up his hand for her to stay back; his smile said everything was all right.

Skip walked over to the police car and told the cops no one needed them. No one's been harmed. Nobody needed to make a report about nothing. You can go. Skip had that kind of power. And the two cops got in the car, turned off the flashing lights, and drove away quietly into the night. "People are trying to sleep, for Christ's sake," Skip said. It was just that simple.

After the cops left, Dad told Mom not to worry; he'd be right up. She went back into the house with Doris while Mike and Jimmy went into the empty bar with Skip. Jimmy poured drinks while Skip examined the lump on John's head, and Dad offered a blow-by-blow. By the end of the story, Skip agreed with Dad: The drunk was lucky Dad didn't kill him. Then Skip finished his drink and shuffled home in the middle of the night.

Lesson: When you're mob adjacent, the police are often nearby. But usually they aren't necessary.

Mickey lost his long battle with cancer in 1957. It was made easier, his wife said, by the medication. He never suffered. Angeline took great comfort in that. She wouldn't be so lucky when her time came.

With a second baby, our family needed more room. We moved a shocking (to Grandma Gentile) ten-minutes west, to an apartment on Maypole Avenue, in an upper unit on a street lined with two-flat apartment buildings. Michael remembers living in Aunt Sim's building on Aberdeen; my earliest memories take place on Maypole.

Mom said I was a hazard for the first five years. If she left toys in the living room, Michael would walk around the pile. I would walk through it, fall, and cut myself. Back on Aberdeen Street, I had my stomach pumped after Mom feared I drank bleach (I hadn't). I also pulled a pot of scalding soup off the stove and down the front of me. Second degree burns, no scars. Decades later, Mom said if the things that happened then happened to a child today, the Department of Child and Family Services would be pounding on the door. But I was not abused; I was clumsy. Years later, Mom said if she had a nickel for every time she found me bleeding and screaming she would have been able to pay off their mortgage.

The good times and hospital visits on Maypole ended abruptly with an eviction notice in 1959. Several of the two-flats were slated for demolition to make room for a school. For my family, the eviction brought an opportunity. In the late 1950s and early 1960s, many Italian families followed the new expressways to the western suburbs. My parents wanted a house, and they wanted to be settled before Michael turned five in July 1960 and started kindergarten the following September.

Aunt Rachel and Uncle Larry were building a new house "out west." Bobby Annerino, Jimmy's son, was building whole blocks of suburban houses in Wood Dale, farther west along I-90, known as the Eisenhower Expressway. Aunt Rachel heard about a three-bedroom, one bath, brick house with a finished basement on 47th Avenue in Bellwood from her friend, Sophia Pantaleo, who lived across the alley. Aunt Rachel told Dad about it, and in 1960 our family left Little Italy and moved to Bellwood.

I remember walking up the concrete steps to what would become our new home – Mom tripped and staggered but didn't fall. I remember Mom packing on Maypole, and moving day. And then all my stuff was in the small front bedroom in Bellwood with white shutters on the windows. Not long after, Aunt Marie and Uncle Joe moved to Bellwood-adjacent Hillside. Relatives weren't the only people drawn to the western suburbs. Quiet townships like Bellwood, Hillside, and Melrose Park became havens for mob connected and mob adjacent families like mine.

7 AIRPORT ADJACENT

Abrief lesson in aviation history: In 1942, Douglas Aircraft built Orchard Field Airport northwest of Chicago to manufacture C-54 airplanes during World War II. In 1949, the airport was renamed to honor U.S. Navy pilot and Medal of Honor winner Edward O'Hare. By the 1950s, America's third largest city had outgrown Midway Airport. When O'Hare Field opened as a commercial facility in 1955, it served as the epicenter of the new global jet age. President John F. Kennedy attended a dedication ceremony for the new main terminal in 1963, such was the force of its national importance. Later that year, the President planned a trip to Dallas. In that uniquely Chicago mob adjacent way, war hero Edward O'Hare was the son of "Artful" Eddie O'Hare, the man responsible for managing the Outfit's Wall Street investments. When the senior O'Hare opened his mouth to the Feds about the Outfit's activities, his reward came in the form of shotgun blasts to oblivion. End of history lesson.

Along Mannheim Road in Schiller Park, a glittering strip of new hotels and motels sprang up almost overnight along the main road leading to O'Hare Airport. The north/south four-lane strip of asphalt transformed from a dusty stretch of nothing into the most swinging street in Chicago, complete with show girls, big name entertainers, world-class amenities, and (discreet, mob-operated) gambling, all within a ten-minute cab ride to or from O'Hare. From North Avenue to the airport, neon signs and blinking lights beckoned travelers, revelers, and convention-goers to the Sahara Inn, the Air Host, the Lido, the Concord, the Guest House, the Golden Cleaver, and other joints up and down the freshly paved street.

The money used to build up Mannheim Road came from guys like Outfit "CEO" Sam Giancana, and he got it from the Outfit's personal piggy bank – union pension funds. Giancana saw a future that looked like Las Vegas, right there on Mannheim Road. For the moment, profits came from discreet gambling and prostitution at the hotels and motels up and down the street. But the bosses fully expected Illinois to legalize open gambling in the near future. They had people down in Springfield working the legislature. Until then, there was plenty of money to be made the old-fashioned way – in secret.

"The Outfit really was the most powerful crime family in the country for the majority of the 20th century," according to former FBI agent Richard Stilling. "The families in New York might have had Chicago on pure numbers and general perception, but on influence and the ability to get things done, the Outfit takes the cake." Chicago's dominance in crime proved an old real estate adage about "location, location, location." Its location on a Great Lake in the heart of the Midwest put Chicago at the crossroads of American commerce. Practically every truck, train, and airplane crossing America passed through Chicago. And the Outfit took a bite out of each one.

Opening a joint was easy; you just needed money, and getting money had never been a problem for the Outfit. Running a place profitably was another story. It took people with brains, people you could trust. By the early 1960s, Jackie Cerone had been serving as Sam Giancana's second-in-command for more than a decade. He'd come up the ranks as Giancana's bodyguard and chauffeur before advancing in the organization, the same route Giancana had taken for mob boss Paul Ricca two decades prior.

Dad met Jackie and his cousins, Skip and Jimmy Cerone, in the late 1940s at Patsy Spilotro's restaurant on Grand and Ogden. They were just guys from the Old Neighborhood. Fifteen years older than Dad, Jackie had an eye for talent, and he liked what he saw. Dad hustled that produce route on the North Side – the Italian Catholic cleaned up in the Jewish neighborhood. And when Skip set him up on the South Side, Dad knocked it out of the park again. Later, his bars on Clybourn Avenue and Dearborn Street made money because he ran a tight, clean ship and took good care of people. Dad didn't drink too much and never fooled with drugs; he didn't gamble or bother the whores, and he kept his mouth shut. Bars and taverns were profitable, but Dad always wanted a nightclub. He got his wish when Jackie mentioned an opportunity and asked Dad if he was interested in buying a new joint in Schiller Park. It was on Mannheim Road, a street the media called "the new Glitter Gulch." Dad bought Orlando's Hideaway practically sight unseen on Jackie's say-so.

[In one of those curious coincidences that follow our family, Dad bought Orlando's Hideaway from Tom Coyne in 1962. Mr. Coyne was friends with Frank Quinn, Michael's future father-in-law, two decades hence. Many years later, Michael met the former owner. Mr. Coyne said it was a very simple transaction: Dad gave Coyne money, Coyne gave Dad keys, and Orlando's Hideaway opened the next night under new ownership without interruption or change.]

In early 1962, Dad left Uncle John behind to run the Bridge and took over Orlando's Hideaway. But Uncle John couldn't make the Bridge work without Dad's magic touch and watchful eye. Within two years the tavern teetered on the brink of ruin. With Dad's consent, Uncle John sold the Bridge at a loss. He then joined Dad's new venture on Glitter Gulch. The family that bought the Bridge changed the name to the Aquarius Pub and owned if for the next forty years.

Chicago Tribune reporter Robert Wiedrich wrote on June 23, 1962, "Inside the night clubs, bars, and theater lounges that line the highway, the jet noises mingle with the primitive beat of drums and the brassy wail of jazz combos. This is the new multimillion dollar "Glitter Gulch" of Chicago – a playground offering wine, women, and song. The prices are high."

Wiedrich made the inevitable Las Vegas comparison and talked about "the flesh traps of Calumet City and Cicero" losing out to their glitzy new cousin in Schiller Park. In actuality, the Outfit simply took its business model – high-priced wine, women, and song – and moved it from one location to another. Sometimes an operation moved to escape overly-ambitious law enforcement, sometimes because of expansion into new territory. Schiller Park was tight as a virgin and ready to be plucked.

What Calumet and Cicero lost, Schiller Park gained, not that it mattered. The money went into the same pocket at the end of the night – to the Boss of Bosses, Sam Giancana. Las Vegas was half a day away by air. It was a lot easier to keep an eye on your operation – and your money – when it was right down the road. Giancana lived in Oak Park, less than ten-miles from the Outfit's investments on Mannheim Road. His gamble paid off big, and the joints printed money. At least for a while.

According to Wiedrich, "On week nights, when night club and tavern owners elsewhere in the Chicago area are standing at their front doors watching the patrons go by, greeters in tuxedos, scantily clad waitresses, and over-worked bartenders of "The Gulch" are packing them in."

Deep-pocketed businessmen were the primary marks of the Outfit operations on Mannheim. Next came the locals from the nearby suburbs, who found dining and nightclubbing on Mannheim Road more convenient than going downtown. And, of course, there were the ever-present hoodlums and hustlers looking for action. Alcohol, prostitution, and gambling continued to drive Outfit profits as they had since the days of Johnny Torrio and Al Capone.

The Air Host Motel opened on December 3, 1962, and advertised rooms for "permanent guests" at $65 per guest, per month. The place was sleek and modern in that uniquely jet age way. A red shield-shaped sign stood on the corner of the property. Horizontal rows of narrow, white motion lines cut through slanting, stacked, white letters spelling out Air Host, as if the two words were flying off the sign. Facing Mannheim Road, an aluminum walkway connected a split-level building containing the nightclub and restaurant with a two-story L-shaped motel. A small swimming pool stood in the center of the property, with parking spaces lining the perimeter. On most nights, there wasn't enough parking. The city didn't make a fuss. There was plenty of parking along Mannheim Road.

Like most of the places along Mannheim, Air Host was new. A dapper weasel who called himself Sol Elegant owned the place – in theory. Dad said Elegant converted a pair of rooms on the top floor into a suite and lived onsite, with "hot and cold running cocktail waitresses" going in and out all day. Elegant's ownership was only on paper. Ultimately, Sam Giancana controlled the Air Host. Fact of the matter, Giancana had a finger in each place, one way or another, and Jackie Cerone kept an eye on the Outfit's money along the Strip, with local help from Rocco Pranno. Orlando's Hideaway was the window-dressing designed to draw crowds to the adjacent Air Host Motel, where the Outfit made its real money. You needed the flash to attract the cash. To get a liquor license to run one of those flashy joints, you needed to be clean. And Mike Gentile was so clean he practically squeaked.

Orlando's Hideaway was Dad's biggest operation in terms of the overhead, inventory, staff, taxes, and the million little details that could add up to big trouble if something went wrong. The link between the adjacent Air Host Motel was first a blessing, then a curse. Food and beverages from

Dad's restaurant kept the high-rollers rolling, and the Air Host hospitality revenue supplemented the cost of the pricey talent he booked in the nightclub.

The design of Orlando's Hideaway was sleek and uncluttered. The name played off the popular song, "Hernando's Hideaway" from the Broadway musical *Pajama Game*. A pair of glass doors facing Mannheim Road led into a small vestibule with gray carpet on the floor and stairs. Photos of the current headline attraction hung on the wall to the left. One set of stairs to the right led up to the white-tablecloth restaurant; another set straight ahead led down to the nightclub. Halfway down the stairs, patrons were enveloped in a silky darkness.

At the foot of the stairs and to the left, the bar ran the length of the club. The stainless-steel surface was padded around the edges with round black bumpers; the same black material covered the front of the bar. The stools (some of which ended up in front of Dad's basement bar in Bellwood) had curved backs made of shiny black spindles, with black padded seats that matched the bar trim. Recessed lights over the bar were hooked up to a dimmer, and a big wall mirror reflected candlelight from small glass globes on the tables and frosted sconces between long, oval mirrors on the opposite wall. A cluster of round deuces and four-tops filled the rest of the space. Black tables. Black chairs. Dark walls.

[Nightclub 101, courtesy of Mike Gentile: You don't need shelves lined with liquor bottles on the wall behind the bar. People don't shop for drinks. They know what they want. When a guy comes in, he expects you'll have what he drinks. If you don't, you're running a bum joint, no matter how many bottles are lined up on dusty shelves.]

Three or four cocktail waitresses in short, black outfits worked each shift, depending on the night. The newspaper ad for waitresses said, "must be attractive." But anybody bothering the girls quickly got shown the door – and not always gently. Dad said one time he threw a guy *up* the stairs after he grabbed a waitress by the ass. He also kept an eight-inch leather-covered cudgel under the bar in case someone needed a crack upside the head. (I have it today, and I've wondered how many heads it cracked over the years.) A small stage to the right jutted into the room, with a clutter of gel-covered spotlights hanging above the edge. Six concrete steps went up to the dressing area behind the stage; six steps down led to the office/storeroom. This simple place minted money over the next few years.

My brother and I thought it was the coolest thing ever. Big name entertainers played in Dad's show room, people like Martha Raye, Phyllis Diller, Louis Prima, and Keely Smith. People I saw on *television!* Eddie Fisher played at Orlando's in 1963. It was a pity booking. Fisher's career was dead in the water after that Elizabeth Taylor business. Sinatra and his Rat Pack were performing next door at the Sahara Inn, and Frank wanted to help his cuckold pal. A request came trickling downstream from Sinatra to Sam Giancana to Jackie Cerone to Dad. And Dad booked Eddie Fisher. He didn't give a shit about a sex scandal. Fisher played a two-week engagement to mostly full houses. Even if people booed – and sometimes they did – they were booing over Orlando's three-drink minimum. Dad asked Mom if she wanted to see Fisher's show. Mom said she wouldn't be caught dead in the same room with Eddie Fisher after what he did to Debbie Reynolds. (There will be more on this later.)

Upstairs, Nick Giannotti ran an Italian restaurant. Giannotti was quickly becoming a celebrity chef long before being a Celebrity Chef became a Thing. Nick worked the room, prompting diners to sprinkle a little Parmesan on the escarole soup, suggesting a slice of homemade ricotta cheesecake, or explaining how a dish was made. A little over a year after Dad bought Orlando's Hideaway, Giannotti started itching for a bigger canvas to paint on, so he took over a place on Roosevelt Road in Forest Park. Naturally, in our mob adjacent world, Giannotti's new location turned out to be the former Armory Lounge.

The Armory had been Sam Giancana's unofficial headquarters for years, until the constant Fed surveillance became too burdensome. (Fun fact: The Armory was so named because it was directly across the street from a former World War II torpedo factory.) Giannotti's new restaurant served as a mainstay of fine Italian cuisine for decades. Nick eventually passed the torch to his son, Vic, who carried the family business into the new millennium, eventually launching a line of premium bottled marinara pasta sauces under the Giannotti brand name.

After Giannotti left, Dad brought Uncle John in to run the restaurant. Under Dad's careful control, the restaurant thrived and began attracting a celebrity crowd. One night, a pair of entertainers walked over from the much larger Sahara Inn next door to have dinner at Orlando's Hideaway. Former TV costars, Jackie Gleason and Art Carney toured the country as a comedy act in the 1960s. They enjoyed their meal so much that they sent for the chef. Uncle John blushed, hemmed, and hawed under the praise of his high-profile diners. Gleason, a dedicated gourmand, couldn't say enough about the veal, which Uncle John promptly re-christened Veal a' la Gleason. "Ralph Kramden" and "Ed Norton" were staples of our childhood. Monday through Friday, WFLD, Channel 32, broadcast reruns of *The Honeymooners* at 10:00 PM. We never missed an episode, and Michael and I were bitterly disappointed we didn't get to see the legends.

There was quite an episode at the restaurant one night. During the afternoon, a load of live snails was delivered for escargot, flown in special and direct from O'Hare for a big dinner party that night. Uncle John put the snails in a pot but neglected to cover it securely. When he came back several hours later to start the evening prep, he discovered the sneaky little mollusks had made a break for it. Hundreds of snails crawled over the stove, counters, floor, even up the walls, leaving slimy trails everywhere. His daughter Tammy said her father tried to cook snails at home years later – and forgot to put the lid on the pot again. His wife nearly fainted when she saw snails crawling all over her kitchen.

Dad maintained a friendly competition with the owner of the motel next to the Air Host. Pint-sized Jewish gangster-wannabe Mandel (Manny) Skar was an ex-con with a dream to dominate Mannheim Road. The Sahara Inn was his $10.8 million crown jewel (built with money milked from the unions, naturally). Stone Park's largest business was the sale of liquor at taverns and lounges. Rocco Pranno controlled the city, as well as nearby Franklin Park, Schiller Park, Melrose Park, and Northlake. He also served as president of Manny Skar's Sahara Motel Corporation. Under his leadership, Skar leveraged nearly $11 million in union loans to build a motel that was later appraised at $2.5 million. The rest of the money, predictably, ended up in the pockets of mob bosses.

Skar gilded the walls of his kingdom, lined the pool with torches, and put in a sky-high diving board that would have intimidated Esther Williams. Girls in hot pink bikinis served drinks while gargoyles on the wall spouted water into an Olympic-size swimming pool – a Hollywood version of Las Vegas dropped in the middle of a western Chicago suburb. Michael and I liked to sneak over and gape at the overdone splendor. Imagine a Technicolor musical set in a Sahara Desert luxury hotel, and you're halfway there. Dad and Manny Skar liked to compare nightclub grosses. The funny thing was that while Skar's Celebrity Lounge at the Sahara was larger, grander and had bigger names, the massive overhead dwarfed Orlando's lean operation. On a per-head basis, Orlando's restaurant and nightclub sometimes out-earned Skar's nightclub. Gilded walls don't fill a cash register.

The Sahara Inn invited controversy before the first guest even signed in. When the 267-room motel opened in 1962, it was already the subject of six – six! – separate ongoing criminal investigations, principally due to interest by the Illinois Director of Public Safety into Skar's mob associations. Schiller Park opened its investigation into the new business to determine the true value of the property for tax purposes. The Illinois Liquor Control

Commission opened their investigation. Because of his previous criminal convictions, Skar was barred from obtaining a liquor license. His solution came in the form of fronts – Larry Roth served as President of Park Inn, Inc., which technically owned the Sahara, along with Park's wife, Ann, serving as secretary. Like Sol Elegant, the Roth's ownership existed only on paper. So, of course, the police also opened an investigation into allegations of fraud. Regardless, the Sahara opened on June 6, and Bobby Darin performed to a sold-out crowd. Once the place was open, Skar immediately broke ground on a massive "convention center" attached to the back of the Sahara. He fully expected to have a license to operate the first open gambling casino in Illinois within two years.

Skar was an old-school impresario who fancied himself somewhere between Florenz Ziegfeld and Mike Todd. He personally hosted "Manny Skar's Sahara Club" in the garish Celebrity Lounge, which he described modestly as a little bit of Broadway, a bit of Hollywood, and a whole lot of Miami Beach and Las Vegas. "Sahara Starlets" in gold harem costumes shimmied for the guests in floor shows that invited scandal. VIPs dined at the Sultan's Table, surrounded by gold carpeting, gold walls and gold chairs.

The scarlet décor in the Sahara's Club Gigi offered high-end dining at high-end prices featuring:

Jumbo Louisiana Shrimp Cocktail Supreme - $1.25 (about $10 in 2017)
Broiled African Lobster Tail, Drawn Butter - $5.50 (about $40 today)
Filet Mignon, Béarnaise Sauce - $6.50 (about $54 today)

The wine list included bottles of 1955 Piper Heidsieck Brut for $5.00 or 1955 Bollinger Brut champagne for $9.00. (A bottle of 1955 Bollinger Brut would cost about $1,200 today – wholesale.)

Big and big-ish names performed. Zsa Zsa Gabor attended the grand opening, where Bobby Darin sang to wife Sandra Dee in the audience. Comedian George Jessel filled the second half of the bill. Future dates were contracted with performers like Patti Page, Johnny Ray, Jackie Mason, Jack Carter, Vic Damone, and Betty Hutton. Fred Waring brought his orchestra, and Frank Sinatra brought his Rat Pack. Eddie Fisher picked up a few dates, too.

Bobby Darin was a hit the second time he played at the Sahara, and he got hit, too. Depending on whose account one reads, Darin was either an innocent victim of thugs, or a deadbeat weakling who owed money to a drug dealer. The incident occurred shortly after midnight when several men, seated at a ringside table, created a disturbance. Darin, who had been singing, walked off the stage and later got into a scuffle. Reports vary as to where the scuffle took place, but everybody agrees Darin got roughed up. The police interceded, and the assailants fled in two cars. The authorities didn't question the victim, nor did Darin sign a complaint.

The Sahara did such great business that an overflow crowd drifted off to fill other spots along Glitter Gulch. The rising tide lifted all joints. But by 1963, what started out golden began to tarnish. Skar lost control of the Sahara and sold it to singing cowboy star Gene Autry, a man he detested. But that was all right; Skar had a plan.

Something else simmered beneath the surface of the glitz and glamour: Crime. Undercover investigations revealed some of the hotels and motels were used for something other than entertaining locals and providing lodging for tired businessmen between flights. Imagine! The local police often preferred to take a mob handout than do the paperwork that came with an arrest. They would have professed to be "shocked, shocked," like Claude Rains' Captain Renault in *Casablanca* to find gambling and prostitution on Mannheim Road. But it was there. You didn't even have to look very hard. Because most of the time, Chicago didn't care.

Dogged mob sleuth Bob Wiedrich described one motel where detectives discovered a string of first-floor rooms reserved by a Chicago madam who provided "intimate services." He wrote, "One newly-opened motel has a wing of rooms with doors that can be opened only by a buzzer from the desk or with a grooved type of cards inserted into special locks." The authorities believed the secret rooms were being used for prostitution, gambling, and Outfit meetings. Shocking.

That same year, Michael started first grade at St. Simeon Grammar School in Bellwood. He appeared in the school play the following year – as a doctor. In his big scene, a mother came running to him with a doll's body in one hand and the doll's head in the other.

She wailed, "Doctor, doctor, my baby's head fell off!"

My brother the doctor said, "There's a lot of that going around these days."

Laughs followed. I remember being pleased for him as I sat in the audience with Mom. Dad didn't come to watch his son's stage debut. He was home – in bed, asleep in the middle of the day. Not long after we moved to Bellwood, a strange new normal descended. Suddenly, Michael and I had to be quiet at home because Dad worked nights and slept during the day. He left the house every night after dinner, always immaculately dressed, the most stylish man we've ever known.

Michael and I had "jobs" now: Dad paid us to polish his shoes. He had a huge walk-in closet in the basement. Cedar-lined and running almost the entire width of the house, two doors opened with a whoosh to reveal rows of suits, sport jackets, top coats, trousers, shirts, and sweaters. The inside looked like a department store – rows of dress shirts arranged chromatically and by style (French cuff, long sleeve, short sleeve, sport), jackets, suits, pants, top coats, car coats, rain coats. Shelves held boxes containing assorted fedoras. Floor-to-ceiling shelves along the sides held shoes – wingtips, cap toe, monk strap, oxfords, and loafers in black, brown, and oxblood. Sometimes I would go in there and close the doors, inhaling the aroma of cedar, feeling the luxurious fabrics, and looking at my distorted reflection in the polished shoes.

When Dad got dressed, he went all out. But there was never anything dandyish about it. Dad dressed like a gentleman, the kind of gentleman who took ladies in mink stoles to fancy nightclubs and usually got laid in the back seat of a Desoto for his efforts. His dresser drawers held dozens of monogrammed handkerchiefs and enough socks and underwear for a platoon. Like any proper Italian man of his era, Dad had a stash of Italian knit sweaters in every color and style from makers like Leonardo Strassi, DaVinci, and other big-name manufacturers.

Dad was flying high, literally and figuratively. He described going to the second fight between Cassius Clay and Sonny Liston. Of the famous first-round knockout, Dad said he went to take a piss and, "By the time I got back, the fight was over." Another time he took a weekend jaunt with his pals to New York for the 1964 World's Fair. His wife stayed home with the children. He brought me a T-shirt. I have a picture of me wearing it.

As the summers wore on, Mom's solution to two, bored, active boys sat in the broiling, asphalt parking lot of the Air Host – a swimming pool. So, she called a cab. Imagine what big shots Michael and I felt like riding alone in the back of a taxi. Think about it: Our mother sent us off alone – ages eight- and nine-years old – in a taxi driven by a man she'd never seen before. Oh yeah, and he's taking us to a motel. Remember this was another time, and in some ways another planet. The cab company was mob-owned and taking us to a mob-friendly joint. We were perfectly safe. The driver dropped us off and Dad paid the fare. Then Michael and I spent the afternoon in the pool while Dad took care of office work. Waitresses fawned over us like little princes and kept a steady stream of snacks coming out to the pool. We were under strict orders from Dad: Our best behavior – or else.

"Would you darling little boys like some ice cream?"

"Yes, please. Thank you very much."

Once, Michael came running back to the pool practically vibrating with excitement. He'd gone down to the club to use the toilet and saw Dad at the bar arguing. A guy was yelling and pointing his finger in Dad's face. Suddenly, Dad grabbed the guy's necktie and pulled until the man's face met the surface of the bar. Michael said the guy's head bounced. Then he went down like a wet noodle. Dad was a skinny guy, but don't fuck with him.

Sometimes Dad got us a room to change clothes or nap in the afternoon. By the time he finished work, Michael and I were usually fried and exhausted. And despite the short ride from the Air Host to our house on 47th Avenue, sometimes we fell asleep in the car. One time, Dad decided to play a joke on Mom. Michael – naturally – went along with the scheme. The two conspirators walked into the house. Mom looked around and asked, "Where's Jeffrey?" Michael and Dad looked at each other and made a big show of pretending they forgot me. Mom spent half a second hysterical before Dad laughed and said I was asleep in the backseat of the car. Wise guys.

Around this time, one of those mob adjacent moments occurred – one of those things that don't happen to other people. Dad's best friends, Johnny DiModica and Sammy Cicero, served as Godfather to Michael and me respectively and were often around. We called them "Goombah Johnny" and "Goombah Sammy." Sammy chose a more traditional path – married, with two daughters, and a Singer sewing machine store – but Johnny hadn't settled down.

He'd blow into the house like a party in custom-made shoes, looking like a million, and ready to lose a million on one toss of the dice. An architect by trade but a gambler by profession, Johnny had style by the bucket. He was the first person I knew with a telephone in his car. Goombah Johnny drove an epic baby blue Cadillac with an enormous antenna on top. The phone was big as a shoebox, wedged between the passenger and driver seats. The car was cool, but cooler was the pair of schnauzers named Buttons and Jo-Jo. Goombah Johnny turned up with them one day, and we fell in love. The dogs wore red, plaid overcoats, because he said they didn't like the cold. I believed him. Streaked shades of silver, gray and black, the hyperactive love muffins only wanted to play. So, while Goombah Johnny visited with Mom and Dad, Michael and I rolled around in the backyard with the dogs. We couldn't decide which was sadder – when Goombah Johnny left, or when he left with Buttons and Jo-Jo.

And then, one day Goombah Johnny disappeared. Gone.

Dad didn't seem especially concerned. We heard him tell Mom, "It probably has something to do with a broad." Most curious was the lack of concern. Goombah Johnny remained "disappeared" for more than a decade.

One day he turned up. Except now he was John Martin, and no one seemed the least puzzled. Now that Michael and I were older, Dad explained what really happened. Johnny had two problems – one concerned a broad (as Dad suspected), and the other involved the broad's husband, who happened to be a mob underboss. (You have to admire a man with the stones to bang a mob underboss' wife.) The broad wanted to leave her husband, but Johnny didn't want to marry her. He just wanted to screw around. That made her mad, so she told her husband she was leaving him – for Johnny DiModica. Naturally, the outraged underboss wanted to kill him, so Goombah Johnny decided it was time to "disappear" himself before someone did it for him.

When he got word that the underboss went to prison, Johnny tested the waters and eased into town with his new name. (He gave Buttons and Jo-Jo to his sister before he "disappeared.") He was John Martin for a few years. Then the underboss had a heart attack in prison, and the vendetta died with him. Johnny DiModica was back. A few years later, he met a beautiful redhead named Syd and married almost immediately. Before long he was a family man with children and settled in Phoenix, where he worked as an architect for the rest of his life.

If I disappeared, I'd like to think someone would be worried. And look for me. I wouldn't want them saying my disappearance "probably had something to do with a broad, and would you pass the salt?"

On Friday, November 22, 1963, something unimaginable happened: Television as I knew it ceased to exist. The day had taken a strange turn. The nun teaching our second-grade class at St. Simeon suddenly left the room and came back shaken, with a radio. That's how we learned the President of the United States had been shot in Dallas. Upon the announcement of his death, classes were cancelled.

When I got home, there was nothing on television. Nothing but news. Everywhere. Even the UHF channels pre-empted regular programming, taken over by unprecedented wall-to-wall, 24-hour-a-day news. All other programming vanished – *Superman* and *I Love Lucy* reruns, even cartoons! During the funeral, the president's dignified widow and her brave, enchanting children became images and icons that defined my youth. Over the next few weeks I learned about life, death, murder, and grief over the mocking Thanksgiving holiday following the young president's slaughter.

J. Edgar Hoover's FBI bungled the investigation so badly that Hoover backed the "lone gunman" theory because it was the only explanation that didn't make his FBI look asleep-at-the-wheel while several gunmen took out the President of the United States. Bobby's murder in 1968 was also an act of mob retribution against the Kennedy clan, according to Chuck Giancana. He claims Sirhan Sirhan played the Lee Harvey Oswald role of designated patsy. But at least in this case, Sirhan actually shot Bobby Kennedy.

Decades after the assassinations, I said something about the tragic murders. Dad shocked me and called the slain Kennedy brothers – I will never forget his exact words – "ass-biters who got what they deserved." This is history as I learned it. The mythic images of Camelot – the family frolics at Hyannis Port, the touch football games on broad expanses of lawn, gleaming white sail boats, and sun-kissed faces – persist today as Ralph Lauren advertisements. The Outfit's reality was not the stuff of high-end fashion ads. When business associates cheated, lied, or went back on their promises, turncoats could – and should – expect deadly consequences. That was the lesson we learned as children.

8 GIANCANA ADJACENT

Michael and I met a new friend at Orlando's Hideaway not long after Dad bought the place. Dad introduced him as Mr. Sam. He was a small, quiet, balding man, always perfectly tailored. We had no idea of his epic backstory. Mr. Sam was simply another face from the old neighborhood who popped into our lives from time to time. He spoke to us as if we were miniature adults and complimented Dad on our manners. He said, "You got a good little crew here, Mike," and laughed.

Over the summer, we saw Mr. Sam meet with Jackie or Skip and some of Dad's other friends in the closed nightclub. After the Armory got too hot from police surveillance and FBI bugs, Sam Giancana started using Orlando's Hideaway for occasional meetings. Frank Sinatra was performing next door at the Sahara Inn. Most of the big names that appeared along Mannheim Road meant nothing to Michael and me. But we knew Frank Sinatra from the movies on late-night television. To our astonishment, one afternoon he walked into Orlando's Hideaway. Mr. Sam was already there. Michael and I had seen him earlier talking to Dad and Jackie.

[We never called him Jackie. He was Mr. Cerone the few times we met. Conversely, Skip and his brother Jimmy were always Skip and Jimmy.]

The tinted glass doors of the vestibule opened, and a flood of afternoon sunlight washed down the stairs. Frank Sinatra came walking down as Michael and I raced to the pool in our swimming trunks. He was short and slight, wearing a gray fedora, sunglasses, and a short-sleeved shirt. Michael kept on running, but I stopped, shocked. He stepped aside and said, "Hey, kid, easy there." Or something like that. Friendly. Playful. But he stood between me, a shimmering pool of cool water, and endless snacks. Our father insisted we behave like gentlemen, so I was not allowed to bark, "Get out of my way!"

When Michael and I went downstairs later, we heard an unforgettable explosion as Mr. Sam raged at Sinatra about how "that lying Irish prick has another guess coming if he thinks we're going to sit still for this." Sinatra started defending President Kennedy, and Mr. Sam exploded. He called the President of the United States' father "a cocksucker." Michael and I agree on this: We have never seen anyone so angry before or since. Snarling, really. Spitting mad. Literally. Red face. Eyes bulging. Insane. Terrifying. Dad hustled us out to the pool. Years later, I asked what Giancana and Sinatra were talking about. Dad shook his head with disgust and said, "That fucking Cal-Neva Lodge."

At the time, Sinatra and Giancana couldn't be seen together. The Sahara Inn was too high profile. But the low-key Air Host offered a convenient alternative right next door. So, Sinatra came to see his business partner about their ill-fated Cal-Neva Lodge venture (where wily old Joe Kennedy also had a piece of the action). Situated directly on the border of California and Nevada on Lake Tahoe, private cabins connected by a series of tunnels that made it perfect for clandestine meetings. The California side had the hotel, restaurant, and showrooms for Sinatra and his big-name pals; the Nevada side had the casino. In the days before open gambling in Nevada, the casino tables could be rolled across the state line in either direction in the event of a raid.

Gambling operations formed the cornerstone of Outfit operations, but Sam Giancana had a casino problem: Enshrined in Nevada's infamous "Black Book," his previous convictions made it unlawful for him to set foot in a Nevada casino. His partnership with Sinatra was intended to be kept in strictest confidence. Eventually the secret of Cal-Neva's ownership came out, and just about everyone lost their investment. Except, of course, Joe Kennedy. He never lost money. He only lost sons.

Like us, Sinatra was mob adjacent, *near* but not *in* the mob. It's been reported that favors passed in both directions between Sinatra and the Outfit. Who knows for sure? What's certain is that Frank Sinatra made an earlier appearance at Mr. Sam's swanky supper club, Villa Venice, in Norridge, Illinois. He brought Dean, Sammy, Eddie Fisher and Jimmy Durante, and their appearances between November 26 and December 2, 1962 caused a sensation.

Will Leonard, writing for the *Chicago Tribune*, reported Sinatra and his pals, "Croon, carol, caper and clown to the biggest cabaret audiences this town has seen in years." The media reported Giancana spared no expense (he only paid his performers scale, not their superstar salaries, though some say the stars performed for free). He tricked out the run-down eight-hundred-seat showroom with red satin ceilings, tapestries, trees, fountains, and half-naked showgirls. Real gondolas and fake gondoliers plied the Des Plaines River (and it was said prostitutes provided "intimate services" in the gondolas). But no one with any sense took a gondola ride. The Des Plaines River connected to an open sewer line.

Giancana kept the gambling discreetly hidden – private cars ferried high rollers to a nearby floating casino set up in a Quonset hut fronted by a fake service station. Skip and Jimmy ran the operation. Enforcer and second-story man, Tony Mastro, worked the door and made sure everybody behaved. This template repeated itself on Mannheim Road – a high-class façade with the best booze, the best broads, and the best performers served as the bait to lure the Outfit's real prey – the deep-pocket gamblers.

The Rat Pack's Villa Venice appearances were wildly successful. *Chicago Tribune* columnist, Herb Lyon, called the scene "Madness at the Villa." He quoted Sinatra saying, "We've never seen anything like it anywhere — Vegas, New York, Paris, you name it." Lyon estimated the total Villa loot for the Rat Pack's seven-day run hit $275,000 to $300,000, "a new night club record."

When Dad told Mom they were going to see the show, she trembled in a state of high agitation for weeks. For her, Christmas came early. As a "Bobby-Soxer" during Sinatra's initial rise to fame as a singer, Mary Ann Dinardi had been among the hoard of girls outside the Chicago Theater screaming, "Oh, Frankie!" To see him up close surpassed any teenage dream.

Mom bought a new dress. It was champagne-colored satin with long sleeves and a sequined lace overdress. We'd never seen her so excited. Mom didn't think there was enough sparkle. So, she added more, hand-sewing clear, iridescent sequins onto the lace. Mom normally only sewed out of emergency – a missing button or a loose hem. That she voluntarily took on a sewing challenge of such magnitude testified to its significance. She sat night after night, watching old movies on TV while she sewed.

Come the big night, Mom left the house in a cloud of perfume and hair spray and wrapped in mink. Dad wore a new suit. Michael and I were left with a babysitter – something that rarely happened – and they went out for a "once in a lifetime night on the town." That's what Mom called it. Michael and I did something more fun: We watched *Bonanza* – Hop-Sing cracked me up! – and the babysitter made Jiffy Pop. It was new, and we watched with amazements as the foil top swelled and spit steam.

It was very late when Mom came into my bedroom. My room was nearest the front door, and I stirred at the sound of it opening. I heard Dad talking to the babysitter in a hushed don't-wake-the-boys voice. Then Mom opened my door. A slash of light crossed the bed, and I squinted. She sat on the edge of the bed and asked softly, "Did you and Michael have fun with the babysitter?"

I told her yes and offered a quick synopsis of *Bonanza*. But I rushed through it for the bigger news: Jiffy Pop. It was magic.

Then she told me all about Frank Sinatra, Dean Martin, and Sammy Davis. I fell asleep as she raked her fingernails gently through my hair and recounted the songs and jokes.

Decades later, Nancy Sinatra confirmed that her father accepted the Villa Venice gig to pay a debt to Sam Giancana after the Outfit helped appoint Jack Kennedy President. The Villa Venice mysteriously burned down after the Rat Pack's appearance.

The night out with Sinatra was a temporary bandage at home. Mom hadn't been entirely happy when Dad bought Orlando's Hideaway. When he ran the Bridge, they led a normal nine-to-five life. After a couple of years, she'd gotten used to having her husband home in the evening and liked seeing him dozing on the couch in front of the television or playing with the boys. Now it was back to lonely nights, quiet days, and a husband who seldom got home before three in the morning. With Michael and me at school, Mom increasingly found herself bored out of her skull and floated a trial balloon about going back to work. She'd kept up with her supervisors at the telephone company and had a standing offer to return. The trouble was dad wouldn't stand for the standing offer. She'd have a baby instead, hoping for that elusive daughter.

The seven-year gap between Lisa Terese (born September 18, 1963) and me largely had to do with the fact that Mom nearly died giving birth when her blood pressure sky-rocketed. They called it toxemia; today the medical community refers to the life-threatening condition as pre-eclampsia. Dad feared being left alone to raise three children if they risked another pregnancy, but perhaps he feared the stigma of people thinking his wife "had to" work more than the fear of being a single parent. So, egg met sperm.

Mom's miserable pregnancy was made worse by Chicago's blistering summer heat and humidity. With a newborn baby, Mom looked forward to getting Michael and me out of the house. As a result, he and I spent many afternoons around the Air Host during the summers between 1963 and 1965. Sometimes Dad let us bring friends. Make no mistake: Nothing made a guy Boss of 47th Avenue faster than taking your neighborhood pals for an afternoon of swimming and snacks at a motel.

One afternoon Michael and I arrived as Keely Smith rehearsed. She and her husband, Louis Prima, were big in the 1950s and 60s, both as a duo and for performing with people like Frank Sinatra, Dean Martin, Count Basie, and Nelson Riddle. Keely Smith was thin, with short, dark hair, and a great shelf of bouncing bosom casting a shadow over a tiny waist. She sang a peppy song in a crisp, clear voice while swinging trim hips and snapping her fingers. Louis Prima blew a horn while he swayed, dipped, and pumped his way across the stage. A six-piece jazz band tried desperately to keep up with him. Between numbers, Miss Smith gave me an autographed copy of *Louis and Keely!* We had no idea who Keely Smith was, but she was awfully nice. I showed the album to Mom when I got into the car. She looked at the cover and curled her nose, "You'd think she could get her hair done for an album cover."

Back then, Mom was devoted to a television soap opera she began following in its original form on the radio, *As the World Turns*. After planning on naming her first two babies Cynthia Louise, only to be presented with sons, Mom decided the name was jinxed. Lisa Hughes was a favorite character on *As the World Turns*. Eileen Fulton portrayed daytime television's first desperate housewife. Her Lisa Hughes character didn't want to sit around the house and change diapers between loads of laundry and coats of floor wax. Faithless, selfish, and deceitful, Lisa served as the moral counterpoint to the devoted, loyal, and maternal Nancy Hughes, her mother-in-law, portrayed by Helen Wagner for and astounding 54 years. But Mom didn't name her treasured daughter after the saint; she named her after the rebel.

Things started heating up in the mid-1960s. Every decade or so, Chicago got a moral bug up its ass and decided to do something about organized crime. It was that time again. Chicago needed a good dose of law and order like castor oil. Unions were the lifeblood of organized crime in Chicago. A campaign began as federal and local authorities tried to get the hotel and nightclub owners to cooperate with investigations. If the Feds could bust open the unions, they could cut off the money and crush the mob. Of course, their plan depended on people cooperating, which they didn't, because Chicago (deep down) loves and protects its mobsters. Around this same time, Sam Giancana was increasingly focused on working with the CIA, developing overseas opportunities, and spending less time in Chicago. Without his strong leadership, the spokes on the wheel of organized crime began to wobble.

The Sahara Inn had nothing but trouble next door. On January 17, 1964, a car bomb blew out ten windows on the north wing. Luckily, there were no injuries or fires. The bomb had been placed in a bag on a courtesy cart between two cars – a message bomb designed to make an expensive mess but not hurt anybody. The blast shook the Sahara Inn, the Air Host and everything within a two-mile radius. Bandleader Fred Waring, performing at the Sahara, was hurled from his bed by the force of the blast. Guests thought the place had been hit by an airplane.

This was the second, bigger bomb. Six months earlier, a smaller explosion did about $1,000 worth of damage. It cost more than $10,000 to clean up after the second explosion. Both bomb blasts were later revealed as part of Manny Skar's plan to damage business at the Sahara Inn and force Gene Autry to sell to a new owner, who would then transfer ownership back to Skar.

Sol Elegant had problems, too. The books weren't balancing, and the bosses had questions. Then a prostitute got arrested at the Air Host, and the cops had questions, too. Elegant high-tailed to Florida without answering anyone's questions. Meanwhile, Dad followed the day-to-day business of running his nightclub and restaurant. It was more than a week before he realized Elegant vacated his suite. Dad assumed he had gone on one of his many vacations. Once Air Host's gambling operation attracted attention from law enforcement, Dad's lot became inextricably linked with the motel's. If the cops shut down Orlando's Hideaway on some trumped-up charge, Dad was screwed. If they shut down the Air Host and he lost the food and beverage revenue, Dad was still screwed.

Many of the problems raining down on Mannheim Road flowed from one source. Richard Scalzitti Cain began his career at the Cook County Sherriff's Police on Day One as a dirty cop. He spent the rest of his life on both sides of the law. But in 1965, Richard Cain had the power to make a pest of himself as the head of the Special Investigations Unit going after vice. Cain took his work seriously – as seriously as he took any work, which is to say he figured out which angle payed off best for him personally and played that one. Richard Cain played many roles in his life: Confidential Informer to the CIA and FBI; body guard to presidential candidate Barry Goldwater; trusted confidant of Illinois Governor Richard B. Ogilvie; suspect in the assassination of President Kennedy, and mercenary in every sense of the word, including training Cuban revolutionaries for Outfit purposes. He was a gem – ask any of his four (or maybe five) wives or his string of abandoned children. Cain focused his attention in 1965 on Mannheim Road. He saw the vice – the gambling, the prostitutes, the perversion, the drugs, the loan sharks (none of which Cain found personally objectionable) and saw it as his professional duty to clean the streets.

None of this meant anything to a pair of young brothers given practically free rein over an entire motel property. Kay Thompson wrote a series of books about a fictional little girl named Eloise who lived at the Plaza Hotel in New York City. Eloise had a hotel. We had a nightclub, restaurant, swimming pool, and a motel as our personal playground. And when we ran out of things to do at the Air Host, we would sneak next door to the Sahara Inn and watch people leap off the 30-foot diving board into the tropical-themed swimming pool, complete with torches and gargoyles. Bite me, Eloise.

Big name entertainers turned up in the hotels and motels along Mannheim Road, some performed in the showrooms, some dined on a special veal dish, and some stayed the night while waiting for a plane out of town. And so it was on the night of August 20, 1965, when the Beatles checked into the Sahara Inn. They slipped in virtually unnoticed, until one of them spoke. A guest heard a British accent, and all hell broke loose. Conveniently, mob adjacent hotels never suffered from a shortage of security, and John, Paul, George, and Ringo were quickly hustled into an elevator moment's ahead of a screaming hoard. The foursome received the best suite in the house – on the fifth floor, for the top-tier price of $105 per night ($1,160 in 2017). They ordered room service and magazines and checked out the next morning for a gig in Minneapolis. From the old guard like Sinatra, to the next generation Beatles, everybody came to Mannheim Road.

Orlando's Hideaway had another big act after Louis Prima and Keely Smith. The sign out front read, "The Criss Cross Revue." Photos in the vestibule showed a devastatingly attractive woman, with the mandatory bouffant helmet of hair, big earrings, a lot of makeup, and a low-cut dress covered in sparkles. Her painted mouth was open slightly as if in mid-song.

It was late afternoon. We were in Dad's office, where Michael and I usually ended up after a day by the pool. We'd wait for Dad and watch the portable television on top of a file cabinet. With the door open, we had a clear line of view to the backstage area. The club was too small for a real dressing room. Wigs on cloth-padded heads lined a folding table surrounded by makeup. Two racks of gowns formed a V-shaped dressing area. Jaded by age ten, having practically grown up in a nightclub, we'd seen lots of pretty girls with helmets of hair and big racks of bosom in sparkly dresses. Nothing about Miss Cross seemed especially noteworthy – except for one thing. And it was kind of a big thing in 1965 – Criss Cross was a man.

As a matter of technical law, it was illegal in the State of Illinois in the Year of Our Lord 1965 for a man to appear in public in female attire. The law prohibiting such behavior stayed on the books in Illinois from 1943 to 1973. Legendary female impersonator Charles Pearce talked about performing with a rack of dresses early in his career. Pearce would hold a gown in front of him and pretend to be Bette Davis or Joan Crawford or whomever – but he couldn't put on the dress, or he might end up in jail. In 1965, Criss Cross courted controversy – and jail time – when he brought his "all girl" revue to Orlando's Hideaway. My brother and I remain shocked that our conservative father booked the act.

The Outfit had a long and profitable relationship with homosexuality. In the mid-1960s, *Chicago Tribune* reporter Bob Wiedrich exposed the role of the Outfit in the gay bars on the Near North Side. The Outfit's plan was to convince owners to convert their fading strip joints and dives into profitable gay nightclubs. According to Wiedrich, these homosexual hangouts pulled in an estimated one million dollars a year. He called the operation "a textbook example of the unholy alliance between crooked police, politicians, and mobsters." With a network of twenty nightclubs and bars catering to homosexuals, "the mutually avaricious interests of these groups are interwoven in a tragic tapestry of corruption." He really laid it on thick.

Beyond skimming profits and selling alcohol and drugs, the Outfit and corrupt members of law enforcement preyed on gays as a source of extortion and blackmail. At the time, homosexuality was still classified as a mental disorder. Being publicly exposed as a homosexual meant scandal and certain ruin. The whiff of impropriety that swirled around homosexuality titillated the public. Titillation breeds curiosity, and curiosity brings money.

That's how it came to pass one afternoon when a man came backstage at Orlando's Hideaway carrying dry cleaning bags. He removed the plastic bag covering several evening gowns and hung them on a rack. Then something extraordinary happened. As Michael and I sat sucking cola through paper straws, the man sat in front of a lighted mirror and began a miraculous transformation. It started with a wig cap. By the time Dad came into the office, Mister Cross's face was nearly gone, and he began to resemble that devastatingly attractive woman in the vestibule photos. Dad got very uncomfortable and hustled us out of the club quickly.

[Decades later, I wrote a novel about a drag queen and a gangster in a nightclub, *Love and Bullets*. I'm sure one event had nothing to do with the other.]

We don't remember how long Criss Cross appeared at Orlando's Hideaway, but the show was a smash. Twice nightly. People lined up for a show that pushed the limits of polite entertainment. Dad said the Criss Cross Revue was the most profitable act to appear on Orlando's stage. Our cousin Marylou Ferrarini and her husband Ted sat in the audience one night. Marylou was shocked, scandalized, and thrilled. "We'd heard all about the show. They were writing about it in the newspaper, and everybody was talking about it. One night your father arranged for a bunch of us to come see the show – Teddy and me, my mother and father, and your mother. I'd never seen anything like it."

The Criss Cross Revue brought a cast of five to Orlando's Hideaway. In addition to Cross, master of ceremonies Marty Lewis kept the show moving with banter and blue jokes and introduced drag performers Criss Cross, Jessica St. John, Libby Reynolds, and Timmy McKay. In the big finale, the "showgirls" danced nearly naked in scanty two-piece gold costumes. Marylou couldn't take her eyes off their nether-regions. "It was completely smooth down there," she said. "I kept asking Teddy where they put it. You couldn't see anything." After the show, the cast mingled with customers. Ferrarini recalls being stunned to see the "girls" making out with men at the bar. It was all so scandalous, naughty, and wrong that she and her party stayed for the second show!

The show also caught the attention of vice cops – in particular, Richard Cain, who vehemently objected to Criss Cross' act. Cain was back in Chicago and up to his old tricks, playing both sides of the law. In the spring of 1965, Richard Cain convinced U.S. Attorney Ed Hanrahan and Attorney General Nicholas Katzenbach that he had the goods to produce indictments and convictions against the Outfit. With their approval, Cain began "a witch hunt the likes of which Chicago had never seen," according to his brother, Michael J. Cain. Richard Cain served subpoenas to everybody and anybody in the Outfit or adjacent to the Outfit. Sam Giancana was eventually sent to jail for contempt for the remainder of the grand jury term after he refused to cooperate, even with immunity. He wasn't the only man not cooperating.

Metal rattled loudly against metal. Someone was knocking on the screen door. Hard. Mom let me watch television in the front room if I promised not to touch anything. Everyone joked that the room was a museum, and she needed a velvet rope to guide people along the thick plastic runner she used to protect the carpet. I liked to watch TV up close, stretched out in front of the RCA console, inches from the glowing tube, elbows on the floor, chin resting in upturned palms, eyes cast upward at the miracle of television. I sat so close Mom yelled I'd ruin my eyes. Warnings about eye damage became a go-to response from Mom as we matured.

I violated all repeated instructions and touched Mom's drapes, parting the heavy brocade panels to see who was banging on the door. Three men in dark suits stood on the cramped, concrete front porch. Mom shot me a look, and I let the curtain panel slip from my hand. I'd hear about it later. She smoothed her dress and hair and opened the front door. Unplanned but perfectly on cue, I stepped next to my mother and looked up. The perfect Madonna and Child moment. My eyes popped open like a waif in a Keane painting when one of the men opened a black bifold leather wallet and flashed a brass badge topped by an eagle. FBI. Mom never took her eyes off the men. She gave my hand a reassuring squeeze and carried on as if she were talking to a stubborn Fuller Brush man. She hadn't watched all those movies for nothing. Those mugs would get nothing out of Mary Ann Gentile.

"Yes? May I help you?" And so, it began. She answered each question with exquisite precision to avoid telling a lie without telling the whole truth and nothing but the truth. What made her performance more impressive was that she made it up on the fly. Mom didn't have training in "What to Do When the FBI Shows Up," and nothing in her background provided the basics for evading questions by law enforcement officers. But she remembered her mother's warning about a liar needing a good memory. So, rather than lie outright, she exercised that old Catholic standby and lied by omission:

"Yes, he lives here *(but he doesn't want to talk to you)*. No, he's not here *(in this room)* right now. No, I don't know when to expect him *(to come up from the basement)*. No, I can't recall ever meeting a man named Sol Elegant *(who was more of a disgusting human being)*. No, I can't recall my husband mentioning his name *(without saying Sol Elegant was nothing but trouble)*."

I remember the screen door opening and Mom taking a business card from one of the men. She glanced at it briefly and stuffed it into the pocket of her dress. "Yes, I'll have him call you *(when hell opens an ice cream parlor)*." Then Mom closed the door on what might have been her first and only criminal act – if lying to the FBI could be considered criminal. She was certainly obstructing justice. And she obstructed it like a pro. If a wife couldn't be forced to testify against her husband in court (which she learned watching *Perry Mason*), then she couldn't be forced to testify against him at her own front door.

If Dad feared the police might bring trouble, he seriously underestimated his wife. Michael and I remember Mom screaming like a banshee that Dad was going to bring trouble and disgrace to the family because of "those people." In the early years, Mom found Dad's Outfit pals colorful and entertaining – plus, they got the best tables at restaurants and nightclubs, rooms full of furniture, and other goods. Then the cops and Feds started asking questions, people started disappearing and dying, and the dark side of the Outfit started getting too close for our nervous mother.

Things started happening fast after that, and Mom pressured Dad to get out of "the business." She was frightened and threatened to leave "and take the kids." Suddenly it was over. Orlando's Hideaway was closed for staging a "lewd show" by order of the Chief Investigator of the Cook County Sherriff's Office, Richard Cain. Dad was out of work, and our playground gone. The lights along Mannheim Road would flash for a few more years, but one by one the lightbulbs started to burn out.

Sol Elegant disappeared, never to be seen again. Dad said many years later he suspected Elegant became "fish food." Manny Skar wanted to get out after his dream crumbled and decided to cooperate with the Feds. On September 11, 1965, forty-two-year old Skar was assassinated behind his apartment building at 3800 N. Lake Shore Drive. No evidence was ever turned over to the federal authorities. Legend says Outfit enforcer Tony Spilotro took care of the wet work. But Spilotro has been blamed for nearly every murder since Abe Lincoln went to the theater.

Upon his murder, a *Daily News* editorial called Manny Skar "a cheap, blustering, boasting, vicious hoodlum...he asked for it." And yet Manny Skar was kind to us and turned a blind eye to two young boys running around his property. Once he caught us sneaking a peek inside the gaudy Club Sahara where Skar opened the show in a red metallic tuxedo. (He had them in black, silver, and gold, too.) Our "punishment" for snooping involved Skar leading us to the coffee shop, where he asked if we preferred a chocolate milkshake or a chocolate soda. Michael and I looked at each other, not knowing the difference. Mr. Skar read our confusion and ordered one of each. Then, the "vicious" hoodlum sat down with us and explained the difference (shakes use milk, sodas use seltzer water) while we taste-tested our way through the variations. He asked if we liked the Beatles, and told us about the time they caused pandemonium in the lobby. On our way out, after saying "Thank you very much, Mr. Skar," we headed back to the Air Host. The "boasting thug" called out, "Tell your father I did two grand last night. Beat that." We never saw him again.

Jackie helped find a buyer for Orlando's Hideaway in 1965. Joe Adornetto (known as Joe Shades) was said to be an Outfit "associate." He also owned the Aragon in Franklin Park and once worked for Manny Skar. Despite the new ownership at Orlando's Hideaway, some things didn't change. Like Dad, Joe Shades had two sons. The younger boy, Rick, recalled seeing mob bosses like Sam Giancana, Joe Accardo, Jackie Cerone, and Joe Aiuppa downstairs in the club. They called him Little Ricky. Joe Shades ran the place until 1971.

By the time Sam Giancana's stint in jail for contempt of court ended in 1966, he was on shaky ground with the Outfit. "Milwaukee" Phil Alderisio had managed things in Sam's absence, but he died of a heart attack when tireless FBI agent Bill Roehmer tried to arrest him. Sensing his precarious position, Giancana left for Mexico – with Richard Cain (of all people) acting as his aid, translator, and accomplice. The Outfit became a rudderless ship.

Richard Cain's rise and fall from good guy to double-crosser to triple-crosser is the stuff of Italian opera. His story came full circle back to the old neighborhood on Grand and Aberdeen, back to the very storefronts where people like Don Vincenzo lived and worked. But we're not ready for that part of the story yet.

The site of the Sahara Inn is now a mid-range chain hotel. The magnificent pool is gone, now a parking lot. The former Air Host still stands at 4101 N. Mannheim Road, with a new name, a new façade and its swimming pool also covered by asphalt. The glass doors into the vestibule – up to the restaurant, down to the nightclub – still face Mannheim Road. I'm sure nobody there knows Sam Giancana once hung out downstairs, or that Frank Sinatra had secret meetings there, or that the place got shut down because of a drag queen.

9 RETAIL ADJACENT

Nothing changes a woman's mind about wanting another baby more than a full-length mink coat. That was Dad's logic during the height of Orlando's Hideaway success. Mom got her figure back nicely after I was born and wore her hair like Elizabeth Taylor – dark, wavy, and almost to the shoulder. Why go through another pregnancy? Dad hoped a fur coat would end the discussion about jobs and babies. The money flowed in those days, and we saw it reflected in trips, cars, clothes, jewelry, and the usual signs of financial success. But when Dad decided to buy Mom a mink coat, he didn't go to a furrier. Retail was for chumps. In our family, you called Aunt Jeanette. She called her friend Millie, and Millie called her son Peter. Peter made a living removing things from the homes of strangers without their permission.

Aunt Jeanette and Millie had been friends since grammar school. Millie was a firecracker. She laughed more than anyone else I've ever met. Practically a smoker from birth, she had a gasping, raspy voice that she often used to tell off-color jokes. Her hair was always dyed Lucille Ball red and piled up in a whirl of curls. She kept herself trim and always dressed to show off her figure. Fun-loving, profane, and completely disrespectful, we adored Millie. But her life was filled with heartache. Her daughter, Fran, married a fellow named Stosh. Like Peter, Stosh also made his living removing things from the homes of strangers without their permission. As a result, Millie had access to a never-ending supply of high-end goods. But despite her casual role as a fence, Peter's criminal career caused her great anguish. Eventually he would be sent to "college" on a thirty-year "scholarship." I remember Dad expressing amazement at the severity of the sentence "for stealing stuff." Murderers got lighter sentences. But all that's ahead.

Peter gave his mother two shopping bags filled with furs. A few nights later, Millie and Aunt Jeanette came over for a pleasant Coffee And. Mom sat with the bags at her feet and pulled out mink coats like rabbits from a magician's hat. This one chestnut brown, that one silver, another black. This one went to the ankle, that one to the knee. Long sleeves, banded sleeves, cuffed sleeves, three-quarter sleeves. There must have been a dozen coats in those bottomless bags. Finally, Mom saw her fawn-colored favorite and modeled it to enthusiastic reviews. She looked so happy. Okay, so someone else's initials were embroidered on the lining. Aunt Jeanette knew a guy who could change the satin lining for a few bucks. And that's how every woman in my family got her furs. Mink. Fox. Rabbit. Persian lamb. All in a bag. Pick what you want. Prices negotiable.

Mom got a mink coat without the bother of going to a store. I thought that's how it worked for everybody. I didn't know Millie's son was a thief, and I never suspected the coats were stolen. In my family, when you needed something or wanted something, you called somebody, and it appeared. What a perfect way to shop, right? My beliefs were shattered by reality.

The Hillside Shopping Center served as a model for the 1960s-shopping experience. This modern marvel immersed the mark (pardon me, the "shopper") in a wall-to-wall retail experience. It was nothing but two parallel rows of stores anchored by the upscale Carson Pirie Scott at one end and low-priced Goldblatt's department store at the other, with the giant parking lots suburbs offered. The Hillside Shopping Center was Chicago's fourth mall. I was nine when they slapped on a roof and created a climate-controlled retail wonderland that kept shoppers cocooned in comfort, safe from Chicago's variable weather. The Hillside Shopping Center offered something for everyone. I loved it.

I remember standing before big display windows and marveling. In each window, shapely female mannequins wore full-length fur coats, and a scattering of torso mannequins showed fur stoles, jackets, wraps, hats, and muffs. It was so swanky inside that you couldn't see a cash register. There were pretty, tufted benches, and velvet chairs in little arrangements, and triple mirrors here and there. I wondered why anyone went to the trouble and expense to build a store devoted to furs. Acquiring a fur didn't require an expensive store; shopping for a fur required a telephone call, a pot of coffee, and dessert.

Fifteen years later, Michael got engaged for the first time. He needed a ring, and an old routine repeated. Dad called Aunt Jeanette, and the curtain went up on another performance of Mob Retail. A few nights later, she and Millie came over for Coffee And. This time Peter came along. Millie's son had always been a mysterious character. We seldom saw him, but heard about his exploits like a character in a soap opera. His action usually occurred off-screen. That night he brought one of those blue, felt, drawstring bags from Crown Royal Scotch. He opened it and dumped out what looked like the crown jewels from a small nation on Mom's kitchen table – diamonds, rubies, emeralds, pearls; he had rings, necklaces, earrings, bracelets, medals, brooches, everything.

Aunt Jeanette pulled out a jeweler's loupe from her handbag and started inspecting stones. She narrowed the selection to two, gaudy, old-lady rings. Michael's fiancé Joan was a thin, dainty, modern young woman. I couldn't imagine her wearing either monstrosity, but I didn't have any lines in this show. Aunt Jeanette finally settled on a set of rings. The engagement ring had a large square stone set in platinum, about a carat-and-a-half; it dropped into a divided wedding band, surrounding the main stone with tapered baguette diamonds. The big question came: "How much?"

Peter looked at the ring and said, "Fifteen-hundred."

Without missing a beat, Aunt Jeanette looked down her nose, scowled, and said, "Peter, I told you my nephew had nine-hundred. He's Junior's boy." Peter opened his mouth, but she gave him The Look. If Aunt Jeanette had been a man, she'd have been a mob boss. She would have negotiated Manhattan from the natives for $16 and a Goldblatt's coupon. "Take the nine hundred," she said. "It's not like you're losing money. The ring is hotter than the coffee!"

Peter sighed and said, "All right. Nine-hundred." He scooped the rejects back into the blue felt bag.

Michael counted off $900 while mom refilled coffee cups and cut a few more slices of cake.

The next day, Aunt Jeanette took the ring to have it reset. She'd been using the same guy at the Jeweler's Building on Wabash Street for decades. He even gave credit for the unused gold. The plan was to make a modern engagement setting and a simple matching wedding band. Then he'd use the leftover diamonds to make a pinkie ring for Dad. Because what's an Italian without a pinkie ring? I told Aunt Jeanette that only in the Gentile family and the British royal family does the concept of "leftover diamonds" and how to use them come into play. She told me to stop being a smart-guy.

Short and plump, Aunt Jeanette was always immaculately dressed and wore her hair pulled up into a dark, ash-blonde, flower pot of petals, curlicues, and tendrils. No matter the occasion, she wore the right outfit and too many rings. With all that extra time on her bejeweled hands, Aunt Jeanette also served as the official family shopper. If you needed something beyond The Hillside Shopping Center's selections or goodies from Millie's magic bags, Aunt Jeanette happily scoured the stores downtown. Wieboldt's, Marshall Field's, Madigan's, Carson's, Goldblatt's, she knew where to find everything – and at the best prices. Dad used to say Aunt Jeanette was a retailer's worst nightmare – she'd spend all day "touching and feeling" the merchandise without spending a penny, storing the knowledge in her vast mental retail database that Wieboldt's had the best prices on cashmere or Carson's had the best selection of handbags.

After decades of devoted service to her family, Aunt Jeanette's siblings decided to throw a party for her sixtieth birthday; and since the official stone celebrating sixty years of anything is a diamond, her brothers and sisters decided to buy a diamond pendant to mark the occasion. Dad then did the unthinkable: He went to a retail store and bought a piece of jewelry. At the party, Aunt Jeanette was both touched and furious. Buying retail? Seriously? Had she taught us nothing? Being mob adjacent means you should never have to buy retail.

10 GAMBLING ADJACENT

Michael and I spent a lot of time with Dad in the immediate aftermath of Orlando's Hideaway closing. At first it was strange. We'd grown accustomed to being quiet during the day while Dad slept, running for the phone so it didn't ring too long, and kissing him goodbye after dinner. It had been our routine for the past three years, practically an eternity in child years. Suddenly Dad was awake during the day and started taking us places. It might be as simple as visiting Aunt Jeanette on a weekday or lunch at Howard Johnson's – the one hovering horizontally *over* the interstate, with tall windows on both sides like a rail car. We went for hamburgers and ice cream and sat by the window. Vertical ribbons of blacktop stretched into infinity as cars zoomed in both directions. Dad told us to look for license plates from other states and offered the princely sum of twenty-five cents for each state spotted. We didn't see any. The cars moved too fast. But it kept us quiet while we ate.

One afternoon at home, Dad announced a field trip. Anthony Cerone was coming over, and we men were going for a ride. To us, he was Uncle Anthony. To everyone else, he was the nephew of Outfit bigshots. Like us, Uncle Anthony was mob adjacent. His father, Louis, was a "straight" man, meaning he worked in a legitimate business – and not a business that served as a cover for illegal activity. But an honest-to-goodness legitimate business – crafting custom leather goods in a tannery. Louis' relatives, however, worked in less legitimate lines.

Dad met Uncle Anthony through Jimmy Cerone in the early 1960s. An electrician by trade, Uncle Anthony once worked with Jimmy at the Rite-Lite Neon Sign Company. Eventually, Mom and Uncle Anthony's wife – Antoinette – became friends, too. But no one called her Antoinette. She was Sis. Michael, Lisa, and I became friendly with their children – Louis, Rosa, Anthony Junior, Mark, and David. Our relationship mirrored what happened in the 1940s at Patsy Spilotro's restaurant when Dad met Jackie, Skip, and Jimmy: Cerones and Gentiles became one big Family.

Tall and broad-shouldered, Aunt Sis had a heart-shaped face, giant eyes, and dark hair cropped in a short, no-fuss style. With her booming voice, Aunt Sis was a force of nature. I thought she was so glamorous. Unlike other women we knew, Aunt Sis worked outside the home. Not only did she work, she owned an upscale women's boutique. Toni's Conversation Clothes brought pricey fashion straight from the runway to sleepy, deep-pocket, west suburban Bensenville, Illinois. A rapturous Bensenville (and beyond) made Aunt Sis wealthy to show their appreciation. Several times a year, she flew to New York and California for fashion shows and buying trips.

Eventually their chain grew to three stores – Hanover Park, Downer's Grove, and the flagship in Bensenville. Mom would later work at Toni's Conversation Clothes when we were in high school. She checked invoices, tagged merchandise, and felt better about herself than she had in years. Eventually Mom worked at two different stores and became an integral part of their operation. But for the time being, Mom cooked for everyone – now that she'd learned how. She became a damn good cook, too. Rather ironic that she became skilled at something she didn't particularly enjoy. Baking skills, on the other hand, remained elusive, and Mom conceded those duties to the supremely gifted Gentile sisters.

As he did practically every time he walked in the door, Uncle Anthony called, "Mare, what have you got to eat?"

"What do you want?"

"Anything. I'm starving."

It was a running joke. The kitchen wasn't Sis' preferred habitat. Even if Sis had the interest in cooking (which she usually did not), she seldom had time. The lady had an empire to run. Who had time to buy groceries? I remember a dinner at the Cerone's. Sis made pasta – but forgot to buy bread. We ate bagels with spaghetti for a truly international dining experience, and everyone had a fine time. It taught us not to get hung up on expectations.

Dad used to say, "Expectation is the first step to disappointment."

Mom asked Uncle Anthony about Sis and the kids while he picked at a plate of cold rigatoni. Then Dad loaded us into the car, and we drove east to

Melrose Park. Michael and I had no idea where we were going, but it was an outing with Dad, and those were usually interesting one way or another.

Skip and Jimmy had a good thing going in the suburbs during the mid-1960s. The Chicago police and the Feds started making like difficult for the mob's established gambling operations within city limits. Several high-profile places were raided and shut down permanently. Since the repeal of Prohibition in 1933, illegal gambling (bookmaking) represented a prime source of profits. The Outfit had been operating with little more than a finger-wagging from the authorities for decades, thanks to generous payoffs. It helped that Mayor Richard Daley seemed to prefer having the Outfit operate quietly rather than expose the layers of corruption in his City Hall. Daley's hand was finally forced, and he reluctantly went after organized crime.

Facing dwindling revenues from its shuttered Chicago gambling dens, the Outfit followed Frank Nitti's Prohibition-era example and hid crime in plain sight. City adjacent western suburbs like Maywood and Melrose Park hosted a bevy of illegal activities in makeshift casinos that generated millions annually. Jimmy and Skip ran one of the best operations around – they had all the poker, craps, broads, and booze the high-rollers wanted. They ran half a dozen houses in Melrose Park, Stone Park, and Northlake.

The operation was magnificent in its simplicity: A modest, single-family residence was purchased through a front. A basement was mandatory, along with a garage, and a long driveway for off-street parking. A split-level with bedrooms upstairs from the main floor was preferred. Those kinds of houses were practically a dime a dozen in the western suburbs – block after block and mile after mile of split-level houses on quiet streets.

Michael and I climbed into the backseat of Dad's Oldsmobile 98 while Uncle Anthony put a toolbox in the trunk and then got in the passenger seat. Melrose Park was less than five miles from Bellwood. We parked in front of a brick house that looked like every other brick house on the street. Uncle Anthony got his toolbox, and we went into the house through a side door along the driveway.

We walked into the spacious kitchen of a split-level home. The owner was a man named Paul. Michael and I didn't recognize him. A pretty woman was making coffee. Paul didn't introduce her. We learned the reason for our visit was so Uncle Anthony could fix an electrical problem. Dad came to visit Paul and dragged Michael and me along for the ride. The woman offered coffee to the men and "pop" to us. Then we men headed to the basement, and the woman shimmied up a back staircase. We heard other female voices upstairs.

The basement wasn't a basement in the usual sense – no sofa, no television, no second kitchen, no bins full of board games. The toys in this basement were of a different variety. A scaled-down casino offered roulette, craps, blackjack, and poker. Half a dozen slot machines lined one wood-paneled wall, each with a black bar stool in front. Along the other wall was a long bar, with another half dozen black stools. This was the new speakeasy. The suburbs were crawling with places like this. When the people with money started moving west, the Outfit followed the money. They found it waiting in the pockets of bored suburbanites.

Dad sat at the bar while Uncle Anthony went about fixing the electrical problem in the dropped ceiling. Paul led Michael and me to the slot machines. First, he opened the back and tinkered with switches. Then he told us to hop up on a bar stool, and handed us each a large waxed paper cup filled with quarters. "Try your luck," he said and left us to our amusement. Michael and I started dropping quarters. My feet dangled in the air, legs not long enough to reach the foot rail. Every few minutes, one slot machine or other spit out a flood of quarters while lights flashed and bells rang. Drop. Pull. Hope. Damn. Again. Drop. Pull. Hope. Ding, ding, ding! Again! Heady stuff for two young boys. Our first exposure to illegal gambling; every boy remembers his first time.

Eventually Uncle Anthony completed his chore, and the outing started winding down. The girls we heard earlier were gathered in the kitchen and dressed fancy. On the way home, I asked Dad why Paul had all that stuff in his basement.

His answer was simple: "He likes to have parties."

"And those girls? Who were they, Dad?"

"Nursing students. They rent the bedrooms upstairs."

"They must work at a very fancy hospital."

Uncle Anthony laughed, reached over the seat, and ruffled my hair.

Decades later, I asked Dad about this fleeting memory. I often made a pest of myself asking about the old days. Most times he would answer my questions, but sometimes he'd dismiss a subject with, "Who the hell remembers?" But he confirmed this recollection and laughed about "the shit you kids remember."

One last thing: When Michael and I hopped off the barstools in front of the over-worked slot machines, Paul told us to keep our "winnings." When you grow up mob adjacent, the odds are often tilted in your favor.

11 DINNER ADJACENT

Uncle John still had the restaurant bug after Richard Cain shut down Orlando's Hideaway. We Gentiles seem to spend most of our lives alternating between the produce business and the hospitality industry. Either way, it's about feeding people. Uncle John opened a restaurant and bar in 1967 in Grayslake, Illinois, called Tammy's, named after his daughter. The menu mixed Italian cuisine with American classics, everything from pasta to burgers and steak and lobster.

From the parking lot, the place looked like a big rustic cabin. In fact, the restaurant adjacent to Tammy's was called The Rustic Manor. According to the restaurant's namesake, our cousin Tammy, the owners of the Rustic Manor fumed when Uncle John's customers parked in their lot when Tammy's lot was full – and it was often full. Customers entered a small foyer with a door to the right leading into the bar. An archway to the left led into the dining room. A large kitchen ran parallel to the dining room. Most nights the bar and restaurant drew big crowds, and the waiters and waitresses in their black and white uniforms moved like monochrome blurs delivering food and drinks.

Aunt Florence helped when needed. On those occasions, Tammy – then about five-years old – accompanied her mother and happily danced on the stage. After all, it was *her* place! Her stepbrothers, Ronny and Wayne Lukow, also worked at *her* place. Like so many Gentile ventures, it turned into a family affair.

Our parents went to Tammy's for dinner one Saturday night with Uncle Anthony and Aunt Sis, Skip and Mary, and Uncle Tony and Aunt Francis. Our parents didn't go out like that often, so it was a big deal for Mom. She bought a new dress, got her hair done, and pulled out that fawn-colored mink coat. They got red carpet treatment coming in the door. Uncle John was busting with pride, walking everyone through the crowded bar and into the nicely populated restaurant. He led them to the best seat in the house – a big, round table toward the back on the right side of the dining room. In a corner, with no one behind them – what you call mob seating.

While everyone else had drinks at the table, Uncle John took Dad to the kitchen. It was hopping in there, and Dad was happy to see the place doing so well. Uncle John got dealt a bad hand when Orlando's Hideaway closed. The "lewd" stage show happened downstairs in the nightclub, not upstairs in the restaurant. But the dominoes fell and both places closed. That put the brothers on the street. Uncle John scraped by for a while before putting together the stake he needed to open Tammy's. Dad was glad to see his brother firmly back on his feet – and glad to see Jackie Gleason's favorite veal dish on the menu.

Their table ate and drank their way up and down the menu. Bottles of wine and champagne, appetizers, main courses, desserts, after dinner drinks. Stingers anyone? Maybe a Brandy Alexander? Uncle John's second wife, Florence, made a brief appearance tableside and charmed everyone. She made a joke about how much fun it was having people for dinner when someone else did the cooking. Mom said Florence wore a light blue dress and commented on how redheads look especially good in blue. Since my mother had never particularly warmed to Florence after Uncle John divorced Doris, it showed a big concession to offer several compliments. Everyone had a wonderful evening, and Dad handed the waiter $500 for their bill. By the time they finished all the handshakes, congratulations, hugs, and kisses, Dad's group didn't leave Tammy's until almost midnight.

Dad called his brother the next afternoon to tell him again how terrific everything turned out. Uncle John said it was the busiest night in a while, cleared almost $700. Immediately, Dad got suspicious and asked where, in the restaurant or bar? Uncle John said both. Remember, Dad handed the waiter $500. The restaurant and bar were both crowded; the math didn't work. He ran enough joints to recognize this routine, and Dad felt sorry for the idiot who pulled it, because that idiot was about to get a nasty surprise.

Uncle John was furious when Dad explained that somebody – most likely the waiter – was robbing him blind. Here's the stupid that walks around among us every day: Uncle John had told the waiter, "Take care of this good-looking so-and-so and his party, he's my baby brother." So, the waiter knew who he was waiting on. And he still decided it was a good idea to steal $500. The idiot apparently never expected the brothers to talk dollars and cents. It was a good bet he'd been stealing since Day Two. Dad said he probably used Day One to figure out how to start stealing on Day Two. Uncle John turned red – more than eight months of stealing, and he hadn't caught it. While he thought people were basically decent, Dad labored under no such illusions and asked Uncle Tony to talk to the waiter. As a professional thief, he'd know how to handle an amateur.

Uncle Tony went back to Tammy's and sat in the bar the next afternoon. Eventually the waiter came to get drinks for a table. Uncle Tony said, "Maybe you remember me from the other night."

The idiot said, "Yeah, you were with Mr. Gentile's brother." And the blood drained out of the guy's face all at once.

Uncle Tony told him to sit down. The waiter sat. Then Uncle Tony explained in a gentle tone what would happen next, while nodding and smiling at anybody looking his way. "You're going to tell me the truth, or you're gonna wake up and see me at the foot of your bed, and you don't want that. Understand?"

A sweaty head bobbed up and down.

"Where's the money you stole?"

A trembling mouth squeaked, "At home."

Uncle Tony shook his empty glass, and the bartender started a fresh drink. "There's a guy out in the parking lot. He's going to watch you get in your car. He knows where you live, and he's going to follow you home." Uncle Tony looked at his watch. "You're going to come back here in thirty-minutes with the money, and you're going to put it right here." He tapped the bar with one meaty finger.

At this point the guy pissed himself. Uncle Tony pretended not to notice to allow the idiot a sliver of dignity. Men who have lost everything stop being cooperative. Mob logic.

Uncle Tony raised one eyebrow. "Go."

Nobody followed the idiot. Uncle Tony worked alone. He sat comfortably at the bar, finished his second drink and waited. The guy was back in less than thirty-minutes, too scared to think about running. He put $500 on the bar, plus another $1,200 and the gold watch Uncle John "lost." He had fresh pants on, but Uncle Tony wasn't holding out hope.

"I'm sorry."

Uncle Tony whispered, "Now get the fuck out of here and don't come back."

"What about my last check?"

Uncle Tony looked at him sideways. "Somebody here owes you money?"

Sputter, sputter, sputter, "No."

"Then why are you still here?"

The barstool toppled over as the guy bolted. Uncle Tony looked at the seat. It was wet.

Tammy's suddenly got a lot more profitable, and Uncle John settled happily into life as a restauranteur. He didn't have his baby brother's sparkle and flash. But Uncle John showed up, suited up, and ran every race like a champion workhorse. The food was good, the drinks were strong, and everybody was having a good time.

About two years into Tammy's run, Uncle John got a call in the middle of the night. His restaurant was on fire, and the place burned to the ground. He said, "Not even a fucking ladle" was left. To make things worse, he didn't have insurance. Busted again. Uncle John always believed the fire was started deliberately, and he didn't look any farther than the jealous competitor in the next building. Nothing was proven, and Uncle John moved on, tending bar for a while before opening another produce market. It was a good thing, too. In about a year his baby brother will need to borrow cooler space to store perishables when he, too, goes back into the produce business.

12 DIVORCE ADJACENT

There's an insulting cliché that says behind every great man is a great woman – as if the women who stood invisibly behind men who didn't achieve greatness amounted to shit, that each wasn't great in her way, if for no other reason than she managed to live with a man. This business of standing invisibly proved especially true for Eisenhower-era brides, having been spoon-fed heaping mounds of bullshit about love, sex, marriage, and taboo. A good wife had no separate identity; she adorned her husband's life like a tattoo – colorful but meaningless in the greater scheme. A good husband cared-for and stage-managed the life of the helpless nitwit he selected as wife and future birth-vessel for his children. In exchange for his support, she deferred on any matter requiring thinking or intelligence. This perverse dynamic served as a template for misery if the husband happened to be a butcher, baker, candlestick maker, or a mob adjacent nightclub owner. The mixture may have been especially potent for the woman who gave up a job she enjoyed to fulfill a role society demanded but she detested. How could she be happy?

Aunt Doris thought she had a good marriage. She and Uncle John wanted children very much, and they'd been trying unsuccessfully. Eventually medical tests proved her unable to bear children, and everything changed. Her infertility presented one of the Catholics' rare get-out-of-marriage free cards.

Uncle John quickly had their marriage annulled. Then he divorced Doris and married Florence Lukow in 1959, rumored to be with child. Decades after their divorce, an exotic visitor arrived at our house in Bellwood. I didn't recognize the beautifully dressed and impeccably coiffed stranger, but Michael remembered her as "Aunt Dodo."

Mom was thrilled by the visit and presented her children. Doris' wide, warm face cracked into happy tears. Michael had been barely three-years old when she moved out of the two-flat on Aberdeen; I'd been an infant. She cried about how we were "all grown up" at twelve and thirteen-years old. As for Lisa, then about seven, Doris cried over her beauty, blue eyes, and blond curls. Then we children were dismissed, and the women sat in the front room gossiping feverishly over soft drinks. I hung back in my bedroom and listened. Doris congratulated Mom on having "everything." Then Mom made a confession: She still missed her job, still hated housework, and often found herself bored senseless by women who based their self-worth on the height of their homemade cakes.

"Could you just kill me?" Mom asked, chuckling darkly.

"But you're glad you didn't leave him, aren't you?" Doris asked.

Mom wanted to leave Dad? It would be years before Mom confessed to me about how she packed her bag one night and asked Aunt Louise to come and get her. She said to Doris, "If my marriage was as good out of bed as it is in bed, we'd have the perfect marriage."

Doris laughed and said it seemed that was the way it always turned out. You got the good relationship or the good sex, but not both.

Imagine how enlightening this was to a twelve-year old boy listening from around the corner.

The conversation ebbed and flowed as Mom brought her former sister-in-law up to date on the extended Gentile family. Doris laughed or gasped as appropriate. She even asked warmly about Uncle John, and Mom told her about Tammy, his and Aunt Florence's blond daughter. Doris laughed about Italians improbably producing blond children. Eavesdropping from the next room, their chatter was like the exposition in movies – the boring stuff that happens before a story gets down to business.

Finally, things started getting interesting. I learned that after Uncle John divorced Doris, she moved to Hollywood. Hollywood! Having grown up sharing Mom's love of old movies and Hollywood legends, I got my first taste of the hard stuff during the Elizabeth Taylor/Eddie Fisher/Richard Burton love triangle that dominated the news and conversations of Bellwood moms in the early-1960s. After that, I was hooked. I leaned against the doorjamb for a long sip of gossip direct and undiluted from Hollywood.

After Doris moved west, she worked as a secretary to big name entertainers like Johnny Carson and Milton Berle. It sounded exciting. Later that night, when Mom repeated the story to Dad, I heard that unmistakable tone when Mom said "secretary" that I heard when people in my family used the word "college." Doris told Mom Johnny Carson liked to wear women's underpants. I remember feeling sorry for him. He was on television nearly every night and seemed so witty and smart. But poor, dumb Johnny Carson couldn't tell the difference between boy underwear and girl underwear. When I folded laundry for Mom, I never mixed up Lisa's ruffled pastel underpants with the tighty-whiteys Michael and I wore. Then Doris mentioned how Milton Berle's penis "deserved its own ZIP code." Neither detail seemed like something a typical secretary would know. But what did I know about Hollywood secretaries?

Doris told Mom everything was different in Hollywood. In the morning, she could walk outside and pick oranges and grapefruit right off the trees. It was seventy-degrees in December, and the sun practically never stopped shining. She'd rented a house right on the beach in Malibu. Pernell Roberts was her next-door neighbor. I knew his name from *Bonanza*. There were so many opportunities, Doris said, that no one was ever out of work long. She drove on things called "freeways" and went on ski trips in the nearby mountains or drove to the desert to enjoy the broiling heat during the "cold weather." It sounded magical.

Doris said getting divorced was the best thing that ever happened to her. Though she loved John and hadn't wanted the divorce at the time, eventually she realized what a lucky break her empty ovaries provided. It didn't destroy or stain Doris. Instead, she got to start life over, and she did it in a town that didn't give a shit if a woman was married, single, or divorced. She walked among palm trees and stood in the shade of great stars. I couldn't imagine anything more exciting.

Doris' visit lit a fire inside me. She provided the first glimpse of a life beyond what I knew at the time. I could be somewhere else; I could be something else. I could be whatever I wanted to be and do what I wanted to do. Learning I had "options" changed everything. Doris told Mom she'd been seeing a writer "with a few credits." She spoke in a foreign language about how a movie studio took an "option" on his book. Then the option "lapsed," and another studio picked up the "project" in "turnaround." The gist was that his book turned around so many times that he made enough money to buy an apartment building. And the book was never made into a movie! But he got paid over and over again. What a great system!

There was a reason for Doris' visit beyond catching up with her former sister-in-law. She was dying of cancer and came back to visit her family. She was being very brave about it, much braver than Mom, who started crying when Doris revealed the fatal diagnosis. I admired the stranger's courage. Here was a dying woman holding up her end of a riotously funny conversation with no sense of "poor me, pity me." Dying was part of life, and she was prepared to face it. Before she left, Doris used our bathroom. Once she had gone, Mom sprayed the toilet seat with Lysol, presumably to kill the cancer germs. Doris died about two years later, but I never forgot the woman I never knew.

13 OCCASIONALLY ADJACENT

The benefits of being mob adjacent popped up in 1972. When I was fourteen-years old, I wanted to go to Spain with the Spanish Club, never mind the fact that I had stubbornly insisted on taking French. The French Club wasn't going to France. But the Spanish Club was going to Spain, and I wanted to go. Over dinner, I casually asked Dad if I could have some cash. He never put much importance on money. If you asked for some, he'd give it to you for a simple "please" and "thank you." He asked how much. I said $500. This was quite a bit of money in 1972 (almost $3,000 today), but he didn't bat an eye. He asked why. I told him. The next day Mom wrote a check.

A few weeks before leaving on the trip, Christmas morning arrived in April when a matched set of luggage miraculously appeared in my bedroom. Amelia Earhart luggage. I wondered in my smart-ass way why they named luggage after a pilot who never reached her final destination. Arriving intact seemed like the minimum requirement for pilots – and luggage. Even by ghastly 1970s standards, it was a particularly ugly set of luggage – dark green, with orange and yellow stripes and piping. Ugly or not, it was brand new and four pieces, just in time for ten days in a foreign country. Mom said someone "dropped it off" that morning, along with something inside the largest suitcase – a camera, camera bag, and a stash of film and flash cubes. It all appeared in a blink of one of those cubes.

I had the kind of parents who said yes when their fourteen-year old son wanted to go to Europe. Sure, we were chaperoned by a nun and one of the moms, but we had plenty of opportunities for mischief. And we took advantage of each. I discovered a preference for gin and an appreciation for paella. As we finished our trip at the Hotel Mare Nostrum in Malaga, Aristotle Onassis' yacht with his wife Jacqueline on board was anchored within sight of the hotel. The paparazzi were going crazy. I climbed the ruins of a Moorish castle on a hill above the hotel and watched the show. I had such a good time in Spain that I went again two years later. That time, I earned most of the money myself working at a tuxedo shop in – where else? – the Hillside Shopping Center. On the second trip, we took a ferry boat from Malaga across the Gibraltar Strait and spent a few days in Tangiers. Three continents in seventeen years seemed like a good start.

By 1974, Dad was long out of anything mob adjacent and enjoyed being his own boss. Luckily, he got out before it all came crashing down in a hell storm of indictments, arrests, and convictions. A rudderless Outfit lurched blindly across a vastly changed terrain as the high cotton days of the 1950s and 1960s receded rapidly into the pages of history. When Dad's pals gathered it became a game of Who? Who got arrested? Who got indicted? Who got convicted? Who went to prison? Who died? (In the last case, the next question always pertained to the method of death – accidental, natural, or induced.)

A nasty piece of business called *Title III of the Omnibus Crime Control and Safe Streets Act of 1968* focused the Federal Government's efforts on squashing organized crime. It got worse with the *Organized Crime Control Act of 1970*, which contained special provisions for *Racketeering-Influenced and Corrupt Organizations (RICO)*. The one-two punch of those pieces of legislation would eventually cripple the Outfit and send a parade of its leaders and followers to prison. Despite sputtering and faltering, the power of the Outfit will remain intact in about a year when Dad needs it to save a beloved idiot from his own stupidity.

I left for college in September 1974 – the kind with dorm rooms instead of prison cells – and became the occasional relative – the son, brother, nephew, and cousin who flew in occasionally and briefly rejoined the family before jetting off to a different orbit on a different trajectory. Dad's produce business was doing great, so great that he refused when I offered to apply for student loans. Dad insisted he didn't want me starting life after graduation saddled with debt. He intended to pay the tuition at Briar Cliff College in Sioux City, Iowa, with cold, hard cash. It wasn't until years later when I saw friends struggling under the weight of debt that seemed more like Outfit loansharking than student loans that I realized the enormity of the gift. On a fruit peddler's earnings, by the way.

Most parents pack the family car or truck with their college-bound child's things. They drive to the school, unload the car, and help their child settle into his or her new environment. Being mob adjacent means things happen differently. Dad knew a guy – Dad *always* knew a guy – and this guy had a four-seater Cessna Skyhawk. Driving eight-hours from Chicago to Sioux City was for chumps. I would be flown in a private plane. The plane belonged to a career thief. He had a reputation for getting stolen goods in the air and out of the state before the theft was discovered. This time the cargo was a teenage boy, his father, and some ugly fucking luggage. A taxi would be waiting at the Sioux City airport.

The flight was bumpy – we didn't fly very high – as we flew over endless miles of farmland and landed uneventfully about two hours later. The waiting driver unloaded the plane's cargo hold and put my things into the trunk of the taxi. Dad and I got into the back seat, and the driver took us to the only hill in Iowa, upon which rested Briar Cliff College (today Briar Cliff University). In the last bit of bizarre theater, the driver carried my stuff into Toller Hall, the men's dormitory, and deposited the bags, boxes, and bundles in my room. My new roommate sat slack-jawed with a "who the hell is this guy?" look on his face. None of this seemed the least bit unusual to me – because it wasn't. It had never occurred to me that there was anything unusual about the way my family lived. College gave me that first glimpse of other-ness.

When the last of my things were stacked in the room, Dad looked around and asked if I needed anything. Nope. I walked him back to the car. Before he got into the taxi, he handed me one of those fat envelopes filled with cash. He told me to hide it and call when it ran out. We hugged, he told me he loved me, and got into the back seat. A moment later the taxi pulled away, and I was completely on my own for the first time in my life. That's when I looked around and saw all the cars and trucks and the families helping their children start on this great new adventure.

Another student asked about my coming to college in a taxi. Did I live in Sioux City? I answered honestly and promptly got a reputation that stuck with me for the next two years.

"A plane?" he repeated incredulously. "You flew here in a private plane?"

"Well, it's not our plane. It belongs to a friend of my father. And I didn't fly it."

"The only planes my dad's friends own are crop dusters."

"It was just a little four-seater," I said almost apologetically.

The story of Jeffrey Gentile arriving by private plane made it around campus by morning. People would look at my nametag during orientation activities, and variations like this occurred:

"Are you the guy who flew here in a private plane?"

"Yeah, that's me."

"What are you? In the Mafia or something?"

"No."

"Well, you wouldn't say, even if you were, right?"

"Right."

"But you're Italian? From Chicago?"

"Yup. Born in Little Italy."

"Oh, okay."

Afterward, everyone assumed I was "connected." I let them.

I look back on Briar Cliff through a forty-year lens and remember it as one of the happiest times of my life so far. So much happiness was being had that I nearly got expelled. Here's what happened: It was bitter cold, dead of winter, and the campus was trapped in a snow globe of cold and ice. I had discovered the great amusement known as marijuana in my senior year of high school. Naturally, Briar Cliff didn't allow students to smoke pot in the dorm, so we normally went outside to commit our crime. But it was too fucking cold.

A trash room at the bottom of the stairs leading to the parking lot offered an alternative. Chutes on each of the four floors sent garbage into the dumpster below. It seemed like the perfect place for four people to share a warm joint one cold winter night. Midway through, the door opened. Busted. The Resident Authority on one of the floors opened the trash chute above, got a whiff of weed, and came to investigate. Had it been another student, we might have got away with it, but this R.A. took his role way too seriously.

We four miscreants were subsequently hauled in front of a disciplinary board of faculty and students, fined a staggering $50, and put on probation for the remainder of the term. The dean warned that any further incidents would result in our immediate expulsion. I was working as a waiter at the time, so the $50 was inconvenient but not troublesome. But the probation presented a problem. I worried a letter might go to my parents and my father would fly back out on that Cessna Skyhawk and kill me. Amazingly, a letter about my crime, fine, and probation appeared – in my mailbox on campus. I paid the $50, and my parents were none the wiser. I still have the letter.

College was the beginning of my adventure. Over the next two years, I made friends and created a new life for myself. Drunk and stoned, we'd share anecdotes late at night about our homes and families. The farm kids told Norman Rockwell stories of hayrides and harvests; I told people about Millie and Aunt Jeanette coming over with shopping bags filled with stolen fur coats. This was my family. This was my history.

PHOTOS

Mickey Gentile and **Angeline Filetti** on their wedding day in 1909. The fifteen-year old bride and her sixteen-year old groom barely knew each other. Neither was especially happy about the union arranged by their parents.

The South Water Market, April 1915, as it looked when Giovani Gentile and his son, Mickey, came first with a horse and wagon and later with trucks to buy fruits and vegetables. Mike Gentile and his sons, and brother John walked these streets across the decades. More than 100 years later, Michael and his sons still work at – or adjacent to – the South Water Market.

Gabby Hartnett (left), catcher for the Chicago Cubs, signs a ball for **Al Capone** (right) at Chicago's Wrigley Field in 1931. Left of Al is his son Albert. Left of Albert is a mob-friendly **Sen. Roland Libonati**. (Photo from the John Binder Collection.)

Eldest brother **John Gentile**, here with wife **Doris**. In his youth, John ran liquor on Frank Nitti's crew until he found himself in the middle of a violent confrontation one night.

(Above) A dapper **Mike Gentile** at the wedding of his sister Rachel to Silver Star recipient Larry Rohlfing, May 6, 1945. (Below) After the wedding of his sister Marie to Joe Difiglio, June 6, 1948, Mike hit the town for a night at the Sky Club at 1630 N. Harlem Avenue, one of the hottest of the hot spots.

Private Mike Gentile (second from right, above, and below right) ran the kitchen – and a bit more – as part of the 59th Engineering Construction Company at Elmendorf Air Force Base.

The person who suffered most during the Korean War was **Angeline Gentile** (center), flanked by sons **John** (left) and **Mike**, known in the family as Junior (right). She missed her baby so much when he was in Alaska that Private Gentile cooked up a scheme worthy of Lucy and Ethel to make it home for Christmas.

(L-R) **Angeline Gentile, Mike Gentile, Ruby Privo, John Gentile, Marie Difiglio** enjoy a family dinner on Aberdeen Street. Ruby played an unwitting – and unhappy – role in introducing Mike to his future wife.

Left, Seventeen-year old **Mary Ann Dinardi** in 1950. Right, the high school graduation photo from 1952 she gave to Mike Gentile once she made up her mind he was the man for her. Below, a glam Mary Ann vacations in Florida in 1953.

Mike and **Mary Ann Gentile** on their wedding day, November 7, 1954. The tall, skinny man smiling behind the happy couple is "Goombah" **Johnny DiModica**. He was the Dean Martin to Dad's Frank Sinatra in their Aberdeen Street Rat Pack.

Mickey and **Angeline** sit in front of their children on "Junior's" wedding day. (Back left to right) **Mike Gentile, Marie Gentile Difiglio, Rachel Gentile Rohlfing, Jeanette Gentile,** and **John Gentile**.

Mike Gentile on his wedding day in 1954. His Outfit connections would remain a constant presence until the last days of his life.

PART TWO: MICHAEL

14 OPPORTUNITY ADJACENT

Post-Orlando's, Jackie Cerone found another place for Dad – a restaurant and bar called the Casa Madrid in Melrose Park. Dad would run the bar. Located on 25th Street, south of Lake Street, Casa Madrid was one of the top-earning gambling joints in the western suburbs. The place was owned by former Al Capone bodyguard Rocco DeGrazia. A short, pudgy, man in glasses, DeGrazia had lost control. He lived upstairs in an apartment with his wife, Margaret, but despite his nearly constant presence onsite, money practically walked out the door. The Outfit wanted it stopped.

The joint was popular with everybody, mob adjacent or not. In its heyday, Casa Madrid hosted shoot-outs, hold-ups, torture, and the occasional murder. For some reason, the place was constantly under surveillance by the authorities. The two-story, brown brick building was likened to a concrete fortress. Nothing that happened inside could be heard outside. By design. In its earlier incarnation as a speakeasy and brothel, Casa Madrid featured a series of secret tunnels that led under 25th Street to an escape hatch out of harm's way. Those passageways came in handy during Prohibition for getting liquor in (and patrons out) and served as mob meeting places thereafter. For those who believe in such things, the tunnels of Casa Madrid are also said to be a hotbed of paranormal activity. Several videos on YouTube document the search for ghosts along its concrete walkways. Psychics talk about sensing dark emotions and fear.

Not long after he started working at Casa Madrid, Dad brought us for lunch. Ma made sure we were dressed like little gentlemen, and Dad took us out for the day. Only fourteen-months apart, some said Michael and I could have been twins. The illusion was helped when Ma sometimes dressed us alike. It had to be tough for a man who worked nights to get up in the middle of the day and take his boys to lunch. But he did. Maybe Dad was trying to make up for the fact that he was never home at night. Lunches out became our thing. He took us to every place he ran during his mob adjacent career. We met Mr. DeGrazia once according to Dad, though neither of us remember. When Rocco died of natural causes in 1978, Dad asked if we remembered going to Casa Madrid. The place and the secret tunnels we remembered, the owner we did not.

When I met with the Outfit Old Lion at the beginning of this project, I mentioned Dad working at the Casa Madrid in the late 1960s. The Old Lion expressed his respect and amazement that Rocco DeGrazia was still whacking people in his eighties. The legend went that DeGrazia caught someone stealing, so he beat the shit out of the guy. But the beating didn't stop the guy from stealing again. What choice did DeGrazia have? He put a bullet between the guy's eyes. The Old Lion tipped his head in respect.

After Dad cleaned up the mess at Casa Madrid, Jackie sent him to a different kind of place, a new concept called a pub. Modeled after its British namesake, the pubs of the late 1960s would morph into the modern sports bar – televisions, food, drinks, broads, and gambling. Dad took us for lunch as usual. The Leather Bottle served beer (and root beer) in frozen mugs, towering hamburgers, and mountains of fries. We ate peanuts from baskets and threw the shells on the floor. We were sold.

Dad repeated the same routine next at the Yorkshire Pub. Jackie bounced him from place to place for almost a year, cleaning up one mess and then moving on to the next. Though grateful to Jackie for throwing work his way, Dad didn't like the jobs or the hours, and the bars didn't pay enough. His wheels started turning for a solution. Jackie's way – bouncing him from one joint to another as a hired hand – put Dad on the end of the organ grinder's chain.

The sound was haunting. Jeffrey and I were in our kitchen-adjacent bedroom. We'd shared a room since Lisa was born. Suddenly, we heard a sound like a wounded animal. It was Dad. Wailing. We'd heard him yell, holler, and scream, but this sound was different. In the kitchen, Ma consoled him. Grandma Gentile had just died after a long battle with cancer. Dad stood next

JEFFREY GENTILE AND MICHAEL GENTILE, JR.

to the phone, holding the receiver. Ma put a hand on his shoulder, took the phone, and hung it up. It was one of the most tender moments I ever saw between them.

After Grandpa died in 1957, Aunt Jeanette continued to live with her mother and later nursed Grandma through a long, terrible illness. I remember her as pudgy, with aprons strings that dipped into her doughy middle. She died a flesh-covered skeleton, crying out in pain night and day, tended by a nurse hired by her children.

We attended our first wake. I was ten, and Jeffrey was nine. I thought the wake was creepy and kind of spooky but it didn't bother me. But when Dad lifted Jeffrey off the ground and held him above the casket, it looked like he was going to scream.

Jeffrey said, "He lowered me slowly toward a gray raisin wearing a black dress. It was the most terrifying moment of my life thus far. The odor of too many flowers swirled around me, and I wanted to scream. But I knew I'd get in trouble. So, I did it. I pressed my trembling lips against the cold, hard, greasy cheek of my dead grandmother's corpse. Mom said I had nightmares for weeks. When Grandma Dinardi died a year later, they didn't make me go."

Often, a story as we knew it turned out to be incomplete. The story of Grandma Gentile's death followed a grand tradition of partial truths. Many years later Ma told me the missing pieces to the story. It was more than children needed to know at the time. Yes, grandma cried out in pain night and day and, yes, she was tended by a nurse. She shouldn't have been in so much pain. The nurse had been giving grandma regular injections of morphine. Then one day Aunt Jeanette came home early and caught the nurse shooting up grandma's morphine, while grandma writhed in agony. Grandma suffered for months while the nurse sat beside her bed, high as a kite on Grandma's dope.

Aunt Jeanette attacked the nurse and beat her to the ground. The bloodied nurse finally escaped the pummeling and ran out of the house. Aunt Jeanette didn't call the police. First, she called Grandma's doctor. Then she called her baby brother, Junior. Dad raced back to the old neighborhood from our house in Bellwood. By the time he arrived, the doctor had properly medicated his patient, and Grandma slept comfortably. Dad asked the mortified doctor questions about the nurse. He'd been the family doctor for years and treated Grandpa Gentile during his battle with cancer, too. The family knew and trusted him.

Ma said the nurse "disappeared" not long after the incident. She didn't say it with quotes around it, not exactly. But her tone changed. All she would say is, "No one knows what happened to her." The nurse was never seen again.

Dad buried his mother and got on with the business of living. Post-Orlando's, his life was up in the air. And if his life was uncertain, so was ours.

McCormick Place opened in 1960. The gleaming white convention center designed by Alfred Shaw served as the epicenter for Chicago's nationally-dominant convention trade. Naturally, the Outfit controlled every single union job. Thousands of jobs, everything from janitors to beverage dispensers. Jackie Cerone got Dad one of those cushy union jobs in 1965 on a crew assigned to tear down the booths after conventions and trade shows. Dad didn't mind the work or the hours. All things considered, it was a good job with good pay at a time when he needed it more than ever.

Fact: Most manufacturers didn't want their crap back after a trade show. They can't sell it as new, and it cost too much to ship back. The de facto policy among the union crews was: Send back what people ask for; do what you want with the rest. In theory (two very large words), the stuff gets tossed.

Fact: That Christmas, Ma and Dad's three sisters each got Noritake china, service for sixteen, Homecoming pattern, with serving pieces down to the last gravy boat, meat platter, and covered vegetable dish.

Jeffrey and I came home one day and did a double-take. Were we in the right house? The living room was filled with completely different furniture – couch, chairs, side tables, coffee table, knickknacks, and our family's first console color television. All of this happened in the time we completed a day of grammar school. Jeffrey nearly cried. Color television! Ma was dusting the new coffee table when we walked in. She moved a large ashtray from one side to another, considered its new position, and then moved it back to its original location. Then Ma looked at our feet and pointed. "Take off your shoes. I just cleaned in here."

She said the whole operation came off like a military maneuver, as if the men were accustomed to quickly moving things in and out of homes. First, the men brought the brown sectional sofa up from the basement and put it on the front lawn. Then the upstairs living room furniture went down to the basement. Once the living room was empty, the new furniture and accessories came in the front door. It took less than an hour. Done. Dad never had anything personally to do with the activities that caused merchandise to fall off the back of the truck. He was simply the beneficiary, gifted with access to goods of virtually every type. It wasn't the first or last time.

Not long after the new living room furniture, Dad got Ma a matched set of kitchen appliances in turquoise – stove, refrigerator, electric can opener, electric knife, electric coffee pot, toaster, waffle iron, even a rechargeable electric cigarette lighter. Everything in the kitchen was turquoise. Even the walls. The color matched the tabletop, seats, and chair backs. Welcome to the sixties!

It typically happened one of two ways: One of Dad's pals would ask if someone would be home next Tuesday afternoon. If so, a truck was going to stop by. We never knew what might be on the truck, so it was always a little bit like Christmas morning. Or, Dad would say to one of his pals: If you happen to come across a desk, I'm looking for one for my son. Next thing I know, two men are carrying a desk into our bedroom. One time we got a new freezer. I remember being way more excited about the fort I planned to make with the cardboard box than about the benefits of firmer frozen food. Another time it was a set of bunk beds for Jeffrey and me and a pair of matching dressers. It would be more than three decades before our mother experienced going into a store and selecting her own furniture. Typically, things simply appeared on an as-needed basis. Off the back of a truck.

Best was the time Dad came home with a kitchen. An entire kitchen – cabinets, countertops, sink, faucet, dishwasher, stove, refrigerator. He shouted from the back door, "Boys! Come out here."

Dad's command was inconvenient. Jeffrey and I were in the middle of watching *Superman*. But when Dad called, we answered. I turned off the TV and hurried outside. We found a big truck idling in the alley, filling the narrow space with gas fumes. Pat Ivanelli stood on the back and sent the rolling door flying upward with a vibrating crash. Inside was a jumble of furniture and appliances. Pat slapped his big hands together as if he couldn't wait to dive in. He was a bigger version of Dad – just as dark and handsome, but taller and broader, with powerful arms and big shoulders.

Dad met Pat at McCormick Place. Like him, Pat grew up mob adjacent. Also like Dad, Pat was a recipient of mob boss generosity in the form of his union job. He was in the carpenter's union when Dad worked in the Teamsters tearing down booths. In the crazy world only unions can create, Pat helped build the displays; Dad helped tear them down. Each worked in different unions. They knew a lot of the same people from the same neighborhoods, too, but never met until fate – and mob patronage – threw them together.

Dad jumped up on the back of the truck, grabbed a wooden drawer and handed it to me. "Here," he said. Then he gave me a couple more. "Take these to the basement. And be careful going up and down the stairs."

I nodded and followed orders. Then it was Jeffrey's turn. He got a stack of drawers, too. I came back and repeated the process. When Jeffrey came back, Dad gave him stacks of cabinet doors. I got doors, too, the next time around. A contingent of uncles arrived a little later – Anthony, Tony, Larry, and Joe. They helped take the rest of the stuff off the truck without a lot of chit-chat and banter. Dad despised chit-chat and banter.

Inside, Ma was all excited. While Frankenstein's kitchen came in through the back door in bits and pieces and went down the basement stairs, she made coffee and sandwiches in what would soon be the *old* kitchen. She could finally hold her head up among relatives. Aunt Marie had a basement kitchen. So did Aunt Rachel. Mom's sisters Louise and Carmella each had basement kitchens, and her brother Pat had a basement kitchen, too. The only ones without a basement kitchen were Ma and Aunt Jeanette, and only because Jeanette was a spinster and barely needed one kitchen. We were finally a two-kitchen family.

Despite the happiness and excitement electrifying the air, tragedy visited. After the last piece of kitchen went into the basement and Dad released Michael and me from service, Jeffrey turned on the television, fully expecting to watch the last few minutes of *Superman*.

It was a heart-breaking moment for my television-obsessed baby brother, and I'll let Jeffrey tell it for himself: "*Superman* was over. I didn't understand. I turned *off* the television. I *stopped* the program. But it hadn't stopped for me. I remember being crushed. It would be more than thirty-years before television learned how to wait."

Meanwhile, over the course of the weekend, one end of our basement was transformed into a working kitchen. Pat helped put the upper and lower cabinets in place and installed the countertops. Uncle Anthony took care of the electrical work, and Uncle Tony lent his expertise with lighting. Jeffrey and I served as the clean-up crew. Thereafter, the basement kitchen became our primary food preparation area. Mom preferred to keep the upstairs kitchen tidy, so she seldom did more than make coffee in a kitchen filled with spanking new appliances. Considering how much stuff fell off the back of a truck while Dad worked at McCormick Place, it's a miracle nothing was ever broken, cracked, or chipped. Then suddenly the bounty ended abruptly.

Designed as a shining temple to American commerce, McCormick Place was built – and advertised – to "outlast Rome's glories." In theory. But in the early hours of a bitter cold Monday, January 16, 1967, a janitor reported smoke at 2:05 AM. By 2:30, Fire Commissioner Robert Quinn upgraded the blaze to a five-alarm fire. Eighteen minutes later, he ordered the first special alarm. Within forty-five minutes, two-thirds of the 320,000-square foot building was fully engulfed in flames that lit the night sky along the lake.

Firefighters tried to thaw nearby hydrants and wasted precious time before discovering they weren't frozen; they weren't hooked up. Expressway workers building an interchange on the Stevenson Expressway and Lake Shore Drive disconnected the hydrants during construction. More than 2,000 firefighters and three fireboats pumped water from the lake onto the fire. It didn't matter. According to Commissioner Quinn, "That fire was out of control when the first units arrived." When the fire was out, McCormick Place's massive houseware show lay in smoldering ashes. Beyond the structure, also lost were millions in one-of-a-kind samples, appliances, show booths, and other merchandise.

The inevitable investigation was inconclusive and dutifully spread the blame among the convention personnel, janitors, and security guards. Naturally. The state-of-the-art building designed to be "unsinkable," so to speak, had serious deficiencies in the wiring, not to mention automatic sprinklers that were neither, disconnected fire hydrants, and the vast array of combustible materials inside the convention hall created the perfect firestorm. The mind circles back to those samples, appliances, and merchandise. It would have been a fine score – millions in easily moveable goods. Back up the truck, load the goods, and torch the joint on the way out. Possible, yes. But not probable. The Outfit played the long game, and it didn't make sense to roast the golden goose. Thousands of mob-controlled union jobs disappeared when McCormick Place burned, and the Outfit lost access to many more millions in goods in the years to come. So, what caused McCormick Place to go up in flames? Sparks. It's always sparks.

Jackie quickly found Dad another union job. Manual labor again, and Dad didn't object. He liked to work hard. But he saw a difference between hard work and working like a Sherpa carrying 15-foot long, 300-pound rolls of carpet up several flights of stairs all day, day-in, and day-out. That was the job Jackie offered, and Dad was expected to be grateful. He wasn't. Considering how much money Dad made for the Outfit through his bars, taverns, pubs and clubs, it was kind of a dick move for Jackie to shove him into a series of back-breaking manual labor jobs on a progressively menial level. But Dad didn't complain. He never complained.

Once Dad accepted the first job offer, he became one of Jackie's guys, one of the many beneficiaries of his generosity. Jackie had hundreds – maybe thousands – of people in jobs because he put them there, people who owed their livelihood and loyalty to him. But Jackie's friendship was a two-way street, with both ends running toward him. The carpet job was short-term, Jackie said. He had something else in mind for Dad – running a bar. And if Jackie wants you to run a bar, that's what you do. Because Jackie is the boss. And you owe him.

Learn the lesson: From Jackie's perspective, Mike Gentile was a reliable asset to be moved around at will – Jackie's will. Whether Mike Gentile liked where he was moved or liked what he was doing amounted to exactly zero. "Beggars can't be choosers" was another of Dad's favorite quotes.

The job moving carpet kept food on the table in the meantime, and Dad shouldered on as always. But he wasn't happy. He nearly lost everything because of Jackie Cerone. Jackie and his Outfit associates had been under investigation by both the FBI and Richard Cain's Special Investigations Unit. When Dad wouldn't talk about unions, gambling, or organized crime, Cain shut down Orlando's Hideaway. The "lewd" drag show had always been a smokescreen. If it hadn't been that, it would have been something else – health code violations in the kitchen maybe. Dad got a few bucks when Jackie engineered the sale of Orlando's Hideaway to another mob adjacent acquaintance. And Dad's reward for keeping his mouth shut? A tin cup with a little cash and a series of back-breaking jobs dancing on the organ grinder's chain.

Everybody needs someone they can talk to about the important stuff, and Dad could be candid with Skip without fear of reprisals. They were genuine friends, compared to Dad's semi-professional relationship with Jackie. Dad told Skip he didn't like the dead-end jobs, didn't like being told where to work, and wanted to go out on his own. For the first time in his mob adjacent life, Dad walked a tricky line. No one wanted to appear ungrateful in Jackie's eyes. It wasn't a winning hand. Dad had made an unspoken and unbreakable commitment when he accepted the first job at Casa Madrid and became one of the people who nibbled crumbs out of Jackie's hand. Fortunately, Skip went to bat for his friend and told Jackie, "Mike Gentile is going out on his own."

Jackie insisted. "My people work wherever I send them."

"If Mike wants out, Mike is out."

Two things worked in Dad's favor: 1) Skip was probably the only person in the world who didn't fear Jackie Cerone's legendary wrath; and 2) while Jackie was technically above Skip on the org chart, there remained a level of respect between the cousins that allowed Skip to have his way on the Mike Gentile issue. Some said if Skip hadn't been so fond of the bottle, he would have been the boss instead of Jackie. Maybe. But Skip never aspired to power. He was too busy living a good life. Thanks to Skip, Dad was out. Just like that.

To show the kind of man Skip was: things were tough financially when Dad went out on his own. After Lisa was born, Dad finally agreed to let Mom get a driver's license. (Amazing to think that a woman in the United States of America needed permission for something so basic.) She got her license, but Dad couldn't afford a second car. So, Skip gave Dad his new Oldsmobile 98. Gave it to him like it was nothing. In some ways, Skip was the older brother Dad never had. I write this with no disrespect to Dad's actual brother. Uncle John was a kind, gentle soul. He just didn't have the rough-and-tumble instincts Dad inherited from their father. More often than not, Dad looked out for his older brother rather than the other way around. In Skip, Dad found that person who could be counted on when things got tough. My brother insists I squished his fingers in the power windows of that Oldsmobile, but I don't remember that.

When Dad mentioned going back into the produce business, Skip said a mob-friendly acquaintance named Bill Dimas had a piece of land Dad could use. It was located at the corner of Higgins Road and Route 83 in Elk Grove Village. Dimas' son-in-law Nick Vangel had a place called Nicky's Round-Up Ranch Burgers on the same piece of land for the first couple of years. Eventually, Vangel sold it and opened a banquet hall in Lombard called The Carlisle, which became the go-to place for mob-related family celebrations. So tight were the ties of mob friendship that around 2010 Nick went to visit his pal, imprisoned mobster James Marcello. On tape recordings of their visit, the Feds refer to Vangel as "Nick the Caterer." Nick Vangel and the Carlisle will pop up in our lives again in about two decades.

It would be hard to start a new business without a stake, but Dad wouldn't ask Skip for money. That would have left Skip involved thereafter. Instead, he turned to another friend from Aberdeen Street, someone not remotely mob adjacent. We only knew him as Georgie, but he was the next man who changed our lives. Georgie worked at one of the produce houses at the Randolph Street Market. In a slick piece of maneuvering, Georgie took $800 from the cash register and lent it to Dad. Then Dad and Georgie went around back to talk to Georgie's partner about a used truck they wanted to sell. Junior from the old neighborhood wants to buy it, Georgie said. It was a piece of junk, and there was a bum sleeping inside, but it ran. Dad offered the $800 Georgie took out of the cash register. Georgie's clueless partner accepted his own money for the truck, and the deal was made. After Dad bought the truck, Georgie handed Dad $2,000 in an envelope. He used the money to buy a load of produce and the essentials to start a business.

Not long after, Dad brought Jeffrey and me to a barren piece of land in the middle of nowhere. There was nothing but dirt, a highway overpass, a hamburger joint surrounded by a dusty asphalt parking lot, a rickety old gas station, and nothing else – nothing except the intersection of two four-lane highways with an endless stream of cars filled with people looking to buy farm-fresh produce, even if it did come from downtown Chicago. Dad planned to build a rudimentary structure to start, a simple lean-to made of army surplus tarps. Folding banquet tables became counters. Jeffrey said it was the "Andy Hardy approach." Instead of putting on a show in the barn, we opened a business in less than a barn. On Monday, April 15, 1968, the morning after Easter, Dad went back into the produce business. And this time he dragged his two sons along, whether they liked it or not. One did. The other didn't.

15 HIGHWAY ADJACENT

It seemed like the middle of the night when Ma came into the bedroom and flicked on the light. She said, "Come on, Michael. Time to get up," and flicked the light a couple more times to make the point. I got out of bed, threw on clothes, and hurried into the kitchen. Today was a big day, and I was excited. Dad sat at the table drinking coffee. Ma sat across from him. No matter what time Dad came home from work or went to work, Ma was always there to say hello or goodbye with a pot of coffee. But she never drank the stuff, couldn't stand it.

Dad and I went out the kitchen door. It was still dark when we walked out the back gate and into the alley. Quiet, too, at 4:00 in the morning, and our work shoes crunched on rocks. The shoes were new. Ma took Jeffrey and me to buy the kind with steel toes. I never wore shoes so heavy. The Village of Bellwood wouldn't let us park the truck on the street. There was a gas station three blocks away, and Dad paid the guy a few bucks to let us park overnight. As we walked, Dad told me how he and Grandpa Mickey used to park their trucks at a gas station near the house on Aberdeen. I felt like a big shot. He always took Jeffrey and me to the places where he worked, but only to visit. Today I was working with Dad. Jeffrey didn't get to go, so he was still at home, asleep in his bed across from mine.

The truck was a beast – green and beat-up, the 1959 Ford had McInerny &

Sons painted on the side. Dad said there was a bum sleeping in the back when he bought it. First thing he did was spray the inside with a hose. Then we scrubbed it down – Dad, Jeffrey, and me. It wasn't bad once we got it cleaned. It started right up, too. I never rode in a truck before, not a big one like this. We roared down St. Charles Road, then south on Mannheim. North on Mannheim used to take us to Orlando's Hideaway, but our life went in a different direction now – literally. It wasn't far to the onramp for the I-90, and I was surprised by the amount of traffic on the expressway at 4:00 in the morning. I'd never been up and out of the house this early before. It would be a day of firsts.

Dad got off the Eisenhower on Racine to Taylor Street, and took Taylor to Morgan. Trucks and tractor-trailers stretched for what seemed like miles, all backed up to loading docks leading to two rows of wholesale produce houses lining the street. I learned later that the South Water Market was a hot-bed of Outfit activity. There wasn't a piece of fruit or a vegetable that came into Chicago without the Outfit getting a taste. Some houses sold everything; some specialized. Al Barnett, for example, only sold "tree and deciduous fruits." Gianukas and Mandolini sold fruit, too. Strube was a vegetable house. Some of the big ones like LaMantia sold everything, with floors of giant coolers filled with wooden pallets. You had Austin Merckel, Auster Brothers, Kemp Brothers, Mushroom Growers, and so many I can't remember all of them. Some houses we bought at all the time, some occasionally, and some never.

The streets, docks and sidewalks were packed with people – buyers, sellers, wholesalers, retailers, drivers, loaders, unloaders – and they were all yelling at each other at the exact same time. Hand trucks and jacks whizzed around carrying stacks and pallets of produce. Dad backed the truck into an available spot and jumped into the thick of things. I followed behind and watched. Dad knew a lot of people at the different houses. Some of the old-timers even remembered Grandpa Mickey. We walked from house to house as he examined the goods. Sometimes Dad bought on the spot; other times he made a mental note. We might compare apples or something at two or three places before he made a final choice. He told me how he used to do this with Grandpa Mickey and Uncle John when he was about my age. I felt so grown-up. Dad gradually checked off his shopping list, and we ended at a paper goods wholesaler, where we bought bales of bags, scales, grease pencils (red and black) and signboards. Last night after we finished cleaning out the truck, we loaded four long, folding tables. Everything we bought went into the back. The sun was fully up as we pulled away from the dock. In a few minutes, we were back on the expressway heading west.

There was one more stop before Elk Grove. Dad drove almost an hour northwest to Hanover Park on Route 59 and Irving Park Road. Uncle John had a market there. Dad planned to store perishables in his brother's cooler for now. Uncle John still bought produce that showed trouble, and Dad still jabbed him about it. Then we doubled back twenty miles to Elk Grove. By 8:00 AM, the tables were loaded and we were ready for business. We'd already done a half day's work before we even started our real work day. Cars started pulling in early and never stopped. Dad paid back his loan from Georgie in six weeks. He said, "You always have to pay your debts in case you want to go back."

From the first day we parked the truck, we were busy, busy, busy. Dust swirled around us as car after car pulled into the dirt lot. We were filthy by the end of the day. It seemed like a special exit on the highway dumped every car into our parking lot. Dad said he hadn't seen anything like this since he started his truck route in Skokie. Apparently, shoppers in Elk Grove Village also never saw onions before! This became our routine: Up before dawn, down to the market, out to Hanover Park, double back to Elk Grove, and then "pile 'em high and watch 'em buy." That's what Dad always said. The higher the display, the more people bought.

After a few weeks, Jeffrey started working, too. He was handy for a few things: He had nice handwriting, so he made the signs. Jeffrey was also kind of artistic and made nice-looking displays. He was smaller and couldn't lift the heavy stuff. Sweeping and cleaning up usually fell to him. And so, at ages twelve and thirteen, we were officially members of the work force, with brand new social security cards (one number apart) and savings accounts at the neighborhood Bank of Commerce.

One of the first things Dad taught us in our new produce career was how to mob count. Over and over, he asked, "What comes after 29?"

The answer will surprise you.

It's not 30. It's 20. Imagine yourself standing next to a mountain of watermelons. You pick one up and toss it to your brother who is standing in the truck. Repeat while counting silently. At the same time, the salesman is counting. You're counting and counting, 27, 28, 29, and 20. You do this a few more times until you get to however many you told the salesman you wanted to buy.

Dad says, "That's 100."

Salesman says, "I counted 120."

Dad says, "Fine. We'll take them off and count again."

Salesman says, "Never mind."

We paid for 100 watermelons. We left with 120. This discount program is known as mob counting.

Back in the Aberdeen Street days, grandpa had Dad take a box of produce to the Benevento's back door every Friday as a sign of respect. A slightly different version happened after Dad went back into the produce business. Every Friday, we dropped off a box with a sampling of the week's best produce for the Sisters of Saint Joseph who lived and worked at St. John Chrysostom Grammar School.

It was weird going into the convent portion of the school – seeing where the nuns ate and watched television, glancing in their sparse bedrooms on the way to their kitchen. We didn't think of nuns as people with lives. They were just scary figures of vengeance and discipline. But I'd walk in with the box, and they'd start gushing about fresh corn or Bing cherries. It was so unexpected. The boxes served the same purpose as the brooches my dad used to give to his mother when he wanted to apologize for something. It turned out Jeffrey and I had a knack for getting in the bad graces of the good Sisters of Saint Joseph. Ma practically had her own designated place on the bench outside the principal's office when she came to discuss the recent misbehavior of Son One or Son Two.

It's one of those moments etched in my memory: Sister Bonafilia was a small woman with a stern face, steel-rimmed glasses, and high standards for behavior. Jeffrey and I ran afoul of those standards on a fairly regular basis. You know how Ingrid Bergman played this warm, kindly nun in *The Bells of Saint Mary?* Sister Bonafilia was no Ingrid Bergman. She started from the premise that all children were wicked and needed to be punished. Ma sat in the chair nearest the door, and I sat next to the window, stealing looks outside while Sister Bonafilia explained how I continually disrupted class with improper questions, like: If God knows everything, why do we have to go to Confession? Sister Bonafilia looked at me with narrowed eyes and warned: "A smart mouth will never get you anywhere, Michael John."

We drove the nuns to extra prayers with years of smart-mouth questions, observations, retorts, and assorted acts of heresy and sacrilege. It wasn't our fault they painted illogic with broad strokes of "faith." In a moment of frustration, Ma once asked, "Did it ever occur to either of you to just sit quietly and listen?"

It didn't. Jeffrey and I looked at each other and wondered what the point was in going to school if you didn't ask questions. The fact that the questions annoyed the nuns was a different matter.

Dad's business grew quickly. At first, we operated off the back of the truck with a few banquet tables borrowed from family members. After a couple of months, Dad stuck 2x4s in oil drums full of cement. (Apparently when you live mob adjacent you know where to get empty oil barrels and large quantities of prepared concrete on short notice.) Once the concrete was set, Dad built a simple lean-to off the side of the truck to prevent the merchandise from baking in the sun. We outgrew that, too. Dad had the power company run a pole. Next, he bought a used refrigerated trailer from Dean's Milk. That meant no more trips to Hanover Park, except the refrigeration unit crapped out after a few weeks. When he called the company to complain, they tried to give him the brush off. Dad promised to paint "Dean's Milk is a Crooked Outfit" in big letters on the side of the trailer facing the highway. A couple days later Dean's Milk sent someone to fix the cooler. It never broke down again. The selections kept growing, too. By the end of the summer, the counters looked like the produce department of a major grocery store.

Now that we had electricity, Dad called in the old crew. Pat Ivanelli, Dad's carpenter pal from the old McCormick Place days, helped build a larger, enclosed wooden structure out of plywood, lumber, and shingles. Uncle Joe and Uncle Larry helped, too. Inside, parallel 50-foot counters ran the length of the trailer. Plywood covered the fronts. Large, hinged doors lifted to form an awning for the customers outside while they shopped the line. Then Uncle Anthony ran BX cable along the ceiling, strung lights and installed outlets. A coat of paint, and we were ready to go. From the minute those big doors went up around 8:00 AM, cars started pouring in. Sometimes they were still pouring in after the doors closed, and sometimes we sold off the back of the open trailer doors as we were closing, just like the "old days" of two summers ago.

We made a good living on that corner (with three kids in private school, by the way), and Dad got to be his own boss instead of dancing on that organ grinder's chain. It was hard, dusty work, and that was fine with him. We did business like a Starbucks. Watermelons had wings. So did 100-lb. sacks of potatoes and 50-pound bags of onions. Every Mother's Day we sold a truckload of flowers. Jeffrey and I took turns standing along the side of Higgins Road hawking bouquets to passing cars. And why not pull in and get a fruit basket? We sold tons of fruit baskets around every holiday.

During the four years we were in that location, no one ever bothered anything or robbed us or vandalized us. Until Saint Jeffrey came up one night to hang out and drink with his high school friends. Someone smoked a cigarette and used a scale pan for an ashtray. Dad started yelling the next morning about how they could have burned the place down.

Eventually, the gas station became available. We spent the next two years there. Dad's crew dismantled the old structure and repurposed the lumber and plywood to make counters and signs in the new location. The tractor trailer was towed over and parked against the back along a brick wall. Dad cleaned the place up inside and out, splashed on a little paint here and there, and converted the double service bays into an open-air market. He'd open those big garage doors, and people would see this long counter with huge displays of fruits and vegetables. Now, we had refrigerated cases for milk and eggs. Fresh bread and packaged bakery goods, too. One thing stayed constant: The ca-ching of the second-hand brass cash register.

One other thing stayed the same: Dad's friends were still his friends even if he didn't work mob adjacent. Every now and then one of his mob pals would turn up to visit with Dad. Sometimes they went for coffee or lunch, and Dad left me in charge. That meant Jeffrey did all the work and waited on all the customers while I read *Sports Illustrated.* After the visit, Dad's friend would walk the length of the counter and buy a lot of everything. Dad always tried to refuse their money, but they always insisted. Business was business. They paid what was due.

Once a week, "Uncle" Tony Mastro pulled up in his gigantic car. Uncle Tony always needed two carts at the produce market. Among Dad's friends, Uncle Tony remained a favorite. He was the teller of dirty jokes and indiscreet stories that my father would try to pre-empt. Uncle Tony would start talking about "this broad" and "tits until you couldn't breathe." I remember that last phrase verbatim because I had recently discovered what "tits" were and wondered how much tit was required before a man couldn't breathe. I looked forward to finding out.

I remember being in Dad's office at Orlando's Hideaway. Uncle Tony patted the surface of the desk and said, "Madone, if this desk could talk!" Dad gave him the same cold eyeball he gave Ma when he wanted her to drop a subject immediately, or he wanted us to behave like gentlemen. What did the desk know? Uncle Tony never said. He was the kind of guy who gave you a $3,000 gold watch when you're 10-years old just because he had it in his pocket. A veteran second-story man, his job was to unlock things that weren't meant for people like him to unlock. Uncle Tony also worked the door at Skip and Jimmy's gambling joints, making sure no one got out of line. He looked like he walked right out of Central Casting. If you needed someone who looked like a mob guy, my Uncle Tony was the guy. Heavy set, balding, with a shirt opened too far and showing too much hairy chest and too many gold chains. He wore polyester double-knit Sansabelt pants – all the rage at the time – in a rainbow of colors. I never saw anyone wear white leather dress shoes without socks before. Rings, chains, watch, gold bracelets. Cologne. He called Dad Mikey – and he called it loudly coming through the door, preceded by, "Yo!"

Uncle Tony needed two carts because he had two families. The idea that one man had two families with two different women at the same time seemed remarkable. But that was the case with Uncle Tony. He filled the carts with identical orders. At the end, he'd pull out a wad of cash bound with an Italian money clip – a thick rubber band. He'd lick his thumb and count off tens and twenties. Then when you took the boxes to his car, he'd push two 10-dollar bills into your back pockets. Dad said Uncle Tony would buy two fur coats. Two diamond bracelets. Two houses. Two whatever. This way he never had to remember what he bought for which woman.

Uncle Tony kept a second family because his wife, "Aunt" Francis, was terminally ill. He would never divorce her. That would be a sin and a shirking of duty. Instead, he set up an alternate arrangement with a nice lady named Pam to make the transition easier when the time came. After Aunt Francis finally passed, he married the woman who kept his other home. Uncle Tony and Pam were married for more than 30 years, until he died.

I hold onto one childhood memory before everything changed. Good at sports from the time we played baseball at the intersection of 47th Avenue and Erie Street, I played little league and was the only eleven-year old alternate on the Bellwood All Star team. Dad came to one of my games. He usually didn't come to anything. But he came this time, and afterwards he took the entire team to Pepe's for lunch. He told the kids to order whatever they wanted. They couldn't believe it. One asked if he could have a second hot dog. Dad told him to get fries, too. The bill must have been $40, which was a lot of money for lunch back in the 1960s. By the end of that meal, every kid wanted a Dad like mine – the big car, the flashy clothes, the wad of cash. I just wanted a Dad who showed up for things all the time. That day, I looked into the stands, and I could see he was proud of me. And it meant everything. Wanting to make Dad proud became a central driver in my life. I failed spectacularly sometimes. Then at twelve-years old, I had to stop playing games and go to work.

In the spring of 1969, I graduated eighth grade. I'd walked to grammar school four blocks from home. For high school, I would take a bus west on St. Charles Road to Cottage Hill Road in Elmhurst, and then north two blocks to Immaculate Conception High School. At St. John Chrysostom, I went to school with kids like me. They looked like me, dressed like me, and lived in houses like mine. But the kids in Elmhurst lived in actual mansions – some had built-in swimming pools and live-in help. I found myself in high school with the children of executives, publishers, industrialists, and entrepreneurs. Their fathers owned the local newspaper, *The Elmhurst Press*, and most of the car dealerships: Elmhurst Ford, Long Chevrolet, Roesch Chevrolet, Bierk Cadillac, and Haggerty Pontiac.

Their kids dressed better, lived better, and got brand new cars for their sixteenth birthdays while I rode the bus. They had white collar fathers. My father's collar was dirty from hard work every day. The Elmhurst kids had all the money and freedom they wanted. I had an allowance and a curfew. I felt different, and I didn't like it. When the school year ended, I went to work because my dad needed me.

I didn't mind the work, but Jeffrey hated it. A born night-owl, he usually had trouble getting up early because he stayed up too late watching movies with Ma. It pissed Dad off. Jeffrey also hated the dirt, dust, and flies. He could barely bring himself to touch a rotten tomato. Sometimes he wore gloves, and Dad teased him about it in Italian. *"Ancora guanti."* "Again gloves!" Jeffrey and I fought like crazy. Sometimes it got physical. I always won. He has the scars to prove it. I had a temper, but he was a mouthy little shit. Sometimes you couldn't help wanting to pop him one. And sometimes I did.

I got tall, lean, and strong as I ripped through my teens. Jeffrey got fat, pimpled, and slow. He was a mama's boy, the good son who never failed to make me look bad. He did well in school without studying and was "college material." We fought constantly. But when he came to Immaculate Conception the year after me, nobody bothered him. I looked out for my little brother – nobody beat him up but me. I was terrible to him then. But ask him today, and he'll say he deserved some of it.

[I did. JG]

When Jeffrey was born, the nuns at the Catholic hospital told Ma to pick a different first name because he needed to be named after a saint. And there was no Saint Jeffrey. Until my fucking brother was born.

Life followed its pattern. Autumn, winter, and early spring meant school. I didn't like school and didn't do especially well (mostly because I didn't try very hard) and got in trouble often. The usual stuff – fighting, mouthing off, not doing my homework. The nuns beat me. A beating now and then was considered good for a child's character. But that didn't work. I did what I wanted to do and didn't worry about the rest. Come the spring, it meant going back to work.

Part of me resented it in the way all kids resented having chores. I didn't like giving up my summers to work in the heat, dust, and rot. I already had chores at home. Did I have to help support the family, too? I had no awareness how at the same age my dad did the same thing with Grandpa Mickey. It was hard not comparing our lives to the rich kids in Elmhurst. We didn't have all the things they had, but we had other things that were irreplaceable, like the deep knowledge that no matter what, "these people" will be there for you. They won't just help you move a dead body, they'll help you dismember it and make dog food out of it so there's no body left to find. That's how Italian family works.

Sometimes I felt like I got cheated out of my childhood, but sometimes the world we lived in delivered unexpected benefits. When Dad worked at McCormick Place, he became friendly with a man named Sam Buongiorno. He was part of a crew that worked under the King of Janitors, Ben Stein – a mob-friendly union boss. After the fire destroyed McCormick Place, Sam and everyone else scrambled for new work. He found it at a place that reached back to the earliest days of my family. Wrigley Field was as close to a holy place as Mickey Gentile ever got outside of a church. Going to Cubs' games with his boys had been a highlight for the hard-working peddler. How could he ever have expected one day his grandson would practically have run of the place?

Not long after we started working in Elk Grove, Dad made a powerful new friend. Orland Busse owned most of Elk Grove before it was Elk Grove. In fact, the stretch of Route 83 that eventually ran through what became Elk Grove was known as Busse Road. His farm produced massive amounts of corn and other grains. He was a big man, with a booming voice. His family lived in a big, white clapboard house on a square of land among fields of corn, corn, and more corn. He took a liking to Dad. Mr. Busse liked people who worked hard. When the Village of Elk Grove started giving Dad grief about licenses, building codes, and health department regulations, Busse told the City to get bent. And they got bent. Nobody in that two-cow town pestered Dad again.

We also met Orland's son, Glenn. He was about thirty and married to Marsha. Following Dad's advice, Glenn set up a produce operation on farm land adjacent to his family's home. It turned into a winner, too. Glenn and Marsha became fixtures in our family. Marsha wasn't much of a cook at the time, and Glenn loved Ma's cooking. So, Ma taught Marsha how to make a few things. Through Marsha, I met her brother, Billy. Get this: Marsha's maiden name was Kidd. That made her brother Billy Kidd. Seriously. Billy was about my age and a big baseball fan like me.

When I mentioned to Dad that I wanted to go to a Cubs' game, I expected to hear about my work schedule and how I couldn't go. To my surprise, he gave me the day off. Billy and I would go, and Glenn would act as driver/chaperone. Then Dad called Sam Buongiorno. After the call, Dad explained how things would work. When you're mob adjacent, there's a procedure. He told me where we were supposed to meet Mr. Buongiorno. Dad's friend would let us into the park without paying (Nice!) and we could sit wherever we wanted (Nice!). Mr. Buongiorno also promised a tour of the park. (Very Nice!) Lastly, Dad pointed a warning finger, and told me to behave. "Don't embarrass me."

Mr. Buongiorno waited outside exactly where Dad said I would find him. "I'd know you were Mike's son anywhere," he said when I introduced myself. A big guy with dark, dark skin, Mr. Buongiorno was Southern Italian, the kind that looked like he got a little too close to Africa. Dad said they called him Black Sam at McCormick Place. He took us past the ticket booths, past the ticket takers, and up into the stands. "We're not very full today. You can sit in one of those boxes," he said pointing.

Glenn was practically sputtering he was so impressed with the treatment. Regular people walked up to the booths and bought tickets. But when you're mob adjacent people escort you to your choice among 40,000 seats. It got better. The vendors wouldn't take my money. Not for hot dogs, popcorn, and not for the beer they shouldn't have been giving underage kids. But the fix was in. I was Sam Buongiorno's guest; Glenn and Billy were my guests, and we owned that fucking place. It was just like the Orlando's Hideaway days when cocktail waitresses brought hot and cold running snacks to Jeffrey and me while we played in the pool. It's good to be the king.

The Gentile family came full circle that day. Mickey and his sons used to get bleacher seats. Whenever I went with friends, we sat in the bleachers, too. Box seats were expensive, especially for a high school kid. Don Vincenzo gave Mickey box seats to show his appreciation for Mickey's help in 1943. Here I was in 1970, and Sam Buongiorno gave me a box seat to show his friendship for my dad.

During the seventh inning stretch, Mr. Buongiorno appeared. "Come with me. I wanna show you guys something."

Whatever Mr. Buongiorno wanted to show me, I couldn't wait to see. Billy and I walked out of the box and followed him down the stairs. Glenn stayed in the seat drinking free beer. Next thing I knew, we're standing ON Wrigley Field. ON the grass. When you're a sports fan, certain ground is sacred. You never expect to walk on it. But there I was in my sneakers standing on Wrigley Field grass. Sure, it felt like grass anywhere. But for that moment, I felt like part of the game. I wondered if the people in the stands wondered who those teenagers were on the field.

We went to the club house first, and I tried not to look like a rube craning my neck in every direction. The club house led directly to the dugout. Billy and I were a pair of tongue-tied morons as we met guys like Ernie Banks, Ron Santo, Roger Metzger, Ken Holtzman, Billy Williams, and Ferguson Jenkins. These guys were my gods and heroes. Coach Leo Durocher scowled, none too happy about Buongiorno leading a tour through the dugout during a game. But the coach knew the score. He knew Buongiorno was connected, and that was that. If I could have played any sport professionally, it would have been baseball. Sometimes when I played on the four corners of 47th and Erie, I imagined myself in a blue and white Cubs' uniform. Now, I stood in front of them shaking hands. I didn't even think to ask for an autograph. Imagine what a ball with all those signatures would be worth today! Stupid!

"Let me show you the scoreboard," Mr. Buongiorno said.

I didn't know what he was talking about. All I had to do was look over my shoulder to see the massive green sign hovering over the outfield bleachers. But we followed Mr. Buongiorno around the rim of the field. He showed us the big doors in left field that opened to get the lawn mowing equipment out. Then we walked through a doorway hidden among the ivy-covered walls lining the field, up some stairs, down a brick-lined hallway and up a long staircase. Holy shit, we weren't going to see the scoreboard; we were going INSIDE. He had a key for the metal door because Sam Buongiorno's job was to work the famous manual scoreboard.

Narrow and bare, wood-paneled walls lined the length of this "backstage" area. All over the walls, big green rectangles with white numbers hung on hooks. The numbers tracked the game inning-by-inning – the balls, strikes, batter uniform number, and outs. He said each number weighed about five pounds. He took a 1 off a hook and handed it to me. Imagine how much I wanted to keep it. But he hung it back on the hook. There were a couple of battered old chairs, a long table, and not much else. Another thing: It was hot in there. This was mid-July. The heat in August must have been awful. No wonder Mr. Buongiorno's skin was so dark – he was roasting in that metal box! He told us about the scoreboard with pride. Apparently, no other ballpark had one like it. Billy and I hung out a couple of the openings and gasped at the park spread out before us. We looked at each other as if to say, "Can you fucking believe THIS?"

The Cubs won – I remember because Mr. Buongiorno had one more job. A flag pole above the scoreboard told the day's story in a single letter. Raising the W flag indicated a win; the dreaded L testified to a different outcome. Mr. Buongiorno let me help raise the white flag with a blue W. I couldn't have felt prouder if I raised the flag over Iwo Jima. Then he walked us back to our seats.

Around this same time, to make work easier, I needed my truck driver's license. But you needed to be eighteen. Also, to get a truck driver's license, you needed to show your birth certificate. My birth certificate – the real, original one issued by Loretto Hospital – says I was born on July 29, 1955. That made me seventeen at the time. But you don't worry about things like licensing procedures when you grow up mob adjacent. Dad knew a "paper guy." This paper guy coincidentally worked at the DMV and had a side business creating fake documents – drivers' licenses, passports, etc. Dad paid him to create a new birth certificate for Michael John Gentile, Junior. Except this Michael John Gentile, Junior was born a year earlier on July 29, 1954. I was suddenly eighteen. I took the new birth certificate from the first guy and went to a second guy at the DMV who didn't know about the first guy; and the second guy gave me a truck driver's license. Just like that. I stayed a year older on paper until I was 39, and the error got discovered when I renewed my driver's license.

Being mob adjacent shows you things that not everyone gets to see. After one of the best afternoons of my life, I went back to that dusty corner. Because my dad needed me.

16 INDICTMENT ADJACENT

E verything changed suddenly. The Chicago papers – the *Sun-Times,* the *Chicago Tribune,* the *Daily News,* and the *Herald* – had a field day when Jackie Cerone was indicted, convicted, and subsequently sent to prison in 1971 on a multimillion dollar interstate gambling rap – all because of a rat named Lou Bombacino. The story played out in the media for months. Scum like Bombacino floated around the Outfit from its inception, people looking to make a quick buck while being unburdened by pesky virtues like principles or loyalty. Mob boss Paul Ricca and others vouched for Bombacino's credibility. In exchange for giving him a job in a phone room taking bets for Jackie, Bombacino repaid the favor by working as an informer for the FBI. We heard about this topic endlessly that year.

Bombacino moved up in the organization until he circulated among the top tier Outfit leaders. He used his position to gather evidence showing Jackie's operation grossing between $300,000 and $400,000 weekly. Bombacino also linked gambling genius Donald Angelini (known as Chicago's Wizard of Odds) with Jackie as a handicapper. He provided Photostats of checks and betting records. For good measure, Bombacino also quoted Jackie as boasting about judges on his payroll "in case he gets arrested." None of those judges came to his aid, and Jackie spent three years in prison.

The story of Jackie's ultimate downfall and prison sentence for skimming millions from Las Vegas casinos is brilliantly charted in *Casino*. (The movie version fictionalizes key events and changes names.) Through a series of bad choices by mob members and sheer, blind, dumb luck, the Feds sent the topmost Outfit bosses to prison after a member of the Kansas City crime family and a Las Vegas casino worker, turned states' evidence. It's a fascinating book and a great movie.

Skip's younger brother Jimmy was also indicted (and later convicted) of conspiring with Jackie to promote interstate gambling in 1970. What a crock of shit! Interstate gambling didn't need "promotion." People came looking for it. Jackie and his associates saw a need and filled it, even though Daddy Government wagged his Federal finger and said no, no, no.

According to his court testimony, the FBI recruited Bombacino while in prison. He spilled his guts on Jackie's operation to avoid being sent back for burglary and robbery. Not only did he squeal on the Outfit, he embarrassed them – in public. During the trial, Paul Ricca was forced to testify from his wheelchair and corroborate Bombacino's sworn testimony that Ricca met at times with Jackie Cerone.

Jackie had been arrested more than nineteen times on charges including loitering, gambling, bookmaking, and robbery; he was also the suspect in four murders. His accomplishments included pleading the Fifth Amendment forty-five times before the McClellan Committee in the late 1950s. Those government assholes got nothing. Finally, they nailed him. Judge Abraham L. Marovitz sentenced Jackie, Jimmy, and three others (Donald Angelini, Joseph Ferriola, and Dominic Cortina) to prison for five years. Another defendant, Frank Aurelio, was sentenced to eighteen months in a separate trial and fined $10,000.

Skip and Tony Mastro got caught up in it, too, when the cops raided their houses in 1971. Uncle Tony, a mere "associate" according to the newspapers, slipped through the noose and avoided jail. Skip wasn't so lucky. He was indicted in 1972 and subsequently convicted. When Jimmy got wind of Bombacino's double-dealing, the FBI whisked their star witness out of town and into the witness protection program, where he lived safely and anonymously – until 1975, when he got greedy and stupid again.

The indictments and convictions of people we knew, the lurid allegations in the newspaper, and the moralizing stories on the evening news were enough to make you lose your faith in journalistic integrity. Nothing we heard or read jibed with the people we knew. Dad took it hard, too. Some of the Outfit guys caught up in the Fed's snare were just names – people dad never met but names he recognized. But Skip and Jimmy were personal friends. Even Jackie – despite Dad's complicated history with the mob boss – was a friend. And friends don't like to see friends sent to prison.

Skip Cerone was like a wishing well. If you wanted something or desired something, the guy you needed was Skip. If Skip could do a favor for a friend, he would. All he asked in return was real and true friendship. Guys like Lou Bombacino showed how tough it could be to find real friends. That's what Skip got from Dad. And that's why over the years Skip helped Dad by giving him a car when Dad couldn't afford one, or helping Dad get out from under Jackie's thumb. Skip never made a big deal out of his generosity.

By the mid-1970s, Dad was comfortably back on his feet financially. Having been cheated out of their honeymoon when Grandpa Mickey took sick on their wedding day, then almost immediately becoming the parents of two boys born fourteen-months apart, Dad decided it was time to give his wife a honeymoon. But when you're mob adjacent, you don't just pick up the phone and make a reservation. You call somebody else. In this case, Dad called Skip. Even when he was knee-deep in indictments, Skip took a minute to do a favor for an old friend. It was a nice distraction from the bullshit, he said. He made a long-distance call to another old friend in Las Vegas. That's all it took – that's all it usually took, one phone call.

Our parents rarely did anything alone. Occasionally they went out to dinner with friends, but they never went away. Ever. Imagine our surprise when Dad announced their trip to Las Vegas. Even more surprising, they were leaving us alone. I was seventeen and Jeffrey was sixteen; he could look after Lisa, so we didn't need a babysitter. Ma packed their bags for a long weekend in the desert. Neither had ever been to Vegas, and Ma was especially excited. I was excited, too. It meant our parents would be gone for the weekend, and I wondered what it would be like not having them underfoot. I seized the opportunity and planned a party for Saturday night.

Nicholas Pileggi quotes a former blackjack dealer in his book *Casino,* "We all knew Chicago ran the Stardust." The top level of management – hotel president Alan Sachs, casino manager Bobby Stella, and casino host Gene Cimorelli – all came from Chicago. "So were dozens of pit bosses, floor men, and dealers." Back then it was called the Stardust Hotel and Golf Course, with no mention of the casino that paid for everything. In the fictionalized movie version of Pileggi's book, Cimorelli's character is called "Billy Sherbert," played by Don Rickles. It was Cimorelli's job to make sure the high rollers had a good time – and left with empty wallets. Skip and Gene Cimorelli had been friends for years. So, if you were a friend of Skip's and mentioned wanting to go to Las Vegas, he could make that happen – and in a style beyond your dreams and

JEFFREY GENTILE AND MICHAEL GENTILE, JR.

your wallet, all with one phone call.

Ma and Dad were met at McCarren Field, the Las Vegas Airport, by a chauffeur in a black suit and cap carrying a sign with "Gentile" written on it. He took the hand luggage and led them to a town car, where a bottle of iced champagne waited in the back seat. When they got to the hotel, Cimorelli escorted them to an enormous suite with a view of the Strip. He asked about Skip and Jimmy and other friends back in Chicago and said a dinner reservation had been made for 8:00 PM. They also had a table reserved for Frank Sinatra's 11:00 PM show. Ma was giddy from the excitement, the two glasses of champagne, and the thought of seeing Frank Sinatra again. Then Cimorelli handed her a small velvet bag containing casino chips ($500 in various denominations). He encouraged her to have fun and left my parents to enjoy their suite.

Half an hour later, there was a knock on the door. Dad opened it, and a waiter pushed in a cart loaded with platters and plates of food and another bottle of champagne they hadn't ordered. Ma said the shrimp were the size of spare ribs and the bowl of caviar was big enough to wash your face in. Dad tried to tip the waiter, but he wouldn't take the money. In fact, Cimorelli warned Dad. He said, "Your money is no good here, Mike."

That night, they sat at a front row table for Sinatra's late show. For the next forty-years, Ma never stopped talking about the time she saw "Frank" at the Stardust. She'd list the songs and repeat the jokes like prayers. Odd details caught her attention – like how there were no wrinkles in Sinatra's tuxedo pants. Ma couldn't figure out how a man put on pants without making even a little wrinkle. He ended the show with "My Kind of Town," a musical tribute to Chicago. To Ma, he was singing to her.

Over the next two days, our parents were the King and Queen of the Stardust. When the breakfast they hadn't ordered arrived the next morning, there was another velvet bag containing another $500 in casino chips. A note from Cimorelli said he hoped they were having a good time and urged them to call if they needed anything.

While our parents saw Phyllis Diller perform on Saturday night (Ma was shocked to realize the comedienne worked with a pre-recorded laugh track), I crammed about thirty people into our house. The party got loud and smoky, and someone found the bar downstairs. Saint Jeffrey was pissed. He said Ma and Dad would find out – there was no way one of the neighbors wouldn't mention a party for thirty loud teenagers – and we'd both be in trouble. Dad told us (meaning me) explicitly: "No parties and nobody in the house." Lisa – then about nine – got so upset by the crowd and the noise that she started crying. Jeffrey took her in the bedroom and closed the door, and that was the last I saw of them. They watched TV, and the party went on past midnight.

Across the country, another breakfast cart arrived at our parents' suite the next morning. And, yes, there was another bag of casino chips among the breakfast goodies. Mom said the Stardust served the most beautiful food she'd ever seen. Everything was perfect, probably thanks to Frank Rosenthal's obsession with consistency and quality. Remember the scene in *Casino* where "Sam 'Ace' Rothstein" complains to the chef about the uneven distribution of blueberries in the muffins? Ma said everything put in front of them looked like it was about to be photographed for a cookbook. When *Casino* came out, Ma howled and said, "It was *just* like that!"

They were passing time in the casino before their flight when Frank Sinatra walked through the room. Ma's heart beat a little faster, especially when Sinatra seemed to tip his head in their direction. Did he remember Dad from Orlando's Hideaway? They never found out. Sinatra kept walking.

When you're mob adjacent, you don't worry about packing bags. You don't worry about carrying your luggage downstairs, checking out, or paying your bill. Because there is no bill, and someone did everything else for you. When it was time to go, Mr. Cimorelli found my parents at a blackjack table, and said, "Your car is ready, Mike."

He walked them outside and handed Mom a little velvet box. "Something to remember your trip," Cimorelli said. Mom gushed and blushed and opened the box. Inside she found a small gold brooch made of pearls and diamond chips, shaped like a starburst. Then he asked Dad to tell that "miserable son of a bitch" hello (meaning Skip).

And in case you're wondering, despite giving them $1,500 in chips and spending all of it in the casino, my parents didn't win a cent. As Dad was fond of saying, "Vegas wasn't built on winners."

Also in case you're wondering, one of the neighbors ratted me out. Dad screamed and hollered, and I got grounded. But it was worth it. Best party of the year.

Many years – and many trips – later, Ma said that weekend to Las Vegas was the best. And it was all because of a man found guilty on gambling charges by a jury of strangers. How's that for a pisser? I'll bet every one of those jurors would have gladly accepted that trip if Skip offered.

17 HOLIDAY ADJACENT

We moved to a bigger location on Addison Road when Dad went into business with Larry Hadley in 1972. Larry had a big operation, but he needed a strong manager. Enter Dad. The building was L-shaped, with 10 garage doors that opened to create a giant outdoor marketplace. An enormous cooler ran the length of one side. When full on a Thursday afternoon, the cooler looked like one of the big produce houses down at the market. The crowds never stopped. Sometimes we got two deliveries a day. Dad had to hire extra help. And kept hiring more. Uncle Joe sometimes came on weekends and stood in the parking lot with a flag, directing cars in and out of the spaces. It was crazy busy. We had two check-out lanes like a grocery store. It wasn't unusual to sell a truck full of watermelons on a Saturday afternoon in July. Dad's knack for making a business pay off never changed.

The other thing that never changed was the respect Dad felt for the people who helped him along the way. Back in the 1970s, Dunkin' Donuts had a popular commercial where a sleepy baker staggers to the shop muttering, "Time to make the donuts." My brother and I called the holidays "time to make the boxes." Every Thanksgiving, Christmas, and Easter, Dad made a special trip to the market for the foods Italians eat at the holidays – fennel, rappini, that kind of stuff – plus all the seasonal fruits and vegetables. Jeffrey would make seven boxes and one of us – it was always me, not one of us, me – would bring the boxes to the DB Lounge in Melrose Park.

I walked in that place seventeen-years old and walked out feeling twenty-five. By the 1970s, Northlake, Melrose Park, and Bellwood were loaded with mob hangouts. A lot of Italians left the city when Mayor Daley knocked down most of Little Italy to build a college campus. He could have got more land cheaper elsewhere, but Daley wanted to destroy Little Italy. Chose to do it deliberately, and threw generations of families out of their homes. For spite, the Italians said. Because those Irish so-and-sos still hated the Italians. Draw your own conclusions.

The DB Lounge was on 25th Street, just south of North Avenue on the east side of the street. It stood in the shadow of the large International Harvester factory on a street lined with retail and commercial businesses. It seated maybe forty to fifty people. Narrow, thin, and deep, it was always smoky and dark. You entered from the street. The bar was on the right, with stand-up tables filling the rest of the space. Nothing special – except for the regulars. The DB Lounge was a prime hangout for the Outfit's old guard and young lions. Because I was Mike's boy, that made me automatically all right. They bought the underage kid drinks and told me stories I probably shouldn't have heard.

Taking the holiday boxes was always a great gig because A) they treated me like a million bucks; and B) think about what a $20 tip was to a seventeen-year old back in the 1970s. It was a lot of money. Now multiply it by seven boxes. I suppose (thinking about it now) I should have given my brother a cut of the tips (he made the boxes after all), but I didn't. My first trip to the DB Lounge started a passionate love affair, and I couldn't get enough of the stories that came out of the old timers. They were worth more than the money.

Uncle Tony retained his title as teller of indiscreet stories. He pointed out one guy at the end of the bar. All day long the guy smoked cigars and drank J&B Scotch, Uncle Tony said. Didn't say much. Just sat there quiet. If you went in one day and he was drinking Mountain Valley Spring Water instead of J&B Scotch, Uncle Tony said, "Don't take no rides with him," because you didn't want to be a participant – or a witness to his work. What kind of stories did you hear around the holidays? Shit about Pilgrims, Santa Claus, and the Easter Bunny? Me? I heard the one about how to tell when a hit man has a contract.

Another time, the same hit man was with his partner in the car waiting for the job to start, and they got hungry. Guy A says, "Why don't you go get some pepper-and-egg sandwiches and coffee, and I'll wait here."

[For those who don't know, a pepper-and-egg sandwich is a classic Chicago specialty: scrambled eggs mixed with sautéed green peppers on French bread. Basically, a scrambled egg sandwich.]

Guy B walks down and brings back the sandwiches and coffee. Guy A opens up the sandwich and goes, "Hey! There's sausage in this. We can't eat sausage. It's Ash Wednesday!"

[For non-Catholics, Lent is a pre-Easter major holiday, and no decent Catholic would think of eating meat on Ash Wednesday, Good Friday, or any Friday during Lent.]

They take the sausage out, throw it on the street, eat the pepper-and-egg sandwiches, and drink the coffee. Because you can't commit a mortal sin even when you're waiting to whack somebody. Being mob adjacent helps you understand how people can put things in tiny little compartments.

I loved being around those guys. It wasn't just the stories or the second-hand thrill that came from being mob adjacent. These guys seemed like they had it all figured out. They didn't work ass-busting jobs in the dogs of August. They sat in an air-conditioned bar while people brought money and merchandise to them. I couldn't figure out why my dad wanted to get away from this world. It looked pretty good to me. It was nice to think about, but I had to get back to Addison Road.

You're not supposed to drive a truck on a boulevard, but I didn't know. On the way back from the DB Lounge, I got a ticket. My first thought was Dad would be really mad. But then I figured he probably wouldn't be. When my brother and I started driving, we got into a few fender-benders. Dad's first question never changed: "Are you all right?" As long as we were safe, nothing else mattered. He was never mad. Never second-guessed. Never accused. From his perspective, you could get a new car any day of the week, a new kid not so much. Given that history, I was pretty sure Dad wouldn't be *really* mad. But he'd be pissed that I got the ticket because I didn't pay attention to the road sign that said no trucks. I expected to hear something about it; I just didn't know how much, how loud, or how long. The other thing when we started driving, Dad said: "Always be respectful to the coppers. Sit in your car, hands on the wheel, yes sir, no sir, even if he's wrong or being an asshole. Take the ticket, and go on your way." He said being a gentleman in a world full of assholes can get a guy out of a jam occasionally. I never forgot that. It's proved true.

I showed Dad the ticket when I got back to the store, and he said, "When the court date comes, just go pay the ticket. It's no big deal." That was it. Then it was back to work. I couldn't have been more surprised. He rode us hard sometimes. Dad had high standards in terms of being Mike Gentile's employees and his sons. Both were hard jobs. I didn't make either easier by discovering gambling, alcohol, and pot in high school.

I went to court, sat in the back, waited, and watched the judge going through the papers. He stops, looks, and puts one on top. Next thing I know, they call me up first. I didn't have to sit there all day! I thought I won the lottery. I'm standing in front of the judge, and he looks at me. He says, "Are you Mike Gentile's son, who used to own the Bridge over there on the corner?"

I said, "Yes, sir, I am."

He banged his gavel down, said, "Case dismissed," and handed me my driver's license. Madone, it was beautiful! I went back to the store and relayed the story to my dad.

He said, "What was the guy's name?"

"The Honorable Charles O'Brien."

Dad looked at me with a crooked head, chuckled, and said, "You know, that drunken Irish so-and-so still owes us $40." Turned out his Honor used to come into the Bridge every day for an Irish coffee before court and bet a $5 daily double.

The ticket was about $40. I guess all debts are paid when you're mob adjacent.

18 TROUBLE ADJACENT

A magnet in Melrose Park kept pulling me back to the DB Lounge, and I started meeting some of the guys my age, the ones just starting up the corporate ladder, so to speak. That's when I started gambling. Nothing big – at first. Ten bucks here, twenty there. Just to make things interesting. I had a job, so I didn't worry about the money. Besides, betting made it more fun – you were literally invested in the outcome. Before long I was betting $50, then $100.

Between working for Dad and placing an occasional bet at the DB Lounge, I was doing pretty well financially for an eighteen-year old. But I was betting most of what came in. I'd lose big and swear off gambling for a while. But watching the game for the sake of the game seemed boring, and eventually I'd be on the phone with a bookie placing a bet or asking about the point spread on Sunday's Jets game.

Dad and I didn't get along very well during this period. You know the thing my dad yelled about more than anything else? Cutting corners. I'd do a half-assed job at school or at work because I wanted to go do something else. He said things would never turn out right with a half-assed effort. I thought he made too big a deal about sweeping the entire floor when only part of the floor needed to be swept.

Aside from our problems at work, I was a problem at home too – mouthing off, fighting with Jeffrey, staying out late, coming home drunk, that kind of stuff. To make things worse, the nuns and dean at Immaculate Conception got so sick of my mouthy bullshit that I got expelled. Oh my God, was Dad mad! My honor-roll brother took pleasure in pointing out that I might not graduate high school. (See – he could be a prick sometimes.) The first time he made a crack about it, Dad shut him down and told him not to say it again. He didn't.

What happened was, during my first three years at I.C., Ken Mazierka was dean of students. He was a great guy, and I always thought he was one of the few people who "got" me. Once he left I.C. for a better opportunity, the principle and the assistant dean, now promoted to dean, decided they didn't appreciate my sense of humor and kicked me out two weeks before my senior year started. Shitty, right? Expelled two weeks before school starts. Ruin a kid's future. And at a Catholic school.

Mr. Mazierka heard about what happened and was particularly disgusted by I.C.'s action. He called Dad and asked about me. Dad wasn't sure what to do. I didn't want to go to the public school, Proviso West; and the other Catholic school, Driscoll, wouldn't take me. Mr. Mazierka said to send me to Notre Dame High School, where he now served as Vice Principle and Dean of Men. Dad gave him permission to do whatever he had to do. Beat him if you have to. Kick his ass up one hallway and down another, Dad said. But get him a diploma.

More headache for Dad: The tuition at I.C. was $300. Notre Dame was $1,100. Plus, to get to Notre Dame I had to have a car because it was twenty-six miles from our house. Although I fucked up in a huge way and got expelled, my punishment was a car and a better school. I remember one time I did something stupid, and Mr. Mazierka got mad. He stood there with his face getting redder, until I practically saw steam coming out. He asked me something like "what were you thinking," and I gave some smart-ass answer. Well, he gave me a smack in the side of the head that practically spun me in a circle – and not for the last time. One thing was for sure: The kind of bullshit I pulled at I.C. wasn't going to fly at Notre Dame. Mr. Mazierka made sure I graduated on time, class of 1973.

The man who shut down Orlando's Hideaway turned up in the news in 1973, too. He turned up dead. After bouncing around on both sides of the law and eventually doing time in prison, Richard Cain's next move was to take over the Outfit. He decided the power vacuum needed to be filled, and he was the man to fill it. Sam Giancana was living in Mexico, and Joe Accardo was essentially retired. Cain crafted a gutsy plan to take out the key Outfit players with multiple hits in Chicago, Las Vegas, and Honolulu, and install himself as Boss of Bosses. Cain's plan mirrored a plot device introduced in Mario Puzo's 1969 novel, *The Godfather*, where Michael Corleone uses the occasion of his niece's baptism to settle family scores simultaneously across the country. Michael Corleone's plan succeeded. Cain's not so much. Here's why:

At present, Marshall Caifano ran the Outfit in Giancana's absence. Though Giancana and Cain had been close in the past, the two men had a falling out over something, or someone, according to Cain's brother. Whatever happened, they were presently estranged. At the time, Caifano ran the best burglary crew in the city. He detested Cain, whom he found cocky, arrogant, and worst of all incompetent. (Cain went to prison over a rookie move in a robbery job.) The loathing was mutual. Cain thought Caifano owed his success to old relationships more than recent results. But Cain needed to join Caifano's crew – badly. He needed money to finance his takeover plan, according to a biography by his brother, *The Tangled Web*, by Michael J. Cain.

On December 20, 1973, Richard Cain arrived for a lunch meeting with Marshall Caifano at Rose's Sandwich Shop on Grand Avenue. It was a popular joint – nothing special to look at, but the food was good, and Sam "Jelly" Cozzo took good care of special guests. Jelly's son, James "Jimmy Boy" Cozzo went to jail young. When he got out, he was Made as a reward for quietly doing his time.

Jeffrey and I knew the sandwich place from its previous incarnation as Eli's Candy Shop. When we were kids, Dad would give us a quarter, and we'd come back with enough candy to rot out our mouths. Jelly and his sister, Rose Polito, owned the building. They previously operated Cozzo's Grocery across the alley from Eli's. As the years went on, competition from bigger grocery stores pushed them out of business, and they turned to Rose's cooking to save the day. The Cozzos were family friends, and we often saw them at celebrations of one kind or other. Aunt Jeanette and Rose were particularly close. Widowed young, Rose kept Aunt Jeanette company. Rose's son, Sammy, looked after both women.

[I know what you're thinking: Another Sam! As we started putting our family history on paper, my brother and I laughed about all the guys in our lives named Mike, Sam, Vince, Joe, Tony and John.]

Of Jelly Cozzo, Michael J. Cain, wrote, "The owner had been described as a "bad hombre" by people in the old neighborhood, a guy who believed his mob associations were paramount in his life." I call bullshit. People around Grand and Aberdeen knew Jelly as kind, funny, generous, and exceptionally profane. Imagine Santa Claus without the gray hair and beard. That's Jelly. The nickname referred to his jolly, jelly belly. A nicer man you wouldn't meet. It wasn't about valuing "mob associations." It was about respecting long friendships and old relationships. That's what people outside Little Italy don't get. Maybe the author confused Jelly with Jimmy Boy, his son. You didn't mess with Jimmy Boy; and if someone messed with you, Jimmy Boy was the guy you wanted in your corner. You'll see why later.

Cain was a regular at Rose's; so was Caifano. He wanted to talk about his takeover plan and get Caifano's blessing – or add him to the hit list. Cain expected to find a receptive audience. With Giancana on shaky ground with Joe Accardo, and Caifano dependent on Accardo to make a living, Richard Cain hoped Caifano would see the wisdom in his plan, according to Cain's brother. Jelly had a routine when VIPs were coming – he left dirty dishes on the corner table so no one would sit there. He cleared the table as soon as Caifano arrived.

On this particular day, Aunt Jeanette was on her way back from D'Amato's Bakery, a block west of Rose's. They made the best bread in town, and my dad joked that D'Amato's coal burning oven hadn't cooled since it was installed almost one-hundred years ago. On her way back from D'Amato's at 1124 W. Grand, Aunt Jeanette stopped at 1117 W. Grand to say hello to Rose and Jelly. She visited for a few minutes and went on her way, paying no attention to the men sitting in the corner.

Here's the puzzling part: At the time, Marshall Caifano lived with nearly constant police surveillance. And he was being watched that day. A member of the Intelligence Division of the Chicago Police Department, Jerry Gladdens, and his partner started their day tailing Caifano and followed him to Rose's. Then Cain arrived. What does Gladdens do when two notorious criminals sit down for a meeting? He decides it's a good time to leave. Gladdens and his partner drove away. After the cops left, Caifano sent Cain on an errand. Cain returned an hour later and found Caifano gone and two masked men holding Jelly, Rose, four customers, and a waitress at gun point.

Michael J. Cain added a dash of crime noir to the scene in his biography: "A walkie-talkie crackled, 'There he is!'"

One man held a sawed-off shotgun. The assailants pretended this was a simple robbery and put everyone against the wall. Then one of the men pulled Cain slightly away from the group. Their eyes met briefly before both barrels blasted through Richard Cain's chin and tore off half of his head. After killing Cain, the walkie-talkie crackled again: "Coast clear." The two men walked out slowly, as if nothing had happened.

According to two different sources, the man holding the shotgun wore one white glove and one black glove. This was said to symbolize the Black Hand of organized crime and the White Hand of organized law – as if there's a difference. In other words, it was a message killing. Cain was interfering with

Outfit/CIA operations. Jelly didn't remember anything about gloves.

In *Mob Cop*, former Chicago police officer and Outfit "associate" Fred Pascente identified Joe Lombardo as one of Richard Cain's killers. Pascente said one of the shooters shouted, "This is a robbery. Everybody against the wall." It had always been speculated that Jelly knew the identities of both shooters. Everybody knew everybody in the Patch. True to protocol, Jelly said nothing. As the masked men lined people up against the wall, Jelly took his sweet time. One of the shooters barked, "Come on, Jelly. Get the fuck in line." Pascente said Lombardo then put a shotgun under Cain's chin and pulled the trigger. After nearly 30 years of treachery, Cain died practically where the Outfit – and my family – began, near Grand and Aberdeen.

One of Dad's pals remarked post-assassination, "They shot off half of Dick Cain's head, and the son of a bitch still had two faces left."

Jelly waited until the men in masks drove off, then called the police. Aunt Jeanette's response became the stuff of family legend. Of Cain's murderers, she said dismissively, "Eh, they weren't going to hurt anybody." She knew how things worked. The men in ski masks were there for a specific job. Killing half a dozen "civilians" wasn't part of it. The worst part, she said, "Jelly was cleaning up for six weeks. He had to paint and re-grout the tile. You can't get that gorp out of grout." Make a note.

19 DEATH ADJACENT

When we moved to Bellwood, nearly every family had a stay-at-home mom. The stay-at-home mom two houses away had a family of five, like ours. Two boys and a girl, like ours. Russell Serritella met Dorothy Bayliss in England during World War II. After the war, she left her sister Violet and brother George in England and came to America as a war bride. Their son – also named Michael (because they aren't enough Michaels in this story!) was five days older than me and liked sports, so we became friends. Our moms got to be friends, too. In the English lady, Ma found a tea-drinking friend in a coffee-drinking world.

I also got along with the older brother, Russell. Everyone called him Butch. He was seven years older, but it didn't matter. I'd hang around in the garage while he tinkered with his 1957 red Chevy Bel Air. Truth told, I used to steal liquor from Dad's bar in our basement and give it to Butch. Before the Chevy, Butch had a Corvair, and he rigged up this genius system. The Corvair had a front-trunk, so he fixed up a holder for a liquor bottle in the trunk that connected to a spigot in the glove compartment. He could pour himself a drink while driving.

Butch, Mike, and I used to load up the trunk of the Bel Air with baseball gloves, bats, and balls and drive over to Jefferson Elementary School on St.

Charles and 46th. We'd pass the afternoon playing Strikeout against the red brick walls. For those who don't know what Strikeout is, it's a three-man game. You start by drawing a strike zone in chalk on the wall. One guy pitches, one bats, one plays outfield. He had a hell of a pitching arm, that Butch.

He was a real ladies' man, too. Banged every girl around. There was a family on 47th with four daughters. He nailed three out of four, and only skipped one because she was underage. He even threw the unattractive sister a pity fuck. That's the kind of decent guy Butch was. Born in 1948, he came of age in the mid-1960s, when everything was falling apart over Vietnam. He smoked weed, had long blond hair past his shoulders, and drove a motorcycle. Tough son-of-a-bitch. Butch wasn't afraid of anybody.

It was October 13, 1973. Butch was at a rough bar in Melrose Park called the Boar's Head. Melrose Park Police Chief Dominic Cimino said a fight and later a shooting started after an unidentified man insulted a woman at the bar. The woman's husband told the man to leave her alone. The unidentified man then pushed the husband, and bartender Frank Belvedere ordered the man to leave. The man was Butch. Then Butch and Frank Belvedere got into a fight, and about twenty-five other patrons joined in.

Eventually the brawl moved outside. Butch beat Belvedere badly. Then Belvedere ran back into the bar and came back with a .38 and started firing randomly at the crowd. Several more shots were fired, hitting Frank Belvedere in the head, chest, and back. The police had no suspect.

Allegedly, Frank Belvedere's brothers, Orest and Buddy, believed Butch pulled the trigger and murdered Frank. The brothers then went to the Outfit bosses in Melrose Park as a matter of mob etiquette and asked for permission to retaliate. Permission granted. Uncle Tony also lived in Melrose Park at the time and worked with the local bosses. He heard about the hit. When he learned Serritella lived on our block, Uncle Tony came over and told Dad. Together, Dad and Uncle Tony walked two houses down to the Serritella's.

They met with Butch and his father. Russell Serritella became enraged that someone dared mark his son for death. Dad suggested Butch leave town for a while and lay low until the business about Belvedere's murder cooled. Butch was concerned but not frightened. His father said, "The Serritellas run from nobody." Having done all they could, Dad and Uncle Tony came back to our house. Over the next three weeks, Butch expected trouble at every turn. He walked to and from his house with one hand on his gun and backed his car into the garage in case he needed to make a fast escape. But running never crossed his mind.

On November 1, 1973, Butch was driving north on Bellwood Avenue around three in the morning. His passenger was Michael DiFronzo, 22, of Melrose Park, the younger brother of reputed Outfit figure, John "No Nose" DiFronzo.

[Welcome to our mob adjacent world: Michael DiFronzo's older brother John went to high school with Dad and Joe Lombardo back in the old neighborhood.]

Another car came up from behind and fired a shotgun at the rear window. Butch sped away, turning east on St. Charles Road toward the Bellwood Police Station. A high-speed chase lasted for more than a mile. His attackers fired repeatedly, eventually pulling up beside the driver's side. When Butch turned to look over his left shoulder, a final shotgun blast blew off the right side of his head. The killers then sped north on 29th Avenue and disappeared into the night.

The bullet-riddled car took seven blasts from a twelve-gauge shotgun and crashed into a parked car less than one-hundred yards from the Bellwood Police Department. DiFronzo suffered cuts from glass shattered by the shotgun blasts. Lieutenant Ken Huntington of the Bellwood PD was unable to provide a description of the killers or their vehicle. He said the "persistence of the killers" suggested the victim was involved in a feud. You think? Seven shotgun blasts weren't accidental?

I heard about Butch's murder on WIND Radio in the morning. The station had a special sound cue like the old-time telegraph for breaking news: beepity, beepity, beepity. "A Bellwood man was shot and killed last night…" I sat stunned. Having practically grown up on bedtime stories about contracts and mob hits, it always felt abstract. Hearing about a stranger being killed was one thing; knowing the person who'd been killed – and having ridden in his death-mobile – was something else. Mom raced to Dorothy's house to comfort her friend.

They fixed Butch up pretty good for his wake, rebuilding the side of his head with whatever undertakers use for jobs like that. You could hardly tell half of his head was gone. It helped that they had him positioned with his right side facing the casket lid. Lesson: When your mob adjacent neighbor gives you some advice, take it.

Orest and Buddy Belvedere would eventually be arrested and tried, but acquitted of Butch's murder. The mother of the Belvedere boys and Dorothy Serritella had a loud, angry confrontation outside the courtroom following the acquittal. Each blamed the other for her son's death. But Orest didn't escape justice completely. Reportedly a member of the Hell's Henchman motorcycle gang, Orest got into another fatal altercation in Melrose Park two years later.

Loyola University student Mark Butterly was in the wrong place on the night of September 17, 1975. Butterly got involved after seeing Belvedere knock a woman off a stool at the Hasty Grill. He later saw Orest Belvedere and Robert Bailey beating the woman in the parking lot, and Butterly came to her aid. Enraged over his interference, Belvedere and Bailey went to their car, came back with a tire iron and a jack, and beat Butterly to death.

At their sentencing in 1977, Judge Frank Wilson called the murder weapons, "instruments of a cruel and inhuman nature," according to the *Chicago Tribune*. "A bullet by a gun to the head would have been more merciful," said Judge Wilson. Belvedere and Bailey were sentenced to seventy-five to two-hundred years in prison. But it didn't make Butch any less dead.

Death visited again in 1973 when Skip Cerone died. After decades of heavy drinking, his liver finally gave out. Two years earlier, on November 1, 1971, Mike Royko wrote an inadvertent tribute to Skip in his syndicated newspaper column. Royko detailed how Skip managed to keep the IRS' hands out of his pockets for decades. "He doesn't pay any income tax. Not a nickel. And he gets away with it. He's been doing it for years; it may be that he has never, in his entire life, payed any income tax." The legendary Chicago columnist wrote of Skip's tax bill, "Officially, the figure is something like $75,000." The method was simple: On paper, officially, Skip and Mary Cerone owned nothing. A few years previously, Skip made the mistake of buying a luxury car and putting it in his name. Royko wrote, "The IRS grabbed it and auctioned it off. That was the last time he owned a car." Skip didn't even have a checking account. He kept his money in portable, spendable cash. By living simply, the government couldn't prove Skip lived beyond his means. The tax liens went back all the way to 1941.

That magnificent bastard went out like a champ – dying on the eve of another gambling indictment! You can arrest him; you can convict him; you can send him to prison; but when he comes out he's going to make a living on gambling. Because people gamble. Willie Sutton robbed banks because that's where the money was; Skip let people bring their money to him. Who had a better system? The newspapers talked about his crimes and allegations of crimes and suggested Chicago was somehow safer with Skip gone to his maker. That might have made great newspaper copy. But it didn't change the fact that Dad lost a good friend, a man who'd been like a brother to him and an uncle to us.

Indirect life lessons come from many sources. Skip and Dad were friends for nearly 30 years. Dad made friends who stayed his friends until the last days of his life. He never squealed. He never ratted. He never cooperated – even when cooperating with an asshole like Richard Cain could have saved Orlando's Hideaway. You don't repay kindness by biting your benefactor on the ass. (See Kennedy, Joseph P; Kennedy, John F; and Kennedy, Robert F.) Remember that. And this:

The quiet town of Tempe, Arizona, was shaken awake on October 6, 1975, when a car bomb exploded and killed a man known to his neighbors as Joseph Nardi. Lou Bombacino, 52, formerly a member of the Chicago Outfit, had been hiding under an assumed name after testifying against Jackie Cerone in 1970, sending Cerone and four others to prison. Bombacino was backing his 1976 Lincoln Continental Mark IV out of the driveway at 8:30 AM when it exploded. The force of the blast blew out seventy-five to one-hundred windows in apartments nearby and sent fragments of the car as far as a quarter mile. The blast blew away all Bombacino's clothes, except a T-shirt, and he was found slumped outside the car where the driver's side door had been.

Clearly the ignition malfunctioned.

I didn't know any of the backstory at the time. All I knew was Uncle Tony came over and said to Dad, "Did you hear? Lou Bombacino died."

Dad asked, "Did he die, or did they die him?"

"Oh, they died him, Mikey. They died him over a quarter mile."

20 PRISON ADJACENT

I made a couple of bad choices in 1975 that caused me to need a lawyer's assistance. Starting in my senior year at Notre Dame High School, I got a part-time job during the fall and winter at a men's clothing store in Elmhurst. There wasn't much to it. Hanging up stock, ringing up orders, telling some jag-off he looks good in pants that don't fit right. One day I saw a bag of money, literally just sitting there. So, I took it. The bag contained thousands, most of it in checks. I ditched the checks and kept the cash. The fact that there was more than $2,000 technically meant I committed a felony. To this day, I can't imagine what made me do something so brazen and so stupid. But I did it. A couple of weeks later I got arrested. The cops bamboozled me into believing they could take a flunked lie detector test to court. But if I confessed, things would go easier. That's what they said. And I believed it. I didn't even know how to call my dad. But I needed to get out of jail.

I called him and said, "You know that thing they were talking about in the newspaper?"

Dad had been suspicious since he read about the theft and warned that he hoped I wasn't involved. "You didn't say anything, did you?"

"Well, yeah, I kind of did."

Here's how the chain goes when you're mob adjacent: I called my dad. He called Romy Lewis, the bail bondsman. Because you know a bail bondsman when you're mob adjacent. Romy came to jail and paid the $20,000 bond, which was two-grand, which was a lot of money back then, and got me out of jail. We sat in his big Lincoln in front of the Elmhurst Police Department, and he asked, "What happened?" Then he looked at me puzzled and said, "I'm under the impression you told these guys you did this."

I gave him the spiel about flunking the lie detector test and the coppers taking it to court.

He said, "You dumb motherfucker. They can't take a lie detector test to court. What are you, stupid? All you had to do was tell them no, no, no. Unless they had evidence, you'd have been fine. And by the way, if you can't trust yourself, who can you trust?" Lesson learned. Deny. Deny. Deny. He let that sink in for minute, then added, "Not for nothing, but maybe this is not the business for you." As we're driving, I sat with my head down. He looked at me straight-faced and said, "By the way, your father is going to kill you."

When I got home, Dad was a madman. "All you had to say was, 'Fuck you, I quit' and walk out the door. Instead, you tell them you did it!" It went like that for half an hour. Then he called Jimmy Cerone and gave him the chain of events.

Jimmy asked, "What the fuck is wrong with your kid? Is he goofy?"

My dad told him, "Yes, he must be. But I've got to get him a lawyer. Who can I use?"

After nearly a decade on his own, a potential felony's worth of bad choices sent Dad back to the mob for help. It was a tough time for our family. I heard my parents arguing about what to do. Dad thought that unless I learned the consequences now, there would be trouble for years to come. Ma begged, cried, pleaded, and said it would kill her if I went to prison. Kill her. Her exact words. Dad relented and asked for a favor. The Outfit's powerful reach smoothed over the mess. But their help came with a price tag that included a future favor. That put the Gentile family right back at Square One – mob adjacent and mob indebted.

Jimmy called a lawyer named Robert J. McDonnell. He had a long history of defending Outfit guys as well as participating in other Outfit activities. But McDonnell had been convicted of something or other and couldn't try cases in DuPage County at the time. Instead, he brought a puppet named John Maloney because Maloney could try cases. McDonnell had been a rising star in the Illinois State's Attorney's office in the 1950s. But he had problems with booze and gambling that loused everything up for him – they said he was deep in debt to juice king Sam DeStefano. Nobody in his right mind wanted to be indebted to "Mad Sam" DeStefano. By the 1970s, McDonnell was basically an Outfit lackey, the guy they called when somebody got arrested. Here's a hell of a detail: It's said McDonnell arranged the meeting between Joe Kennedy and Sam Giancana to get Outfit support for Jack Kennedy's crooked presidential run. I just knew McDonnell as the guy helping to save my ass.

At the time I got arrested, the head judge of DuPage County in 1975 was Alfred Woodward. You know who his son is? The guy who uncovered Watergate, Bob Woodward, the man who sunk President Nixon – his father was Chief Judge in DuPage County, and I got him. If Bob Woodward had followed the money in my case, it would have led directly to his father's courthouse. Who's connected to whom didn't mean shit to me at the time. I'm trying to figure out how I'm going to do five years. My Dad tells me don't worry about it. Don't worry about it? Don't worry about it, he said.

However it worked – and I don't exactly know how it worked – $20,000 and a future favor bought a sentence that included probation and six weeks' work release. I learned a lesson that day in Judge Bernstein's courtroom: Justice is served a' la carte. The more one pays, the less Justice served.

Under the terms of my punishment, I had to be in jail by 2:00 AM every morning. But because I had to go to work at 6:00 AM, I only spent four hours a day in "custody." The first day, I walked into the work release section scared to death. The only thing I knew about prison was the bullshit I saw in movies and television shows. I was sweating and shivering and feeling like I had to shit all at the same time. I'd never been in jail before this situation. Then I looked at the guard's name tag, and it was a name I recognized. I couldn't have been safer in my mother's arms. I didn't even have to go upstairs into the jail. Every night, the same officer checked me in. I'd leave on my street clothes, and he'd let me lay down in a holding cell. At six o'clock, he sent me home. Six weeks, done, over. Mob adjacent means even when you're in jail, they take care of you.

The whole thing turned into a family affair. The guard was related to Patsy Spilotro, whose restaurant served as a meeting place for future Outfit members back in the late 1940s, and where Dad first met members of the Cerone family. My attorney, Bob McDonnell, later married Antoinette Giancana, Mr. Sam's entitled daughter. And every Friday for the next year, Dad went to see Jimmy with another payment on the cost of my sentence. The future favor was a different story.

Looking back on fatherhood, Dad said, "If I had known how much trouble you would cause, I would have hit my prick with a hammer."

Meanwhile, the operation on Addison Road got too big and too complicated. Hugely profitable, a bigger business brought bigger headaches, and Dad had enough headaches, thanks to me. I didn't realize until years later that he sold his piece of the business because he needed the money to save my ass. All I knew was he leased a new spot on North York Road in Elmhurst. Once we got this operation going, the other favor came due: Jimmy Cerone would be our partner. I'd known Jimmy my whole life, so I was pretty sure everything would work out fine. Why should I worry, right? I wasn't the one who had to fork over $20,000 and half of his business.

Jimmy Cerone was in his mid-sixties in the mid-seventies. He was a small, thin, wiry man with a fringe of gray and white hair wrapped around his otherwise bald head, typically covered by a canvas fishing hat. Full of energy and jacked on caffeine, Jimmy worked as hard as anybody. Being Dad's "partner" was technically a euphemism for taking half the profits. Jimmy could have come every Sunday and picked up his cut. Actually working was never part of the deal. But because it was my father, Jimmy did his share of the work for his share of the profits. He waited on customers, stocked the counters, swept the floors, and took out trash. I don't care what anybody prints or says about Jimmy Cerone; I know the kind of man he was. I used to wonder what those rich Elmhurst housewives would have thought if they knew the man weighing out tomatoes was a convicted criminal.

While we were on York Road, a man named Ned Bakes started showing up every day or so. He was an old friend of Jimmy's. Ned was about seventy, heavy-set, nearly bald, and recently out of prison for his role in a stock swindle. He was working for Brighton Krug Construction at the time, which back then was a mob influenced construction company that did lots of road work. When Dad took the lease in Elmhurst, the parking lot was gravel. Jimmy complained about the dust whenever someone drove away too fast. Ned solved the problem by sending over a Brighton crew. One day, all of a sudden, we had an asphalt parking lot. Sure cut down on the dust – and Jimmy's complaining. Even better was the deal Ned worked out for Jimmy. A Brighton crew showed up at Jimmy's house in Elmwood Park, ripped up the driveway and installed a new one – with heating coils embedded in the asphalt. Jimmy never had to worry about shoveling a driveway again. Like Dad, Jimmy hated the cold weather, and particularly hated being inconvenienced by it.

We later learned Ned Bakes' real name was Ignatius Spachessi. He'd been a driver for Al Capone in the 1920s, like another mobster we met, Rocco DeGrazia. Back in the 1940s, Spachessi/Bakes had a headache with another mobster. But his watchdog was Paul Ricca, right up near the top of the Outfit. As long as Paul Ricca was alive, Ned Bakes was fine. In 1975, Paul Ricca died. About six weeks later, Ned's wife called looking for him. She called him "Nedsie." Had we seen Nedsie? No. He didn't visit every day, so we didn't think much about it. Ned was last seen leaving his home at 8:30 AM, Saturday,

November 29. They found him in the trunk of his 1975 Chevrolet Caprice on December 3, parked at the Torch Lite Restaurant in Addison, a half mile from his home. He was shot twice in the top of the head with a large caliber handgun and strangled. Because one or the other wasn't dead enough.

We never met the man who was Ignatius Spachessi. We didn't know about his conviction for tax evasion in 1965, or that he drove for Al Capone, or that he once worked as a county bailiff and deputy sheriff. Hell, he might have been one of the dirty cops Richard Cain paid off for Sam Giancana. My brother and I only knew Ned, a big guy with a fringe of white hair who came to visit with Jimmy and my dad and always brought a big box of donuts. To this day, we don't know where he got those donuts. They were the best donuts we ever had. We took another lesson from the experience: Being mob adjacent means not seeing people as gangsters and criminals, just nice guys who bring donuts.

Ned's murder wasn't the only shocking death that year. After years as absentee boss, Sam Giancana returned to Chicago in 1975. He had spent the past decade mainly based in Mexico, working international deals to set up legal casino operations in Europe, the Middle East, South America, and other locations, that is until Mexico rudely deported him in his pajamas and bedroom slippers into the hands of the FBI waiting across the border in Texas.

Because Jackie Cerone served as Giancana's number two, we heard a lot about Mr. Sam's global adventures from Jimmy during the time he worked with Dad in Elmhurst. Jimmy could be candid with Dad because Dad was like Fort Knox when it came to information. Nothing got out. But Jeffrey and I overheard bits and pieces. Those bits and pieces were always clouded in euphemisms. We'd hear "that guy is in Monte Carlo" or "those two just got back from Lebanon."

People expressed two points of view: One side admired Giancana for moving the Outfit in legitimate directions. Post-JFK, newly installed President Johnson showed no interest in the Outfit operations, and the heat cooled as quickly as JFK's corpse. With the country distracted by Vietnam, Giancana took the Outfit global. Forget backroom bookies and floating craps games. Legal casinos were the future. The other side felt Giancana's absence meant no one kept an eye on operations in Chicago. Joe Accardo in particular was said to nurse a giant grudge because Giancana declined to share his lush, legitimate, global gambling profits.

Among conflicting theories, a few facts are certain: On June 19, 1975, Sam Giancana was in the basement kitchen of his home at 1147 S. Wenonah Avenue in Oak Park, Illinois. A pan of sausage and peppers was frying on the stove. A person likely known to Giancana entered through the basement door (no sign of forced entry). This person placed a gun against the back of Sam Giancana's head and fired. The killer then placed the gun in the corpse's mouth and fired again. Five more shots were fired under the dead man's chin. The killer vanished without being seen and left the pan sizzling on the stove.

Francine Giancana, Sam's daughter, said she saw his "longtime aide" Butch Blasi pull into the driveway as she left around 10:00 PM after visiting her father. Was Blasi the shooter, or did he clear the path for another assassin, possibly the often-accused Tony Spilotro? Was the hit sanctioned by Joe Accardo, or was it over something else entirely?

"Something else" sounds right when one considers that same day – June 19, 1975 – members of the Senate Select Committee on Intelligence arrived in Chicago. Their job was to transport Sam Giancana to Washington, D.C., where in five days he was scheduled to testify about the CIA's Fidel Castro assassination plot – a plot in which Sam Giancana and Richard Cain actively participated.

The go-to explanation blames Giancana's killing on a mob hit. But if I'm playing armchair detective, Giancana could have inflicted far greater damage on the CIA than his Outfit brethren, most of whom were already dead or in prison. His murder shocked me, even though many murders were blamed on Giancana. The man was nice to us when we were kids. Gangsters were only gangsters at work; they were just people the rest of the time. We knew the people, not the gangsters. Jeffrey said our experiences growing up left us with "cognitive dissonance." All I know is growing up mob adjacent leaves you with happy memories, often untouched by ugly realities.

21 BOWLING ALLEY ADJACENT

There was a bar in Elmhurst that wasn't too fussy about checking IDs, and on any given night most of the people drinking were probably underage. It didn't matter to me. I turned twenty-one a year ago, but my driver's license said I was twenty-two. And it didn't matter to the cops because the place was "connected," so they tended to stay away. Legal or illegal, come 2:00 AM the bars in Elmhurst closed. But when you've been drinking all night and you've got a nose full of blow, you're not ready for the night to end. It's not a problem. You head to Northlake, where the Town & Country Bowl stayed open until four.

I was still on three years' probation after my conviction, and probably shouldn't have been drinking in a bar in the first place. Then there was the whole smoking pot and doing blow thing. But I never thought about shit like that back then. I was still ready to party when I got to the Town & Country. They had a nice bar adjacent to the bowling alley, and it started filling up every night after the bars around town closed. At the time, I was seeing a girl named Donna. We were having a drink, and she wanted to play the jukebox, so we walked over. Another guy and some rough-looking broad were standing in front of it, talking. Donna tried to get around them, and the guy started getting mouthy.

I wasn't in the mood for a fight, so I said something like, "Come on, she just wants to play a song."

The guy started getting loud and obnoxious, and I repeated that I didn't want any trouble.

Next, he growled and pointed his finger. "I'm not fucking moving, and if you want me to move, you try to move me."

At this point, Donna tugged at my arm and said, "Let's go, Mike."

The guy started mocking her, "Let's go, Mike." Then he switched to his voice and says, "Listen to your girlfriend, asshole, and get lost."

"Why do you have to be such a prick? All she wanted to do is play the jukebox. We're all here to have a good time, okay? Don't be a jag-off."

You know how we all have a thing (or things) that set you off? For me it's someone poking me in the chest. It's the red cape in front of the bull. Do that, and I can't be responsible for what happens next. Now the rough-looking broad decided it's her turn to get in a few shots.

She looked at her scumbag date and says, "Are you going to let him talk to you like that?"

That's when he did it. He stood up, took a step closer, poked his fat finger into the middle of my chest three times and said, "Get the fuck out of here."

A bomb went off in my head, and it was like I was watching somebody else. This Somebody Else grabbed the guy's finger with one hand and bent it backward. Then, this Somebody Else grabbed the guy's hair and smashed his head through the glass top of the jukebox. I heard people screaming when he lifted his head. Jagged shards of broken glass cut open both cheeks like meat flaps and blood rained down. His girl started screaming for someone to call the police, call an ambulance.

[Coincidence: My future wife was at the Town & Country Bowl that night. She saw the whole thing. When we meet in a few years, she'll tell this story, not realizing she was talking about me.]

I decided it was time to leave. We were almost out the door when the Northlake cops pull up in front. The other girl is pointing and screaming, "That's him, that's him."

The cop car pulled away with me in the backseat just as the ambulance arrived. Donna stood with a sour expression on her face and waved from the steps as the cop car drove off. Sitting handcuffed in the backseat, I'm sure of one thing: I'm going to jail. I got in a violent bar fight while on probation, and now I am royally screwed. Turned out the cops knew the guy I got in the fight with, and he'd been in trouble before. The cops couldn't have been nicer, all things considered. I got the feeling they didn't really want to arrest me, but they had to because that broad was making a scene. So, they took me to the Northlake Police Department.

I also decided in the cop car that I was not calling my dad, because I was pretty sure he'd leave me in jail. He wanted me to go to jail that first time. He said it was the only way I would learn. But he bought me out of trouble for Ma's sake, and I didn't learn anything. Clearly. Because here I was at five in the morning at the police station about to get my one phone call. I'm stupid sometimes, but I'm no fool. I called Uncle Tony. He'd know what to do.

If Uncle Tony was surprised that someone called his house at five in the morning, you couldn't hear it in his voice. It might as well have been five in the evening. I told him I got arrested, and he started yelling, "Don't let them fingerprint you. Tell the cops you gotta take a shit. Whatever you do, don't let them fingerprint you! I'll be right there." He lived in Stone Park then, maybe ten minutes away.

I told the desk sergeant I had to use the toilet. The cop who brought me in led me to a bathroom and took off one of the cuffs. I went into the stall, pulled down my pants, and sat – in case somebody came in to check. While I pretended to shit, I thought about my call with Uncle Tony. He didn't ask why I'd been arrested. He didn't say he was sending a bail bondsman. No, he was coming himself. Maybe he's trying to get me released on my own recognizance. Maybe he's pleading self-defense. The desk sergeant is calling for me to hurry up, but I'm not moving.

Finally, I hear the voice of salvation – and it's pissed. I come out of the toilet to see Uncle Tony barreling in. He saw me with the cuffs on, and his face turned bright red. He screamed: "Get those fucking cuffs off that kid RIGHT NOW!" Then he walked right into the shift commander's office and slammed the door.

Let's back up. We're standing in the Northlake Police Department at almost six in the morning. Northlake is a Westside suburb. Skip and Jimmy Cerone's gambling operation (where Uncle Tony worked the door) couldn't operate without mob friendly cops agreeing to look the other way in exchange for – you know how the rest of this goes. The Northlake police know Tony Mastro. He was friends with Rocco Pranno, the man who ran Stone Park, Schiller Park, Melrose Park, and Northlake. He was also friends with Pranno's cousin, Daniel Provenzo, Northlake Chief of Police. If anybody could get a guy out of trouble in Northlake, it was Tony Mastro. A few minutes later, he and the commander walked out. The commander nodded at the cop who brought me in, and the handcuffs came off. Then the commander took the report that the desk cop started filling out and handed it to Uncle Tony.

"Let's go, Michael." We walk out a side door, and it was light outside. Uncle Tony had the half-completed arrest report in his hand, crumpled it into a ball, and tossed it at me.

I asked nervously, "So, what's next?"

"There is no next. They lost your paperwork. Get in the car. I'm gonna drive you home. Don't tell your father about this." Then he cracked me in the head really hard. "What the fuck is wrong with you? You could have killed that guy."

I didn't even think about making the "but he poked me" excuse because Uncle Tony probably would have killed me. Instead I apologized for calling him so late and thanked him for getting me out of trouble. Growing up mob adjacent means you know who to call when you need to get out of a dicey situation.

For the rest of the day and for several days after, I kept hearing Uncle Tony's booming, disgusted voice: "You could have killed that guy." I didn't want something like that on my conscience, not ever. I made a vow: That night at Town & Country Bowl was the last bar fight I'd ever get into. After that, when things started heating up I walked away. I didn't care if some douche tried to bait me by calling me a pussy. I almost killed a guy. I wasn't looking for a second chance.

22 RAILROAD ADJACENT

We had to leave the York Road location in 1976 when the farmer sold the land under our building, and we moved to another location on Irving Park Road in Wood Dale, again at a busy intersection. The end of the York Road business also marked the end of Dad's partnership with Jimmy. The new store sat directly across from the commuter railroad lines that dumped people in front of our store practically every hour on the half hour. Business boomed from day one.

As our business operation gradually changed over the years, one thing stayed the same – at every place Dad owned, he painted the top third of the windows with black chalkboard paint. When Jeffrey was in town over summer breaks from college, Mr. Nice Handwriting painted the daily specials on the windows and made signs for inside. If my brother was away at school, Dad painted the signs.

I didn't paint signs because I had a system for getting out of things I didn't want to do. Here's my system: (Write this down – it worked like a charm): If you're asked to do something you don't want to do, do it really badly. I painted the signs exactly once. Dad came outside, looked at the window, and said, "There's a U in cantaloupe. Fix it." Now, he didn't say, "Wash the window and repaint it." He said, "Fix it." So, I fixed it. I painted a little "u" in between and sort of above the "o" and "p." Now it said "Cantaloupe." Done. Then Dad came out, looked at the window, and gave me the spiel about how you're guaranteed to get half-assed results if you make a half-assed effort. He told me to wash the window, which I did. Then he painted the sign, and never asked me again. At home, after I broke a few dishes and glasses, Ma stopped asking me to clean up after dinner. That's why it's called a system, people.

Business was great that first summer. There were still a lot of local farms in the area back then. Now it's all housing developments and big box stores. But back then we got stuff fresh from the farms – corn and tomatoes still warm from the field, stuff you never got in grocery stores. Today they'd call it "artisanal produce" or some bullshit and charge $8 a pound. Whatever you call it, we sold it by the trailer full.

Once the store was up and running, Dad decided to open a restaurant. He found a location in nearby Elmhurst, and the plan was that I would run the market; he would run the restaurant, and Jeffrey (about to graduate from Southern Illinois University) would swing between both places until he found a "real" job. Dad named the place Lisa's. He had very specific ideas about food. For example, Dad insisted on fresh-cut fries and real milkshakes. Obsessed with cleanliness, he filtered the oil and cleaned the fryer twice a day.

Across Lake Street, half a dozen factories spit out an endless line of hungry workers, and a nearby industrial park meant every day we had lines out the door. Dad even "allowed" Ma to work. She made "gravy" in what we called the "Oh My God" pot – a pot large enough to poach a three-year old child. Her pasta and meatball take-out dinners on Fridays practically flew out the door. It's a tough call which was more popular – the top round of beef Dad slow-roasted in a bath of garlic juice, water, and herbs, or Ma's meatball sandwiches. We siblings keep an image in our heads: Ma is standing in the restaurant kitchen at the stove, rolling endless meatballs in her tiny hands. She kept an old toothbrush by the sink to clean the gunk out of her rings.

While running the produce market on Irving Park Road, I got into some trouble over gambling and had to borrow from a juice guy – a loan shark. Stupid, I know. But I managed to pay the guy every week, and I paid him on the come-down. For those who don't know what the come-down is, it means you pay the juice (the interest), plus a little bit of the principle, and before long you pay down the whole thing. I paid everything off, but Lou the juice guy says to me, "You still owe."

I said, "But no, I don't."

"Yeah, you do. Make sure you're here with the payment next week."

Officially screwed, I turned to Uncle Tony for help. Again. I explained what happened. First, he gave me another hard crack upside the head for going on the juice. I mean he really hit me. Not like a playful smack. Which is fine, I can take a crack. But I didn't want to have to pay any more than I owed.

Uncle Tony asked, "When do you go see this guy again?"

"Wednesday."

On Wednesday, Uncle Tony came with me to a joint in Melrose Park. We walked in, and saw the loan shark at the bar. I walked up to Lou and said, "I'd like you to meet my Uncle Tony."

Uncle Tony took it from there. He was semi-retired by that point, but his reputation still held. "Look, I understand you had this kid on the come-down, and he paid everything he owes. What are you doing telling him he still owes?"

The juice guy looked Uncle Tony in the eye, and he said, "I had no idea he knew anybody. I'm sorry." In other words, Lou was screwing me over because he thought he could get away with it.

Lou and I became friends after that. Today, he's a relic of another era. In his seventies, Lou is the kind of man who sends you and your wife birthday cards and brings you a tin of cookies when you meet for lunch. He's Lou, the Friendly Juice Guy – as long as you pay him on time.

Being mob adjacent means you only had to pay the juice you're due. But that didn't get me off the hook with Uncle Tony. When we got into the car, he reached in the pocket of his black leather coat and took out a .25 caliber Beretta. He held it to my thigh, and he said, "Listen, the next time you borrow money from one of these guys, I promise you I will shoot you in the thigh myself. I won't break a bone. I'll only go through the meat, but it'll hurt like hell, and you'll remember for the rest of your life. There's nothing worse than a rat. But if I hear you go on the juice again, I'm going to your father. Do you hear me?"

I looked at the gun pressed against my thigh. The barrel was short and surprisingly thick. I nodded.

Uncle Tony put the gun in his coat pocket and started the car. As he pulled out of the parking lot, he checked both ways and said, "Watch out with all this gambling, big shot. Remember what your father says: Vegas wasn't built on winners."

I wasn't going to Vegas. What the fuck was he talking about? But he had that Beretta in his pocket, so I nodded again and kept my big mouth shut.

23 POWER ADJACENT

I was going out a lot in the late 1970s. With plenty of cash, catching girls was easy when you're fishing with green bait. Usually I picked up a girl like you'd pick up a pizza on the way home after a night of drinking. Quality wasn't a consideration. When you're half-drunk at three in the morning, do you worry about whether it's a good pizza? Or do you just want it to be hot and ready to stuff in your mouth?

If I told Dad about going to this place or that place, he'd narrow his eyes and say, "Big shot." It was never a compliment. Sometimes he'd get on me about staying out late.

Ma would look at him sideways and ask, "You never stayed out late showing a girl the town? Was that somebody else I went out with?"

He'd look down his nose and growl playfully. "Shut up, Mare."

I continued doing whatever I wanted. But one thing I couldn't do was stay out all night unless I wanted to fight it out every time. My parents didn't care that I was eighteen, nineteen, or twenty. As long as I lived in their house, Ma stayed up waiting for me to come home, no matter how late. When Dad heard the front door close, he'd come flying out of their bedroom in boxer shorts and a white T-shirt and start yelling about scaring "your poor mother" half to death – while she watched the late, late show and nibbled on snacks. If I came home while it was still dark outside, the grief stayed in check. But come on, who wants to get out of a warm bed at the Holiday Inn or the Addison Motel or wherever he spent the night fucking and go home to his parents? When I turned twenty-one, I moved out.

Bill McGuirk was a bartender at the Elmhurst Gardens, so I saw him several times a week. Between the Gardens and the DB Lounge, I probably went to one bar or the other five or six nights a week. Bill and I became friends, and we eventually rented a two-bedroom house in Elmhurst. I was in the kitchen late one night after a couple of girls left. Bill came in stark naked and sat down at the table while I made a sandwich. I saw something out of the corner of my eye. It was moving. And it was on Bill's naked, upper thigh. I said, "I don't want you thinking I'm the kind of guy who checks out other guys, but are freckles supposed to move?"

I did him a favor and went to buy crab cream. Bill spent the rest of the night doing laundry and soaking his junk in kerosene. I got two bottles – one for him, one for me, just in case. Who knew how far those little fuckers could jump. Good times.

Joan Strasser and I started dating after she graduated from high school in 1976. She was two years younger, but Joan and I had a lot in common – we knew a lot of the same people. She dated my best friend for two years, so we spent a lot of time together in high school as friends. We both loved sports; and we both liked to have fun. Oh, God, we had fun! Every night was a party. She could match me beer-for-beer and stat-for-stat on any sport. We'd get into passionate arguments about the relative uselessness of the Cubs' starting line-up or the ham-hands of the Bears' quarterback. After we'd been dating for a while, I brought Joan to two family events.

In May 1977, I took her to a birthday dinner for Ma at a mob-connected restaurant called Meo's in west suburban Addison. Joan was confused by the men kissing each other on the cheek. She kept looking at me like "who are these guys?" But one thing remains constant: Old men like pretty, young girls. So, they flattered Joan, called her "pretty lady," told her she was too good for a bum like me, and treated her with the "old school" gentlemanly behavior my generation barely recognized. By the time we left, Joan was under their spell. The whole drive home she talked about how "sweet" everyone was. I didn't bother telling her that at least one of those sweet men was a contract killer. Why dull her buzz?

The second event was dinner at Tom's Steak House in Melrose Park. We met my parents, along with Uncle Anthony, Aunt Sis, Jimmy, and Nina. Nobody sat still. Either Jimmy visited friends at other tables or someone walked up to ours. Dad, too. He knew everybody. He always did. And everybody greeted him like a long-lost friend. Places didn't get more connected than Tom's.

During the 2007 "Family Secrets" mob trial, Nick Calabrese claimed that he, his brother Frank, and John Fecarotta threw a bomb on the roof of Tom's Steak House in 1982. Calabrese testified that he didn't know why mob higher-ups targeted the restaurant. He just blew it up. After the bombing, police said they found "no evidence that mobsters meet at Tom's." Really? The night we walked into the dining room, it was a who's who of Outfit guys.

Jackie and Clara Cerone were there. I hadn't seen him since Orlando's Hideaway. I was a kid then and didn't understand who – and what – Jackie Cerone was. Back then, he was just one of Dad's friends. In the years since, I learned plenty about John Phillip "Jackie" Cerone and his life one step below the most powerful criminal boss in America. It was said Jackie could go from humorous to murderous in a blink. One of the most feared and volatile Outfit guys, he commanded the room just by being in it. This was real power. Quiet power. Jackie smiled or didn't smile, and you somehow knew what it meant, who he liked, and who he didn't like. Dapper as ever and always the best dressed man in the room, Jackie only wore custom-made suits and shoes.

Clara was decked out, too, with red hair shellacked into a curly helmet, and a lot of big jewelry. In her youth, she'd been a dancer. She and Jackie met four decades ago at a gambling club called the Rock Garden in Cicero, where she danced as part of the supper club entertainment. Clara's father Frank had been a close friend of Al Capone, and she was probably as close to mob royalty as one got in Chicago.

Jackie and Clara sat at a table near the back of the room. Occasionally, someone approached to pay their respects. No one sat down, and no one lingered. Still beautiful in middle age, Clara smiled at everyone but kissed no one. Jackie shook with his right hand, then cupped his left hand over the other person's hand, and held it. The gesture seemed intimate and commanding at the same time. He's holding you by the hand, so you're not getting away until he lets go. But he's smiling. The media called him the smiling gambler. Jimmy and Nina made a pilgrimage to Jackie and Clara's table. Later, Uncle Anthony went over to visit with Dad.

Conveniently, Ma and Aunt Sis kept Joan engaged in chit-chat while I tried to gawk discreetly. A few moments into each visit, Clara picked up her water glass. This served as a cue that their meal was about to begin, and the visitor should depart. People with good manners understood the gesture and acted accordingly. Jackie took care of people who didn't take the cue. He said goodnight and turned away. Jackie had moved on, and so should you.

The lesson came with dinner: Power doesn't make a big show of itself. It doesn't have to be loud, and it doesn't have to be aggressive. You can't see the electric running through the power lines. You only see what happens when the line breaks. Then the sparks fly.

Over the years, I'd heard and read stories about things he did or might have done. None of it seemed possible looking at the well-dressed gentleman dining with his elegant wife. Jackie Cerone was a perfect example of the difference between what can be proven and what can be alleged. Jackie had a gruesome list of *alleged* crimes, but he was only *convicted* for gambling. Jackie was a perfect contradiction in his personal life, too. Privately, he offered friendly advice and business opportunities to Mike Gentile. The friendly business advisor once violently beat another man who used a filthy word in front of Clara.

Looking at Jackie Cerone, it was hard to believe he was the savage monster the media sometimes made him out to be. Some of the allegations had to be the stuff of urban legend, right? He wasn't really the "top-rated executioner" people made him out to be, was he? Dad was always quick to puncture my delusions about "gentlemen" hoodlums and gangsters. "Don't think just because he gets a manicure Jackie Cerone doesn't know how to get his hands dirty."

Having grown up hearing (or overhearing) stories about mob "celebrities," it was fun seeing one of the stars in person. I'd heard people talk about Jackie Cerone and automatically lower their voices. He had that kind of power. And nobody ever, ever called him "Jackie the Lackie." I didn't care what Dad said. Running into mob guys was cool.

As I learned and continued to learn into my trouble-making twenties, if you didn't see a mobster at one joint, you went to the next. Somebody would be there. No matter where an Outfit guy stood on the org chart, quality was important. Second-rate was dead last. The mob guys went to the best places, and that's where I wanted to be. Hang out with the hoodlums. Have drinks with gangsters. I wanted to be part of their world without – you know – being part of their world. It sounds stupid and shallow looking in the rearview mirror. And it was. But it was fun in the moment.

Beyond Meo's in Addison and Tom's Steak House in Melrose Park, there was Rocky's (owned by Jackie Cerone and Joe Lombardo's brother, Rocky), Auroi's on Lake Street, Slicker Sam's (owned by mob-connected Salvatore Rosa) on Rice Avenue, The Come Back Inn on Belmont, and Leoni's on Lake. If I felt like going downtown, I could pick among Agostino's, The Tavern on Rush, Carmine's, Billy's, and Tiodori's (also known as the Division Street Lounge).

Spread out across the city, I could choose from mob places like The Golden Horn, Gene & Georgetti's, Horwath's, or Nick Giannotti's place – Nick's Village. Paul Lee owned King Wah in Chinatown. Lee was mobbed up with the Tong – the Chinese version of the Outfit. Dad used to take us on special occasions when we were kids. Jeffrey and I would split a giant slab of beef called Hong Kong Steak.

I hadn't planned on asking Joan to marry me. I loved being with her, and we'd been tossing "I love you" back and forth for months. We'd been together for over a year, and we lived like a married couple, meaning she sometimes spent the nights at my house. But Joan got the same grief from her parents that I used to get when I stayed out all night, so the overnight stays were few and far between. Plenty of nights I pulled myself out of bed, put on my pants, and drove Joan home. I'd see her mother or father glaring from the other side of their living room window at the bastard soiling their little girl.

One night we were in bed, and it was getting late. I said, "I don't want you to go home anymore. I think we should get married."

She never made it home that night, and the next morning we broke the news to her parents. I don't think they were entirely happy about it. Luckily, they didn't have a say. Sure, we were young. And, yeah, we were stupid. But we were in love. And we knew everything. When did anything go wrong because two people were in love, other than all the time?

My wedding to Joan was set for September 4, 1978 – until the pregnancy test came back positive and pushed up the timing. It was a scramble to find a hall to accommodate a last-minute reception. Every place was booked. But my dad is resourceful. He relied on his connected friends. Next thing Joan and I knew, a slot opened at Louis' Restaurant on Lake Street in Addison. We booked a church and made plans for a February 5 wedding. Invitations went to 150 friends and family members. Naturally, this included a table of Dad's pals from the old neighborhood.

Three children followed in four years: Kristyn Marie made her debut on July 4, 1977. Michael John III on January 19, 1979. Jason Donald on April 10, 1980. To her credit, Joan threw herself into being a wife and mother. The most generous word I can find for my behavior is "distracted," as in distracted by the massive amount of fun I was having running around town. Somehow in a warped, wannabee echo chamber in my head, I convinced myself that spending time with mob guys meant I was like them. After all, I bought drinks for them; they bought drinks for me. I played a doctor in a grammar school play; I cannot actually sew on someone's head. I knew one thing, but not the other.

Things started going wrong about a year after Kristyn was born. Everything else in my life was good, so naturally that was the time to develop a really bad gambling habit. At least before Kristyn was born, Joan had a full-time job. Two salaries helped if I hit a losing streak. Joan didn't complain. It was small amounts at first, and she didn't notice.

One morning at the store I heard the bell over the front door. Instead of a customer, Danny the bookie stood there. He didn't look mad; he looked disappointed. I'd been letting the phone ring all morning. Practically every time it stopped, I called Dad at the restaurant to see if he'd just called. I didn't want him thinking I wasn't there. The bullshit was that I was waiting on a customer and couldn't get to the phone. He'd ask about the take, and I'd run a total. Then I'd hang up, and the phone would ring again. After I called Dad the third time, he asked, "Who the hell is calling the store so many times?" I heard a whiff of accusation. When it finally stopped ringing, I thought I bought another day.

Danny stood in the doorway and asked, "Doesn't your phone work? I've been trying to call you all morning. I expected to see you last night."

I was supposed to bring $500 to the DB Lounge. But I didn't for several reasons, the main reason being I didn't have $500. Ladies and gentlemen, this is the situation in which every gambler eventually finds himself or herself: Behind the eight-ball with no way to pay. I offered bullshit instead – my wife and kid were sick, and I couldn't get out last night.

Danny nodded. "You gotta take care of your family." I hoped that meant an extension (with interest) until payday. Then he said, "I have a family to take care of, too. And you owe me money." He turned his head to the left, and his eyes rested on the cash register.

I knew what I had to do, but I didn't know how to explain it to Dad later. I opened the register and counted out $500. But now he wanted $750 – to cover the cost of coming to me. Between what was in the drawer and what was in the bank bag, I had enough to cover my debt. After Danny left, my hands felt clammy and cold, and I stood there shaking. How the hell could I explain $750 missing without admitting the truth? First, I put all the money in my pocket into the register – that reduced the missing amount by a whopping $85. Maybe if I told Dad business dropped off in the afternoon...

Today, I can see I had a gambling problem. But back then I just thought I was gambling. Because it was fun. There's an old saying about how God takes care of drunks and fools. God took care of one degenerate gambler that day, too. The store got busy. When I locked the door, I'd made back the missing $665, plus a little more. It would look like an off day. But it was robbing Peter to pay Paul. At the end of the week when Dad did the books, he'd realize the amount of money we took in didn't reconcile with the amount of produce purchased. There was no way to explain the missing $750, short of the truth. And I couldn't take the money out of our savings account without Joan asking questions. The truth wasn't an option on two fronts. But if I placed a couple of bets, and if I won, I could replace the money before the end of the week, and Dad would be none the wiser. Want to know the worst part? I won. By the end of the week I was up $900, with enough to pay back the register and a little profit. A smart man would have recognized his narrow escape and stopped gambling. But I wasn't smart. I was on a roll! When the roll stopped, I robbed Peter to pay Paul again.

My dad eventually realized what I'd been doing. And he fired me. He not only fired me; he shut down the market in 1978. I scrambled to support my family, and rescue came through my father-in-law. Don Strasser worked at Budweiser for decades and helped me get a job delivering beer in the city. It was good pay with good benefits, just what a family man needed. Because Joan was pregnant again. I talked it over with Dad, and he agreed that taking the job was the right choice. He said, "Do the smart thing. It'll be a new experience." Cold. But true.

By the time Michael III was born, I was working with Dad at the restaurant. I hated that job at Budweiser. Dad gave me another chance, but watched me like a hawk. Meanwhile, after two babies in less than three years, Joan didn't have the time or energy for my irresponsible behavior. It came to a head on a perfectly ordinary night after a perfectly ordinary dinner. Joan was doing the dishes when I said I wanted to go out.

She said, "We don't have a babysitter."

"I meant me. I'm going out."

The battle began with a barrage of "how dare you" and continued through an explosion of "are you fucking kidding me?" I spent the next hour dodging bullets as my wife fired off a list of my shortcomings in excruciating detail. Clearly, she'd been compiling it for a while. As she kept going on and on, I started getting pissed. She wasn't exactly Mary Poppins-perfect. But I had no defense when she said: "I look after five people – you, me, and the three kids. You look after *you*." Then she went nuclear with, "I can take the kids and go live with my parents."

The words hit like a hammer in the throat. I saw myself coming home to an empty apartment with an empty bed and the empty cribs of my missing children. I apologized. Then I apologized again. I didn't begrudge Joan a night out and wouldn't have stopped her from having one. But at that particular moment, I wasn't thinking about her at all. And that was exactly the problem. I convinced Joan to stay and we put that argument to bed – for the night anyway.

The next day at the restaurant I made the mistake of telling Ma about the argument when she asked why I was so crabby. I thought she'd take my side. Instead, she slapped my shoulder and said, "You're just like your father. He didn't see why he should have to stay home because I had two babies. Like they were just mine and not his, too."

Dad shook his head at me and asked, "What kind of jag-off tells a woman with an infant and an eighteen-month old he's going out?"

Ma's mouth dropped open and she pointed at me. "Apple," she said. Then she pointed at Dad. "Meet your tree."

He looked at me and shook a finger. "If that girl kicks you out, you're not coming to live with us."

Ma waved him away. "If you need a place to stay, you've always got a home."

"That's why he's like this, Mare. You baby him."

Ma wasn't having it. "Oh, yeah. It's my fault he gambles with hoodlums." Then she fired the last shot. "You're never going to convince me there's something wrong with taking care of my son." And he never did.

You've seen the scene in every gangster movie – the one where the guy walks into the restaurant or the nightclub or wherever, and the crowd parts. It's all a Frank Sinatra Rat Pack ringy-ding-ding of a time. I lived that scene over and over. You know where you don't get treated like a hero? At home. Because your wife is tired of being ignored while you're out having a good time. Is going out three or four times a week a lot? It didn't seem like it. I started accumulating phone numbers. Instead of broads, bookies, and loan sharks, I had nightclub managers and maître d's all over town. I even knew a guy on one of those dinner cruises off Navy Pier, but I get seasick.

I never once thought: "Why don't I go home and watch the kids while Joan gets her hair done?" Back then, I had a lot of friends from high school, some married with kids like me. We were big shots ten years ago. Some went to college, some didn't. The quarterback on the high school football team – the one who didn't go to college because he blew out his knee at seventeen – worked for his father-in-law's insurance company. The center on the basketball team flunked out of Northwestern and worked at his father's car dealership.

I loved my wife and kids. But I wasn't ready to be a husband and father. Some of my friends weren't either, and that made us a pack. When my dad was my age, he ran with Goombah Sammy, Goombah Johnny, Frankie, Uncle Tony, Skip, and Jimmy. I had Bob, Ed, Dave, Billy, and half a dozen other guys. We spent our time being irresponsible. Because we could. Dad and I argued about it all the time. He didn't like when I hung out with Outfit guys. Once he taunted me about whether I'd "declared a mob major." He said that was the next step for "bums." A bum was defined as "one of those guys with no job who's always got money."

Some bums "majored" in things like driving. Historically, driving served as a stepping stone to leadership, starting first with Big Jim Colosimo's driver (Al Capone) and continuing through Al Capone's driver (Joe Accardo) to Paul Ricca's driver (Sam Giancana) to Sam Giancana's driver (Jackie Cerone), and to Jackie Cerone's driver (John DiFronzo). Dad said I used to like burning trash at the market. Maybe I could mob major in arson. Or maybe bombing. Juicing? Collecting? Forging? Painting? Boosting? The Outfit offered lots of career paths.

But I never wanted to be a gangster. I was just looking to have a good time. I also had a wife, parents, and in-laws who considered me a bad husband and a marginal father. With good cause. In early 1981, Joan left and took the kids to live at her parents' house. When she filed for divorce, I didn't fight it. We'd both had enough by that point. The final papers arrived in November 1981, and I signed them without a second thought. And where did I sign those papers? At my parents' house, where I was living in Jeffrey's old bedroom. I had no plan, an angry ex-wife, and three kids I saw less each month. I could barely look my dad in the eye. He was so disgusted and disappointed. Join the club.

On Saint Patrick's Day 1982, my cousin called and said we needed to go out. He was another in the long list of Michaels in our family. Michael Joseph Difiglio was the son of Dad's sister Marie and her husband Joe. I called him Fig. I didn't feel like going out, but he wasn't having my excuses. I worked at a flea market produce concession and hung out in Jeffrey's old bedroom blowing pot smoke out the window. That was about it. Fig said he was coming to get me, so I better be ready.

We went to a place in Lombard called Sweet Peppers. It was packed with drunks drinking green beer, and I started having a good time despite myself. Fig saw a girl he knew from high school and started talking to her. They both grew up in Hillside and had known each other forever. She was short and busty, with a round face, pale skin, brown eyes, and curly, brown hair. She had the bawdy, easy laugh of a woman who wasn't accustomed to taking shit from anybody. Lou Ann Griffin was on a date, but that didn't matter. I liked her immediately. In fact, I tried to convince her to ditch her date and leave with me. But she wouldn't. I even kissed her in the hallway and made another "let's blow this joint" pitch. No dice. The only thing I got was a phone number.

Two nights later, Lou Ann and I had our first date. We went to see *On Golden Pond*. What a stupid fucking movie! After, we went out for sandwiches and realized how much we had in common and how many of the same people we knew. She told me about her two kids (Shannon and Patrick were the same ages as Kristyn and Michael). Her marriage went off the rails, too, so we also had that in common. After I took her home, I thought about Lou Ann, her kids, my kids, and saw the beginning of something that looked like *The Brady Bunch.*

My mob adjacent all-access pass got us into the best places. We had a terrific date at Café Bohemia. Jim Janek had been running the restaurant and jazz lounge on Clinton for decades. His restaurant offered meals served nowhere else. Café Bohemia was famous for game meats – but game meats that would shock modern diners. They served hippopotamus, elk, and lion. Broiled northern moose steak. Braised bear chops. Bengal tiger strips. Lions and tigers and bears. On the menu! Dad went for dinner during the 1968 Democratic National Convention. Some people remember the riots. I remember Café Bohemia served donkey and elephant meat. Dad came home and said he refused to eat the donkey steak. When Janek said it tasted like beef, Dad said, "You know what tastes like beef? Beef, jag-off."

By the time Lou Ann and I went to Café Bohemia in the mid-1980s, the crispy duck with wild rice was probably the most adventurous thing on the menu. It looked like a hunting lodge inside, all dark corners, dark wood, and old leather. Animal heads mounted on the walls, carcasses hanging. I asked the maître d' for Jim Janek, like my dad told me to do. The maître d made a call and a few moments later, Janek appeared. Salt and pepper hair, tan, big smile, stocky and solid but not fat, tweed sport jacket, brown tie. He looked like the kind of man who owned a hunting lodge and hunted big game, like something out of a Hemingway story.

"Mr. Janek, my name is Mike Gentile, Junior. My father sends his regards. And he wanted to know if you still served donkey steak."

We shook hands and Janek laughed. "Tell that son of a bitch I said hello. And there's no donkey on the menu." I introduced Lou Ann, and Janek talked to us for a couple of minutes about the old days. I always loved hearing about the old days.

"I used to go to the Bridge. The business he did in that place!" He laughed and said, "The mobsters were worried about being around the cops, so they drank to calm their nerves. The cops worried about getting whacked by the mobsters, so they drank to calm their nerves. The lawyers worried that the judges would see them, so they drank to calm their nerves. The judges worried that the lawyers, cops, and mobsters would see them, so they drank to calm their nerves, too. Between all those nerve-calming drinks, your father filled that cash register until it begged for mercy." Finally, he shook my hand again, turned to the maître d' and said, "Carl, take my guests to a table."

Carl snapped to attention and grabbed menus. We followed. Lou Ann barely had her purse on the chair when a waiter showed up with an ice bucket and a bottle of champagne we hadn't ordered. Pop! Pour! Cheers! Normally, I'm not a champagne drinker. Little bubbles. Agita. Vodka's my drink. On the rocks. Turned out that was her drink, too. A shared interest in imported vodka seemed a fine way to build a relationship.

Lou Ann looked over the top of her glass and asked, "Do you always get treated like this?"

"What do you mean?"

"All these people fussing." She leaned closer. "Who ARE you?"

"Me? I'm just a guy from Bellwood."

"And I'm just a girl from Hillside, but I don't get free champagne just for walking into a restaurant."

"My dad used to be in the business, so he knows a lot of people." Then I told her about the time in 1968 when Jim Janek tried to get Dad to eat donkey steak. Lou Ann was disgusted. A good relationship needs a solid baseline, and we found ours: Neither wanted to eat anything we might see at a zoo.

Appetizers we hadn't order appeared at the table – an enormous tureen of shrimp cocktail and a plate of Shrimp de Jonghe, basically shrimp sautéed in butter, garlic, herbs, and white wine with a crunchy topping. It's been Lou Ann's favorite dish ever since. We hadn't looked at the menus. Café Bohemia was famous for its crispy duck with wild rice. Janek's gimmick was that he numbered each serving to demonstrate how many times people ordered it – sort of like McDonald's and its hamburgers. The number was well over a million, but I can't remember exactly. That's a lot of dead ducks. We finished the champagne, ordered a couple of vodka rocks, and tucked into the shrimp.

She looked me hard in the eye and asked, "Are you one of those guys? I'm not judging. I just want to know."

I knew what she meant. Bellwood, Hillside, and Melrose Park were filled with third-generation mobbed-up guys around my age. Maybe their grandfather cooked alky for Al Capone, and their uncle or father worked on a crew with Joe Accardo. Fifty years later, they moved into the family business like I moved into Dad's. They sort of had jobs, but mostly they ran with crews robbing and stealing or doing leg work for juice guys. A girl didn't plan a future with one of those guys. Good news: I had a regular job, just like my dad. Lou Ann seemed relieved.

We talked about our families over dinner. She'd known Fig since grammar school, and she knew his family, too. Her parents played cards once a week with Uncle Joe and Aunt Marie. Lou Ann didn't know anything about my family's Grand and Aberdeen backstory, so I told her how my dad grew up with the guys who became the next generation of mobsters after Al Capone. They were just guys from the neighborhood. "We don't know hoodlums and gangsters on a professional basis."

"Okay." Then she asked about my dad.

It's not a complicated story. If the Outfit was the varsity team, my dad was the mascot – the guy who hung around the team but didn't play the game. His job was to make sure everybody had a good time – at his bar on Clybourn, the tavern on Dearborn, the nightclub on Mannheim, and places like Casa Madrid, The Leather Bottle, The Yorkshire Pub, and all the other joints. When Dad wasn't entertaining various levels of mobdom, he palled around with guys like Skip, Jimmy, Uncle Tony, and the rest of his Rat Pack. After nearly forty years of mob adjacency, Dad knew just about everybody. And I wanted to know everybody Dad knew. It was our thing. Jeffrey and Ma had movies as their thing. It was gangsters for Dad and me.

Lou Ann shrugged. "Some fathers and sons fish."

The waiter brought a plate of desserts – a wedge a cheesecake, a hunk of chocolate cake, and these little cookies. She had coffee. But I'm like Ma. Can't stand the stuff. After the busboy took away the plates, the waiter returned. "Mr. Janek sends his regards to your father." He walked away and I started to get up.

Lou Ann shot me a look. "You didn't pay the bill."

"What bill? Get your purse." I learned this from my dad: If the owner comps you, leave a tip equal to your bill, plus twenty percent. That's what he said. And that's what I did. Pay the good time forward. It's good for the soul.

On the way to the lounge, she asked, "Am I going to regret getting involved with you?"

"Probably. Some of the time anyway. But I won't do it on purpose."

"Is that supposed to help?"

It wasn't long before I moved into her house. I liked being part of a family and coming home to kids again. But I felt unsettled. Shannon, Kris, Patrick, and Michael became friends almost immediately, with Jason tagging along like the dutiful younger brother. The more time my kids spent with her kids, the closer everybody became. I wanted to know we were building something real – that I wasn't just the guy living at his girlfriend's house with no rights and no real place. Something that felt like a romantic idea had been percolating in my head for a few weeks. It was coming up on the anniversary of the day we met. I wanted to get married. On St. Patrick's Day.

A few weeks in advance of March 17, I proposed. Her eyebrows knitted together, and she looked at me like I just shit on the carpet – shock and then horror and disgust. Having had one failed marriage made her hesitate. I'd been honest about why my marriage to Joan failed, so she knew where the land mines were buried. Lou Ann kept me waiting a good, long time for an answer.

She talked it over with Shannon and Patrick, since it affected them, too. Her kids were crazy about me. Finally, she said yes. We got married on St. Patrick's Day 1988 at City Hall. We didn't want the trouble and expense of a second big wedding. We both did the formal wedding thing already with a different cast, and neither had a happy ending.

Lou Ann had worked hard to support herself and two small kids after her marriage fell apart. Recently separated in 1977, she got a job working in the coat room at The Carlisle through Nick Vangel – the man the FBI called "Nick the Caterer." It was a good gig. The hours were flexible, and she got tips in addition to the hourly pay.

"All you had to do was hang up coats and give them back later," Lou Ann said. It was wintertime, and the place was hosting a big, Italian wedding. "You always knew when it was a mob wedding because the FBI was in the parking lot; and when you made the table arrangements, everyone was seated against the back wall."

During the reception, an old man came out of the ballroom and sat in a chair next to the coat room. He asked if she minded if he smoked a cigar. His wife wouldn't let him smoke around her. Lou Ann didn't mind and happily passed the time chatting. The man said how proud he'd been to walk his granddaughter Alicia down the aisle. As they talked, Lou Ann noticed Nick giving her the eye.

When she walked to the other side of the lobby, Nick asked, "Do you know who that man is?"

She said, "Yeah, he's the bride's grandpa."

Nick looked at her sideways when she didn't react. "That's Tony Accardo. Tony Accardo!" He stared wide-eyed in disbelief. "He's the mob boss of Chicago."

Lou Ann didn't follow the who's who of mob hierarchy. But she humored her boss. "Should I call him Mr. Accardo?"

At the end of the night, the old man gave her a $100 bill when he retrieved his wife's mink coat.

When my brother and I started working on this memoir, we agreed it was a shame Dad never met Accardo. It would have added another dimension to our history, but their paths never crossed. Turns out Lou Ann took care of that checkbox.

24 KITCHEN ADJACENT

I was living with Lou Ann in 1982 before we got married, and the phone rang around 10:00 PM. It was Dad. I heard trouble in his voice. He said, "Get over here right away. Bring a gun. And make sure it's loaded." I hung up the phone and started throwing on clothes like a lunatic and grabbed the gun hidden in the closet. Lou Ann panicked and tried to stop me from leaving.

"My dad has never said anything like that to me. I gotta go."

Dad stood at the end of the driveway and jumped into the car practically before I stopped. Right away he started to cry. "It's your Aunt Jeanette."

I had a destination and started driving.

Dad continued, "Somebody tried to break into her house. She's been attacked and beaten up." He sat in silence the rest of the drive.

Somebody beat up a 65-year old spinster? What the fuck? Then I realized why Dad called me. Lou Ann's house was on the way to Aunt Jeanette's, and it meant doubling back to pick up Dad. But he didn't trust himself to drive. My dad needed me.

Chicago's Westside had seen better days. Since the death of longtime boss Fiore "Fifi" Buccieri in 1973 (from natural causes), Dad's old school chum Joe Lombardo controlled the Westside. When Lombardo went to prison in 1982, Jimmy Boy Cozzo assumed many of his boss' responsibilities. Later in his career, he helped open casinos in other cities and countries and may have been the first man in history to lose money on a casino, until Donald Trump proved conclusively it's still possible to be a loser in the casino business. But on that night in 1982, Jimmy Boy was firmly in charge of Chicago's Westside. Among his personal responsibilities was making sure no one fucked with his father and aunt, nestled safely in their brick three-flat on Grand Avenue near Aberdeen. Aunt Jeanette's attack was practically a shot across Jimmy Boy's bow.

Jimmy Boy's cousin Sammy Polito (Rose's son) waited on Aunt Jeanette's front porch. The first thing Sammy said was, "Mom called five minutes ago from the hospital. Jeanette is fine."

At those words, Dad uncoiled.

We walked up the curved staircase in the foyer to Aunt Jeanette's second-floor apartment. She had rented out the large main floor after Grandma Gentile died and lived upstairs in a small two-bedroom unit. The kitchen looked like a slaughterhouse, bloody hand prints on the walls, blood everywhere. Toppled furniture. Like something from a horror movie. You can't imagine anybody survived from the look of it. Dad gasped and choked up all over again.

Sammy explained what happened: Around 8:00 PM, Jeanette was watching television and heard a noise on the enclosed back porch adjacent to her kitchen. She opened the door, and a masked man pushed his way in and started hitting her with a pipe. He split her head wide open. She couldn't see for all the blood running down her face, but she fought back, pushing her attacker out the door and down the back stairs. He tumbled head over heels, then got up and limped away while Jeanette ran into her apartment and locked the door. She called Junior and the police. In that order.

Rosie and Sammy lived around the corner. Sammy had his own apartment. He was about my age. They heard the police cars and ambulances and walked to the corner of Grand and Aberdeen to see what was going on. They saw the commotion in front of Jeanette's house and raced down. When the paramedics brought Jeanette down on a stretcher, Rosie got in the ambulance while Sammy waited for us. He went up to the apartment after everybody left.

Sammy later said he hadn't seen that much blood since "you know – that day." (He meant the day Richard Cain was executed in the sandwich shop.) Half an hour or so later, Rosie called to say Jeanette would be fine. The doctors stitched her head, and the nurses were cleaning her up. She told Sammy to get a change of clothes for Jeanette and give it to Junior.

Sammy said he wasn't sure what he put in the bag. He grabbed what looked like an everyday dress and some shoes, but it got too embarrassing when he opened a drawer full of old lady underpants and brassieres. He handed Dad the paper bag, and we headed to Saint Ann's Hospital. Sammy said he'd call some people to come over and start cleaning up. When you grow up mob adjacent, you know people who can get rid of stubborn blood stains and other unsightly evidence.

Aunt Jeanette was sitting up in bed watching television when we arrived. Rosie sat in a chair beside the bed. Both were drinking coffee. All they needed was a plate of cookies to make their impromptu Coffee And complete. Color returned to Dad's face when he saw his sister with his own eyes. There wasn't a spot of blood anywhere, just a wide bandage on the left side of her head. Her hair was washed, and she was in a clean hospital gown. Dad hugged her, and I waved from the doorway.

"Nice work, Aunt. All the way down the stairs, huh?"

She said, "The bastard should have broken his neck."

I went into the hallway and called Ma and Lou Ann while Dad talked to the doctor.

Rosie came out of the room and squeezed my arm. "Tough as nails, that one." She looked exhausted. "The neighborhood is changing," she said softly. Rosie was right. And it wasn't changing for the better. I told her I remembered Eli's Candy Shop, and she smiled.

The doctor wanted Aunt Jeanette to stay overnight. She started to give him lip about staying, but Dad told her to be quiet. Then we drove Rosie home, and Dad walked her up to her apartment. Sammy was waiting. He said the cleaning people were already at Jeanette's. We went around the corner to check on the house. The residents at 460 North Aberdeen were awake – the young family on the main floor and the two singles who lived in a pair of studios upstairs behind Aunt Jeanette's apartment. All were relieved to learn Jeanette was safe. Upstairs, three men with buckets, mobs, rags, and spray bottles scrubbed Aunt Jeanette's kitchen and back porch. Another was installing a lock on the door at the bottom of the stairs.

On the way back to Itasca, Dad said they'd been trying to get Aunt Jeanette to move closer to the rest of the family for years. A bad element was moving into her neighborhood, and he didn't like it. She had trouble once before. The problem, according to Dad, was "once upon a time." Once upon a time, Grand and Aberdeen was a safe neighborhood filled with families who knew each other over generations. Those families dwindled over the decades, and a rougher crowd moved in. She wouldn't discuss moving. Not even after "what happened at the bus stop."

Once upon a time, a nicely dressed woman could stand safely on the corner of Grand and Aberdeen and wait for a bus to carry her into the city for a pleasant afternoon of shopping. That same woman standing on that same bus stop in the 1980s wearing a fur coat, gold necklaces, and diamond rings attracted attention she didn't want. Dad had been warning her about going out looking like she was "dipped in egg and rolled in diamonds." He told her she had no business walking around in a mink coat and jewelry in "that neighborhood." Aunt Jeanette took offense to the idea that she lived in "that neighborhood" and did exactly as she pleased.

He said, "According to my sister, she was waiting for the bus when a colored guy ran up, grabbed her gold necklaces and pulled them off her neck. She grabbed hold of his arms and tried to stop him. Because her goddamned necklaces were worth getting hurt over! He knocked her on her ass and ran off." Dad stared out the window and grumbled. "Now this." I expected a formal sit-down between the Gentile siblings soon. Screws would be turned to convince Jeanette to leave the old neighborhood. Without success.

That was also the night Dad told me about Grandpa Mickey, Don Vincenzo, and the engine crank that changed Gentile family history. He told me how different Aberdeen Street was back then, how nobody locked their doors. When Aunt Jeanette rented out the main floor in 1966, she had to put a new lock on the front door because no one could find the original key. Dad said he never had a key to the house, never needed one. Now people put steel bars on their windows. He talked the whole way back, and it was the first time I got a look at the man my dad was before he met Ma and became a father.

Back in the old neighborhood, Jimmy Boy took great offense to his aunt's friend being attacked and decided to look into the matter. Turned out there'd been a junkie hanging around in the neighborhood, and he'd been chased away trying to break into another house. He matched the description Jeanette gave – tall, thin, long hair peeking under a ski mask. A few days later, a tall, thin, long-haired man was found in a nearby alley with both arms and legs broken. Dad said the only reason they didn't find a dead body was because the junkie didn't kill Jeanette. She still refused to move.

25 RETIREMENT ADJACENT

The lasting effects of a childhood bout with pleurisy and decades of damage caused by smoking left Dad with emphysema. The man who loved nothing more than hard work had trouble catching his breath and tying his shoes. He caught colds almost constantly, and at fifty-three his health situation seemed closer to a man twenty years older. Despite his health problems, business continued to grow at the restaurant after Dad put in a deli case and started selling cold cuts. It was hard for him to admit the work was becoming too much. He started talking about selling, but nobody thought he was serious. If he had a slow day or a piece of equipment broke, he'd grumble about selling "the fucking place." Then it would be busy the next day or the repair turned out to be minor, and that would be it on the subject of selling.

Without much discussion, he put Lisa's up for sale, and it sold almost immediately. Those factories weren't going anywhere, and neither were the people working in the industrial park and at the car dealerships lining Lake Street. You could have sold shit sandwiches and still made good money off the lunch business. He took a few things – including the Oh My God pot – and basically handed the keys to the new owner – lock, stock, and lunch business. But he kept the recipes.

Dad had been using the same accountant since Orlando's Hideaway. Marshall Samler was more than a CPA; he and his wife, Ruth, had become part of our family. He advised Dad on investments and helped Dad grow his money. On his advice, Dad had been buying stock in power plants, public utilities, and telecommunications. He bought pharmaceutical stock, too – a lot of it. Once a month, Dad and Marshall met at the same kosher deli for lunch. Lisa ribbed Dad about being cheap because he and Marshall split a giant corned beef sandwich and a slice of cheesecake. Dad never stuffed himself. He'd leave the last bite of steak or cake on the plate because he'd had enough. Over lunch, Marshall and Dad talked business.

Marshall happened to be Jewish, a fact that made no difference to Dad. But in the same way Dad irrationally believed Italians had a better head for organized crime, he believed Jews had a better head for finance, so Dad always followed his accountant friend's advice. Marshall would say something like, "I've been thinking, Mike. Electronics. They're going to be big." When Dad sold the restaurant, he invested in electronics just as the technology market exploded. For a man who owned small businesses most of his life, my dad retired comfortably.

Having tasted the workplace after decades as a reluctant homemaker, Ma told Dad she intended to keep working after he sold the restaurant. Telemarketing sounded interesting. You got to sit down and talk on the phone. She was good at both. At fifty-two, Ma started a new career in telemarketing. She got a job with Montgomery Ward's selling life insurance over the phone. After a couple of years, she parlayed her experience into a new job. The woman with a high school diploma was going to sell industrial chemicals. Over the phone.

Around the same time Ma went to work for United Laboratories, Dad started getting restless. A man who'd been working since thirteen didn't take well to sitting home with the newspaper and television. He started fixing dinner to pass the time, then shopping for ingredients. Ma teased him about going to the store to buy one tomato. Before long, he was mopping the kitchen floor. The 1954 Mike Gentile wouldn't have recognized his 1984 self. We teased him about being Suzie Homemaker, and he teased Ma. He'd ask if she wanted him to cut up her pork chop. Since he'd already shopped for it, cooked it, and cleaned up after it, did she need him to cut it into little pieces, too? He and Ma were never happier than during that period.

I had a produce concession in a warehouse-type store. Dad helped – he was glad to have something to do. He wanted me to succeed; and I needed the help. The store wanted all pre-packed, pre-priced trays. Okay, fine. I wanted to make four-packs; Dad wanted six-packs. I said: If somebody only needs two tomatoes, they'll buy a four-pack. But they won't buy a six-pack, so you don't sell any tomatoes. If they need six tomatoes, they'll buy two four-packs. Now you've sold two extra tomatoes by packaging them in smaller quantities. Dad insisted it was faster to make six-packs. He was right. And I was right. It turned into an argument because we both needed to be right. We made both. The four-packs sold better. But the business failed anyway.

Retirement was like sitting naked on sandpaper for a man like my dad. It grated his ass. After the gutters were cleaned, the garage painted, and dinner prepared, he was still bored out of his skull. Dad got restless, and the boredom got him thinking about the old days off the back of the truck. He started exploring flea markets and swap meets. Dad found the Holy Grail one Sunday afternoon at the biggest indoor/outdoor flea market in Cicero. The Great American Flea Market was packed. Dad hadn't seen an operation on this scale since the stalls on Maxwell Street forty-years ago. He walked around counting the fruit and vegetable stands – ten. Right away he wanted to go out and buy a truck like it was 1948 and he was eighteen. But he was fifty-three, and his emphysema wasn't getting any better. But you had about as much luck reminding Mike Gentile of that fact as you had getting Jeanette Gentile to move off Aberdeen Street. Still not happening.

Here's where it helps to be mob adjacent: When Dad saw the competition, he decided they needed to go. Somehow, he learned the flea market was owned by Don Horowitz. And Don Horowitz had a friend named Ben Stein, formerly known as the Janitor King of Chicago. Once upon a time, Stein managed the janitorial work at McCormick Place, where Jackie Cerone got Dad a job in the Teamsters' union. Because just about everything in Chicago traces back to a crooked union one way or another.

Dad called Jimmy. Jimmy called somebody else, and the next thing you know Don Horowitz kicked out all ten vendors and gave the exclusive produce concession to Dad for the next six years at a flea market with seven-thousand visitors on weekends. When you're mob adjacent, competition mysteriously disappears. It was just Saturdays and Sundays, but for a while it seemed to take years off Dad. It was just him, Uncle Joe, Uncle Anthony, and me. Overnight the flea market went from a couple of tables behind the back of a van to this major operation.

Old friends at the market split pallets and bent the rules. The sellers at the big houses usually looked to get rid of broken boxes of produce on the cheap. Dad goes in and asks if they have any "broken pears." His pal says no – and hands Dad a hammer. Then Dad goes into the cooler, busts up a dozen or so boxes, and his pal sells them to Dad for half price. We had a special on pears that weekend.

The first time Lou Ann met my dad, she came to the flea market and saw two gray-haired men behind a make-shift counter. One was my dad, and the other was Uncle Anthony. A customer started picking through the tomatoes, and one of the gray-haired men yelled, "I don't touch your tomatoes, don't touch mine. You want to play with the tomatoes, go to the grocery store."

Lou Ann later said she kept praying, "Please let Mike's dad be the other guy. Please let Mike's dad be the other guy." It wasn't.

26 MARKET ADJACENT

I started working at the South Water Market and took one step closer into the lion's den when I opened a restaurant in 1984. The Old Lion and I met in early 1983. I saw him at the market and introduced myself saying, "Maybe you remember my dad, Mike Gentile." He did. Aunt Jeanette had worked in the bookkeeping office at American Main Lingerie with the Old Lion's mother, Anna. I'd see Anna occasionally at Aunt Jeanette's. She'd laugh and say, "You tell your father, Anna said he's no good." It was her way of saying hello.

The Old Lion and I struck up a friendship. To my surprise, when I mentioned an idea for a restaurant, he was interested. He already had a location in mind at the corner of Morgan and 14th Street. It was the perfect spot. Trucks came in from all over the country day and night, and there were thousands of people working in and around the market. They all needed to be fed. A well-run joint would be a gold mine. The Old Lion offered to bankroll me with his son-in-law, Vince. A guy named Chuck looked out for the Old Lion's interests like they were his own. He'd be at the restaurant, too, keeping an eye on things. With Outfit backing and protection, What's Your Beef? opened in 1984. Dad warned me about getting mixed up with The Old Lion, but I knew better. I always knew better.

On our second day in business, I came in, and all the meat was gone – four hams, three top rounds of beef, and two boxes of Vienna hot dogs. We couldn't open. We had nothing to sell. Chuck grabbed a club he kept behind the counter and said, "Let's go."

Around that time there were a lot of what I called "lost boys" around the market. Young kids in their early twenties, usually strung out on something, and looking to make a few quick bucks to feed their habit. One was a kid named Bobby. Now, I'm not sure how Chuck knew it was Bobby who stole the meat, but it was. Turned out Bobby sold $400 worth of meat for $20 to another restaurant around the corner. We found Bobby nearby, and he admitted what he did and why. He wanted the $20 for a hooker. Chuck took that club and started beating that kid everywhere but on the head.

I heard the wood cracking against bone, and Bobby just took it like he knew he had it coming. The kid never made a sound. After about twenty whacks, I started getting sick to my stomach. I grabbed Chuck's arm and yelled, "That's enough."

Chuck whirled around and hit me across the back with the club for interfering. It hurt like a motherfucker. It was the first time I'd been on the receiving end of an Outfit guy's wrath, and I didn't like it. Chuck went back to hitting Bobby. Finally, he stopped. There wasn't a drop of blood anywhere, but I knew Bobby would be bruised from neck to ankles. But he got up and hobbled with Chuck and me to the restaurant where he sold the meat. We went in with a club and a busted-up junkie and came out with a club, a busted-up junkie, and $400 worth of meat. Then we went back to the restaurant and opened. That was Day Two.

There was a lot of political stuff going on down at the market in the early 1980s, mostly involving the Teamsters. There were a couple of union stewards named Jimmy and Vincent. Nice guys. Mob adjacent, like me. They came in for lunch nearly every day with a guy from Strube Produce named Nick Chiusolo. A simmering pot of resentment had started coming to a boil among the union and non-union drivers as they tried to get organized. One day, Jimmy and Vincent were getting pushed around by a couple of drivers when Nick and I happened along. We jumped into the mix without thinking about it. I grabbed one of the guys and pitched him head-first off the loading dock and onto the street six feet below. Trouble ended, Nick and I continued on our way.

We were standing in front of Strube when the guy I tossed off the dock came running after me with a cop and pointing his finger. Next thing you know, I'm in handcuffs. Dad had come to the restaurant earlier and happened to be at Strube visiting friends. I looked at him when the cop cuffed me, and he just stood there. I expected him to do something or say something. But Dad just crossed his arms and waited. I got into bed with these guys; he wanted to see how they were going to get me out of it.

A voice came blasting out of nowhere. "What the fuck are you doing, you stupid son of a bitch?" It was the lieutenant in charge of the South Water Market district, a mob friendly guy.

I thought he was yelling at me. But no. He was yelling at the cop. The lieutenant knew I worked with the Old Lion. And just like that, I was out of trouble. I looked at Dad and smiled. It could have gone the other way just as easily. But I'm rubbing my wrists and loving being mob adjacent. People were standing around watching, and my dad shook his head at the shit I manage to get myself into. The truck driver started yelling about how he wanted me arrested for assault. That's when Vincent and Jimmy arrived and told the cop what really happened. The story ended with the truck driver limping away after the cop threatened to arrest him.

The neighborhood around the market changed by the 1980s. People got robbed, beaten, and killed. That's when Dad and I bought guns. He said something that stuck with me. Maybe I was going a little overboard about the cool factor of buying a gun. He said, "That gun is like your prick. You don't take it out unless you're ready to use it." That's how Dad knew I had a gun when he called about Aunt Jeanette getting attacked.

The time I worked with the Old Lion and Chuck turned into one of the best times of my life. Besides the restaurant, Chuck and I had a side business selling trailer loads of produce on Maxwell Street on the weekends. The money flowed in – and flowed out just as fast. One of Chuck's favorite places was the Division Street Baths, an old world-style Russian bath owned by Joe Colucci, another Capone-era gangster. The place looked like a seedy palace in a bad neighborhood of ancient Rome. John and Jim Belushi were regulars. In fact, John wanted to shoot part of *Blues Brothers* inside. Colucci said no: "We were busy that day."

Chuck parked on the sidewalk. Everybody did in front of the Division Street Baths. And nobody ever bothered Joe's customers. There was a story that a mob guy came in to explain a mistake, ended up getting whacked, burned up in the oven, and left the building as smoke from the chimney. I doubt this story. The average oven isn't hot enough to burn up a body. But that's the legend the place had.

We'd go two or three times a week. Here's how it worked: We'd walk in and Chuck would shout upstairs how many people were in his party. Joe would make sure someone started lunch. Then came the steam bath. First you took off all your clothes. This was weird for me, being in a room full of naked men.

They'd hand you a bucket filled with boiling water. Floating in the water is a whole bar of Ivory soap and a small branch of oak leaves. You'd go into the steam room while the soap slowly melts. Then someone comes in, swirls the leaves in the soapy water, and beats you with them. It felt good, and it felt strange. Once the steam bath was over, we went upstairs for lunch. You could at least wear towels or robes then. I didn't care for the nudity. But the lunch was always good.

The other thing that happened over lunch was betting. Lots of betting. If there was a game or a race or two cockroaches running up the wall, I'd bet on it. Chuck didn't mind that we were spending so much time on Division Street. Vince took care of the restaurant, so I didn't worry. But I should have. Owning a small business means being there day after day. Dad always understood that. But I didn't. I wanted to hang out with Outfit guys, place bets, and do some recreational cocaine to keep the days humming along. You know what happens when you live like that? Eventually your business goes broke, which is exactly what happened.

27 WEDDING ADJACENT

Our sister Lisa married Jerry King in 1986. She had the church, the music, the big dress, the flowers, and all the stuff that goes with a Catholic, Italian wedding. And in true Italian style, the lavender mother-of-the-bride dress cost almost as much as Lisa's wedding gown. Lou Ann planned their reception, and it came off beautifully. She had plenty of experience from her days working for "Nick the Caterer" at The Carlisle. What made the day memorable to me wasn't the fact that our only sister got married. No. It was that my father came armed. To a church.

Dad tucked a small handgun with a mother-of-pearl handle in his waistband. I felt it when I bumped against him and asked what the hell? Was the gun in case Jerry didn't say "I do" on cue? There was going to be a wedding or a funeral; and either way, Dad was prepared? He gave me a cold eyeball. In fact, he carried the gun because he had an envelope with $10,000 in cash to pay for his daughter's reception pinned inside his dove-gray tuxedo jacket. Why didn't he write a check? Decades of being mob adjacent made Dad prefer paying cash. Personally, I love that my dad came to church heavy, whatever the reason.

While I didn't know Jerry very well yet, he seemed like a nice guy – quiet, hard-working, respectful. His family seemed like good people, too. They were Irish immigrants who worked hard for their slice of the American pie, just like the Gentiles. In private conversations, Dad gave Mr. and Mrs. King the highest compliment – he said they were "respectable people." In other words, Irish or not, they were all right. High praise from a man who grew up hating the Irish. After Lisa left nursing school, she met Jerry at a nursing home in Franklin Park, where they both worked. She took care of patients; he worked maintenance. One thing led to another; next thing she's walking up the aisle in this huge dress with a train that reached halfway to Elk Grove.

On Saturday, September 12, 1986, two-hundred people gathered at St. Peter's Church in Itasca for a wedding mass, followed by a reception at Sharko's Restaurant in Villa Park. Growing up, we only went to Italian weddings because everybody we knew was Italian. When my friends from high school started getting married, I experienced "American" weddings for the first time. At each reception, I'd see a table loaded with gift-wrapped presents, something I found inconceivable. Italians don't bring gifts to a wedding; they bring envelopes.

After a series of strategic bridal showers with different guest lists, my sister had already successfully shaken down close to 100 people and filled her new apartment with every manner of linen, small appliances, intimate apparel, kitchen and bathroom accessories, not to mention the obligatory set of china, silver flatware, and crystal glass ware. With enough loot to open a small department store, the last thing Lisa and Jerry needed was a gift-wrapped anything.

Dad made sure the kids were set up in a nice apartment. Lisa and Jerry had dinner at our parents' house a couple of times a week – just like Dad and Ma went to Grandma Gentile's when they were newlyweds. I don't think Lisa knew much about the kitchen then. But she knew how to clean a house because Ma believed in "training" her children. Ma taught each of us how to clean toilets, floors, walls, dishes, and dirty laundry. She said we needed to know how to do those things because someday we'd have to do them for ourselves. It didn't hurt that in the moment she got to pawn off the housekeeping chores she detested under the heading of "life skills." Turned out Ma had a system, too.

Seven years younger, Lisa was a baby in the 1960s when dad's mob connected and mob adjacent pals were most active in our lives. She didn't swim in Orlando's pool or explore the Sahara Inn and didn't work at the markets, so she never met some of Dad's friends. He didn't talk about the old days with Lisa. By the time she was old enough to understand what was going on, the Outfit was sputtering on empty. Reading an early draft of this book was a revelation. She'd call practically gasping and say things like, "That nice man who brought the donuts drove for Al Capone?" Yup. Or, "Grandpa Mickey gave some guy a beating with a tire iron?" Technically, he only hit the guy once. I wouldn't necessarily call it a "beating." But yeah. While our parents, family, and friends tended to be discreet in conversations about who went to "college" and whatnot, Lisa grew up and filled in the blanks from television and newspaper stories just like Jeffrey and me.

At her wedding reception, waiters in uniforms circulated with trays of hors d'oeuvres. While guests milled around, Aunt Marie pulled up to Dad and lodged a complaint. She wanted to know why those people at the table against the back wall got trays of hors d'oeuvres delivered to them while everyone else had to grab snacks from passing waiters like beggars. Dad said nothing. He raised his hand and pressed his nose sideways in what I imagine is the universal gesture for "mobster." The lightbulb lit over Aunt Marie's head, and she smiled toward the table of mobsters. When she looked again, she recognized some of their faces from the old neighborhood and waved.

By the end of the evening, my sister had a satin bag filled with envelopes. One of the guys at the "special" table was Pat Ivanelli. But no one called him Pat; they called him Elbows. Elbows was legendary among Dad's crew for being cheap. My dad said they called him Elbows because Pat's arms didn't bend far enough to pick up a check. When Lisa opened the fat envelopes the next day, the fattest one came from Elbows. It just goes to show you.

28 LOSS ADJACENT

By 1995, my boys were teenagers, and they'd been hearing stories all their lives about the South Water Market and Elk Grove Village and all the joints over the years. They were on board with helping grandpa get an operation going at the flea market. So were Uncle Joe and Uncle Anthony. My brother-in-law Jerry was in, too. So was my future son-in-law Joe. And me, of course. We're all in. Dad bought a van, and he was ready to go. My boys loved it. One of their friends – a kid named Matt – joined up for the adventure. Dad would pull the second-hand van into my driveway in Hillside, and his pit crew of half-asleep teenagers piled in. We started in early May. For three weeks, Dad put the boys through the same paces that Jeffrey and I marched more than twenty-five years ago.

Dad used to talk about how you could always make a living with a case of apples in the trunk of your car. You sell the apples to buy dinner tonight and buy another case tomorrow. He said you could always convince someone at the market to spot you a case. From there, the future was limitless. Perpetual economic security hinged on one case of apples. That's how it started for our family. Giovanni Gentile came to Chicago and sold fruits and vegetables along the neighborhood streets. So did Grandpa Mickey. So did Dad and Uncle John. When Uncle John died suddenly of a heart attack in 1989, he still had the same produce market in Hanover Park. And when necessity demanded, Jeffrey and I entered the produce business, too. It left an indelible mark on us.

My son, Mike, still talks about sorting rotten oranges. He'd open a box and a puff of green mold would come out like smoke. Then he'd dip the good oranges in a bucket of filthy green water and use a disgusting rag to wash off the mold residue. Jeffrey said his first memory of the produce business was sitting in the back of the green truck separating rotten and good Jaffa oranges from Israel. Dad was training the next generation of fruit peddlers. This was the operation we grew up with, I told the boys – a truck, a couple of tables, cases of fruit, and boxes of vegetables. For the next three weeks, Dad, the boys, and I had the time of our lives. It was 1968 all over again.

Then on May 21, Dad took me aside and said, "I can't do it anymore. I can't work at the flea market." There were tears in his eyes. Dad enjoyed owning restaurants and nightclubs, but he loved the produce business. It broke my heart when that fucking emphysema stole his joy. To see him, you'd think he was perfectly healthy for a man of sixty-five. He was tan and robust and walked shoulders up, chest out, like the soldier he was so many decades ago. His hair was thick, with a fair amount of pepper mixed in with the salty gray. People said he looked like Anthony Quinn. To me, he looked more like Robert De Niro.

In the early hours of Friday, May 26, 1995, my dad had a heart attack and died a couple of hours later at Alexian Brothers Hospital in Elk Grove Village – the place I thought was a million miles away the first time Dad took us there. For Dad and me, it was a perfectly ordinary day. I was working at one of the big produce houses down at the South Water Market. It wasn't unusual for me to talk to Dad half a dozen times a day on the phone. Nothing important. It would go like this:

Me: What are you doing?

Dad: Same thing I was doing an hour ago when you called. What are you doing?

Me: Working.

Dad: How can you be working if you're talking on the phone? Call me later, jag-off.

An hour later, I'd call him again. It was our routine. He'd joke about me bothering him, but he always wanted to talk. A son remembers his father's last words. He said: "Call me later, jag-off." Then he laughed and hung up the phone. Perfectly ordinary.

I asked Jeffrey, and his experience was perfectly ordinary, too. He was living in Redondo Beach and talked to Dad on Tuesday. His thing with Dad was complaining about his job. My Depression era father would listen to Jeffrey's corporate woes patiently. When Jeffrey stopped complaining, my dad would ask, "And when do you get paid?" He got Dad laughing so hard that he started coughing. Dad said, "You're a pain in the ass. Talk to you later."

Lisa, too, nothing out of the ordinary. She was five months pregnant with her second baby and felt like shit most of the time. She and Dad were supposed to have breakfast, but she didn't feel up to it and cancelled. He asked if she wanted to have lunch. She wasn't sure, maybe tomorrow. Dad said it didn't matter if he paid for lunch today or tomorrow. He called later to see how she was feeling. His last words to his only daughter: "Okay you curly-haired little witch. I'll talk to you later." He planned on talking to each of us – later.

Ma said it was a perfectly ordinary Thursday. They ate shrimp and pasta for dinner. Later she went to visit Lisa and got home around 11:00 PM. Dad was in bed. Ma was watching television when he got up around 2:15 in the morning and leaned against the railing. Ma asked what was wrong. He said he was having trouble breathing. She asked if she should do something.

"Yeah, I think you better call 9-1-1. And don't get excited."

She made the call, all the while Dad stood at the top of the stairs, making slow exhalations. He said, "Turn on the kitchen lights." Puff, puff, puff. "Turn on the driveway light." Puff, puff, puff. "Turn on the garage light, so they can see where we are." Puff, puff, puff. She did all this. Said nothing. Didn't get excited. "Now get dressed."

She hurried up the stairs past him and said nothing. She stayed calm – at least on the outside. Her husband of forty-years never said another word to her. The paramedics arrived soon after. Ma stood silently in the kitchen doorway wringing her hands. They put Dad on a stretcher and whisked him to Alexian Brothers. Mom prayed the whole way, fingering rosary beads on an ambulance ride that seemed to take forever.

"They worked on him a long time," she said later. "The more time that passed, the worse it looked. I barely got to see your father once we got there. They just whisked that curtain around him." A little while later a nurse asked her to move to a private room. Ma knew this was a bad sign. The next time she saw her husband, he was dead. It was 3:41 AM Saturday, May 26, 1995. That's what it says on the death certificate. Cardiorespiratory arrest. Ventricular tachycardia. Myocardial infarction. Fancy names for heart failure. Dad's lungs filled with fluid, and he didn't have the strength to get a good breath. He was drowning internally. Finally, his heart couldn't take it. So, it stopped.

Here's something to think about: Dad signed a Do Not Resuscitate order after his last serious hospitalization. And the paramedics – doing their duty to stabilize the patient – intubated him anyway. They prolonged his suffering and forced his terrified wife to watch him struggle. Because it was their job. As I drove to the hospital, I remembered our talk a few days earlier and expected he might die. But I wasn't prepared to find him dead.

When I walked into Dad's room, the tube was still rammed down his throat, and there was tape on his face. It looked grotesque. I called the nurse and made her remove the tube. Then I took the tape off his face and straightened his hair. Dad looked like he was sleeping. The heavy, gold St. Christopher medal around his neck came into his life decades ago, hotter than coffee, a little something Uncle Tony picked up "at work." I took it off and put it around my neck. It's been there ever since. Then Ma, Uncle Joe, and Aunt Marie came in. Ma said she called Jeffrey, and he was on his way from California.

We'd planned to work the flea market that weekend. The trucks were full, and I wasn't going to let several thousand dollars of produce rot. My dad would haunt me! I did something I don't think anybody ever did in the history of the South Water Market: I returned a truckload of produce, and every single vendor refunded every single penny. Dad had been a fixture around the market since the 1940s. People knew him, remembered him, and admired him. I heard lots of nice things, and it made me proud. I had always been proud to be Mike Gentile's son, even if I didn't always make him proud to be my father. We'd spent the greater part of the last twenty-years arguing about shit that didn't matter. Take that lesson.

He looked good. A little color in his cheeks. Not too much. His salt and pepper hair nicely combed back. Snazzy sports jacket. Black and white hounds tooth. Double-breasted. The first choice had been the black suit. Beautiful, summer weight wool. Very sharp. Also double-breasted. He'd bought it for the cruise this past September. Should he wear the black suit? No. Black suits, he always said, were "funeral suits." So, the black was passed over in favor of the natty hound's tooth jacket with a white on white shirt, nicely pressed and crisp to the touch. The red silk tie shimmered. There were black pleated pants. All things considered, he looked good. This was shocking, all things considered. Dad was as handsome and robust as I'd ever seen him. And dead.

My father died on Friday, but owing to the holiday weekend – Memorial Day, for lovers of irony – he couldn't be buried until the following Tuesday. They wouldn't prepare Dad until Monday. He'd spend the holiday weekend in a refrigerated box. I envied him.

First thing I think when I walk into the funeral parlor: Madone! He looks pretty good for a dead guy. I couldn't take my eyes off him. He hadn't wasted and withered. He looked handsome and healthy. He looked good. For a dead guy. That's what Dad always said after someone else's funeral. If you asked how the deceased looked, that was your answer: "Pretty good for a dead guy." If you were driving and a funeral procession passed and you wondered out loud who died, you could count on my dad to say, "The guy in the first car." He had no fear or awe where death was concerned.

For the next seven hours, I fought the urge to laugh several times. My dad had a wicked sense of humor, and all I had to do was look at someone and remember things he said: This one looks like an old suitcase. That one is so cheap he still has his Baptism money. That one would fuck a warm cantaloupe. And they all came to pay their respects.

As we stood praying at the end of the long, awful night, in walked Jimmy Cerone. He had to be in his eighties. They'd been friends for nearly four decades. Throughout all the mob adjacent years, Jimmy had been a constant – a pal, partner, and occasional savior. He was old and hobbled and using a cane, but everyone knew who he was. Leaning on his son James' arm, Jimmy walked up to the coffin and looked at my dad. Just looked at him. Then he patted Dad on the cheek and said, "You're a good boy, Mikey." He prayed silently and made the Sign of the Cross. Ritual done, Jimmy walked over to Ma, kissed her forehead, and said, "You've got to understand, your husband was the best." And there was one of those fat envelopes. It was $5,000. The money didn't mean anything to Jimmy. It was just his way of showing respect.

Crazy as it may sound, that was the best tribute I could want for my dad. You know why Outfit guys succeeded? Because they could read the human need. As businessmen, they exploited those needs. You might be able to fool a preacher with false piety, but you're not going to get anything over on a mob boss. And if they decide you're good, you're good. And my dad was the best.

Jimmy shook my hand and kissed me on the cheek. I said hello to his son, and James said something nice about my dad. They left right after.

That's when Aunt Jeanette grabbed Jeffrey's arm and said, "Your father was never a gangster. He just knew people." She was right. You didn't grow up on Aberdeen Street back in the day and not know people. Some of the people – well – they had jobs. Just jobs.

We gathered at nine the following day. I was still numb from the night before. This was our Last Goodbye. The priest finished a prayer and family members filed past the coffin. Ma went first. She kissed Dad's forehead and ran her fingers gently through his hair, then she walked away crying softly. They loaded the casket into the back of the hearse and headed to the funeral mass at Saint Peter's, then on to Mary Queen of Heaven Cemetery in Hillside, where so many mobsters, hoodlums, and gangsters spend eternity. One thing was certain: Dad would have plenty of company from the old neighborhood. Within a few hours, it was all over. My father's soul was commended to a Catholic God and his body to a patch of earth. What the fuck were the rest of us supposed to do?

The week after Dad's funeral, we brought two trailer loads out to the flea market as a tribute. We sold out in what turned into our biggest single day ever. All day we talked about how generations of Gentile men were guiding customers to our stall from the great produce market in the sky. We continued there for another three years, eventually growing so big that we had fifteen people behind the counter. But my boys never forgot those three weeks with their grandpa.

After spending more than a decade behind bars, Jackie Cerone was released from prison in 1996. Shortly after being paroled at age eighty-two, the Outfit boss died of natural causes – maybe. The most outrageous story purports that Cerone was "murdered" on orders from Outfit competitor Joe Aiuppa. A mob friendly doctor allegedly gave Jackie blood pressure medication known to cause ulcerated sores in the intestines. Those sores were said to have caused the intestinal cancer that killed Cerone six days after his release from prison. Sounds like a fairly complicated "murder" scheme – with no guarantee of success. But some people look for a conspiracy in a case of the sniffles.

Jimmy Cerone died in 1997. He was a fine man, a hard worker, and a loyal and true friend.

Our father was the son of a humble fruit peddler. By most measures, he wasn't a man who warranted a book about his life. He only did what millions of people have done for millions of years: He made sure his family was secure. Through it all, he was guided by a personal code that stressed hard work, commitment, and keeping your mouth shut. It's not a bad code by any measure.

In August 2002, the phone rang. Opportunity was calling. My old boss at a produce house presented the offer of a lifetime – a job running the entire department at one of the biggest wholesale houses in the city. Today, I walk the same pavement Giovani and Mickey Gentile walked at the South Water Market. Some of the old timers remember Dad with the friendly profanity that is the currency of the market: "That motherfucker was one hell of a guy."

Dad had been seeing a pulmonary specialist for several years and kept saying he had seventy-percent breathing capacity. We later learned it was only seventeen percent. Every step, every breath had been an effort. But Mike Gentile never let a little thing like breathing get in the way of the work that needed to be done.

When Jeffrey and I started this book, our objective was to memorialize and even celebrate the mob adjacent days of our youth. But as the story went on, Dad's past bled into our past, and long-buried ghosts reappeared. I couldn't tell

Dad's story about the mob connections that enabled our comfortable life without talking about the unintended consequences that spilled into my life and my family's life.

I did terrible things, selfish things, and thoughtless things that deeply hurt the people I love. I can't change the past. I have to live with it. Each decision – good and bad (so many bad) – made me the man I am today. Would my life have been easier if I hadn't fallen victim to the shiny illusion of a mob adjacent life? Absolutely. I would have been free to make a whole new set of bad decisions. That's the thing about being mob adjacent – it gets you close, but not too close. It lets you walk away while others pay a price, but it doesn't let you off free. I'm not the same guy who pushed a mouthy asshole's face through a plate of glass. All that shit served as the fertilizer that helped me grow into a better person. Dad would be proud of the man I am today, just like I'm proud to be his son.

For decades, our lives had been cocooned in safety and our family's well-being assured under the protective wing of successive mob bosses. Even my felony was erased with a wrist slap. Dad's markets should have been prime targets for robberies. Most of the money was in cash, and often one of us was alone in the store. It would have been an easy boost. Likewise, Dad's bars and nightclubs were cash enterprises back in the days before credit cards. Same for the restaurant. Cash and lots of it, especially after those epic lunch rushes. No one bothered us. Not ever. There might as well have been blinking neon signs over each of Dad's enterprises reading "Fuhgeddaboudit." We didn't need alarms or security companies. We had the Outfit watching over us.

Living mob adjacent taught us about seeing things differently. The nice man with the donuts might be a convicted thief or the biggest crime boss in the world. The ordinary split-level home might be a suburban brothel and casino. The attractive lady might be a man. We see and do things differently; we live differently. The attitudes of Little Italy and the legacy of family marked us and made us the people we are today.

I'm happier than I ever thought I had a right to be. I'm surrounded by people who love me. A "family" dinner means 30 people, and that's before I include my sister's family or my brother's. Most of our children live close enough to visit weekly. I'm the Dad who helps his kids financially as they build families of their own, just like Dad helped me so many times. And I'm the grandfather shouting from the bleachers at baseball, soccer, and football games. None of my kids took up my bad habits, and I don't even know a bail bondsman. I call that success.

PHOTOS

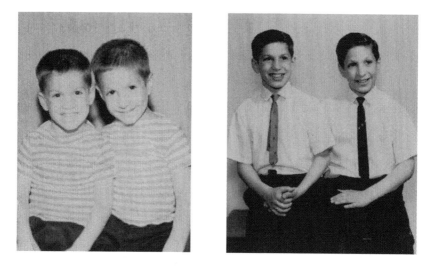

Jeffrey (left) and **Michael** (right). Mom had a thing about dressing us like twins. Technically, we're fourteen-months apart. But as long as she had to do the work of twins, she might as well get the fawning and flattery of strangers to make up for the drudgery of mothering two boys.

Above, perfect little gentleman. **Jeffrey**, age four, and **Michael**, age five, on Aberdeen Street, 1960. The occasion was Michael's kindergarten graduation from St. Patrick's Academy.

It was always about the kids. Above, **Mike Gentile** and **Michael John Jr.** in 1955 and with **Ashely King** in 1991. Below, **Mary Ann** with her treasured baby girl, **Lisa Terese**, on her Christening day in 1963.

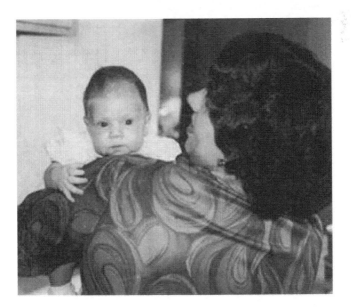

Tony "Joe Batters" Accardo was the Chicago Outfit's Chairman of the Board. The man called the most powerful criminal in America famously never spent a night in jail and died quietly of natural causes at age 86 in 1992. (Photo from the John Binder Collection)

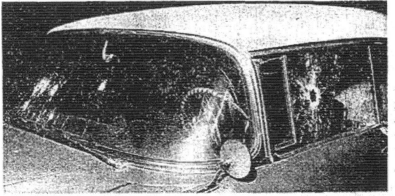

Tribune Photo by Gerald West

Bullet-riddled car of Russell Serritella, who was killed by gunfire from passing car at 2700 W. St. Charles Rd., Bellwood.

Bellwood man is chased in car, killed by blasts from shotgun

A 25-YEAR-OLD Bellwood man was s l a i n by shotgun blasts early yesterday after gunmen in another car chased his auto at high speeds for a mile thru the suburb.

Russell P. Serritella, 117 N. 47th Av., Bellwood, died of head wounds a short time later in Westlake Community Hospital.

His auto, riddled by pellets from up to seven blasts from a 12-gauge shotgun, went out of control and crashed into a car parked in a lot at 29th Avenue and St. Charles Road, about a block from the Bellwood police station, 2726 St. Charles Rd.

A COMPANION in Serritella's car, Michael Di Fronzo, 22, of 1636 N. 33d Av., Melrose Park, suffered cuts from glass s h a t t e r e d by the shotgun blasts.

Because of the persistence of the killers, police were attempting to learn if Serritella had been engaged in a feud.

Lt. Ken Huntington of the Bellwood police said Di Fronzo was unable to provide a description of the gunmen or the car in which they were riding.

AS POLICE pieced together events, Serritella and Di Fronzo were driving north on Bellwood Avenue in the suburb about 3 a. m. when another

car came up behind them and fired a shot into the rear window of Serritella's car.

Serritella tried to speed away and turned eastward on St. Charles Road, possibly trying to reach the police station.

But before Serritella could do so, the killers pulled their car beside Serritella's and fired their final shotgun blast directly at him.

The killers then sped northward on 29th Avenue, police said.

They'll drink to that!

Or will they? The final results of the Great Tee Hut Lounge Women's Lib Referendum, William Petrad's report is sure to have you raising your stein in salute or drowning yourself in sorrow. Look for the tally this Sunday, November 4th in the Chicago Tribune Magazine.

Russell "Butch" Serritella, Junior lived with his family two houses down from the Gentiles on 47th Avenue in Bellwood. Mike Gentile heard about a contract on his neighbor and offered a warning. Butch ignored it. When your mob adjacent neighbor offers advice, take it. (Photo courtesy of the *Chicago Tribune*).

205

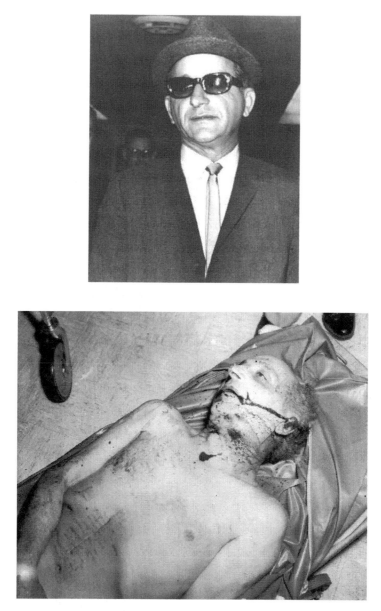

Sam Giancana was known as "Mr. Sam" whenever he visited Orlando's Hideaway between 1962-65. Upon returning to Chicago in 1975, Giancana was murdered in the basement of his home by an unknown assailant (Bottom photo from the John Binder Collection).

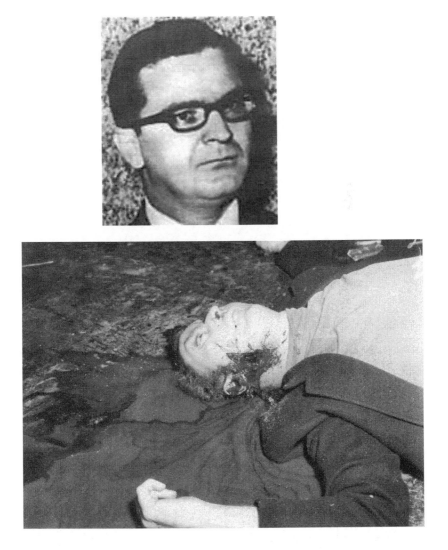

Richard Scalzitti Cain (above) started his career in the Chicago Sheriff's Department as a dirty cop. He spent the rest of his life switching sides, working as easily with the Outfit as the CIA. Chuck Giancana (brother of Sam) fingers Cain as the real shooter responsible for JFK's murder in Dallas – as part of a joint Outfit/CIA hit. He had a date with fate at a sandwich shop run by Gentile family friends in 1973. (Bottom photo from the John Binder Collection)

James "Jelly" Cozzo, and his sister Rose Polito ran a sandwich shop that was popular with Westside mob bosses. In 1973, it served as the sight of a brutal gangland killing when crooked cop Richard Cain met a messy end practically where the Outfit – and the Gentile family – started, on Grand Avenue near Aberdeen Street.

Above: An always dapper **John Phillip Cerone, Sr.**, with wife **Clara Russo Cerone** attending the wedding of Paul Ricca's son in 1964. (Photo from the John Binder Collection)

Jackie Cerone's downfall, conviction, and imprisonment for his role in Las Vegas money skimming operations were documented in Nicholas Pileggi's book *Casino* and fictionalized in Martin Scorcese's 1995 film version. It was said he could go from humorous to murderous in the blink of an eye.

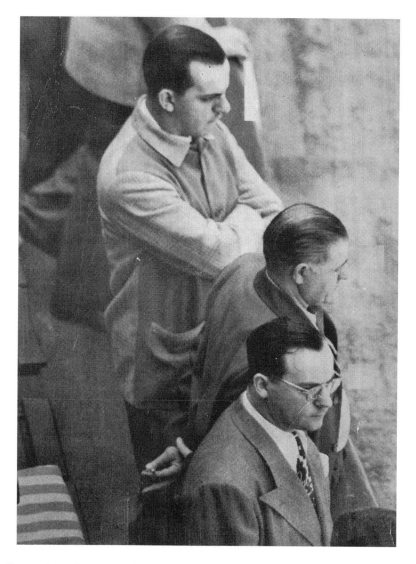

Above, a day at the racetrack in 1945 for **Jimmy Cerone** (top) and **Frank "Skip" Cerone** (bottom). (Photo from the John Binder Collection)

Busted. **Don (The Wizard of Odds) Angelini** (left front), cuffed to **Dominic Cortina**. **Jackie Cerone** (right front), cuffed to **James Cerone.** All were subsequently convicted for running a major gambling ring in 1970. (Photos from the John Binder Collection)

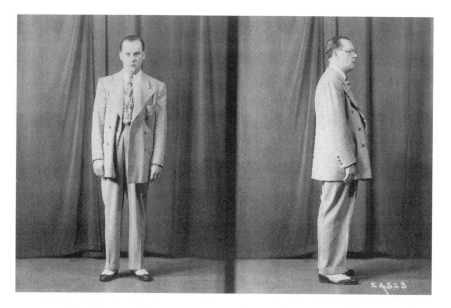

Above: **Frank "Skip" Cerone** was arrested and convicted for selling draft deferments in 1944 (Photo from the John Binder Collection)

Above, **Skip Cerone** and wife, **Mary**, were frequent faces at family gatherings. Fun fact: as a young woman, Mary Ann (Mamie) Rehberger was a Ziegfeld girl before her marriage. (Perhaps that explains the hat.)

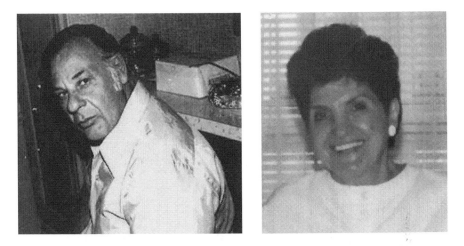

"Uncle" **Anthony Cerone** (left), was the nephew of Outfit bigshot, Jackie Cerone. He and wife **Antoinette "Sis" Cerone** (right) owned a chain of upscale women's boutiques. The Cerone and Gentile families were indivisible for decades. (Photos courtesy of Rosa Cerone)

Mike and **Mary Ann Gentile** as we will always remember them. Whenever she saw this photo, she remarked, "I liked that hairstyle."

The Aberdeen Street crew in 1978: (back left to right) **Jeanette Gentile, Rachel Gentile Rohlfing,** and **Marie Gentile Difiglio;** (front left to right) **John Gentile,** and **Mike Gentile.**

The Mannheim Road crew in 1965: **Criss Cross** brought his "all girl" revue to Orlando's Hideaway and literally brought the house down. (Photo taken at Orlando's Hideaway, 1965)

Big name entertainers performed, played, and stayed at Manny Skar's Sahara Inn, the jewel of the Mannheim Strip in the 1960s. Orlando's Hideaway was next door, adjacent to the Air Host Motel. With his empire in ruins, **Manny Skar** (below) decided to testify against his Outfit benefactors in 1965. It didn't go as planned. (Photos from the John Binder Collection)

A surprise, sixty-fifth birthday party in October 1995. In seven months, this vital man will be gone, the victim of lungs and a heart that failed him. (Left to right) **Jeffrey Gentile, Mike Gentile, Lisa Gentile King,** and **Michael Gentile.**

PART III: JEFFREY

29 CHANGE ADJACENT

In 1959, Liberace sued the *Daily Mirror* when a columnist hinted that the flamboyant (homosexual) piano player was a homosexual. A jury found in favor of the (homosexual) piano player and agreed that his reputation had been impugned – and more importantly libeled – by the allegation of homosexuality. Liberace got $10,000 when the case settled (about $87,000 today). The verdict sent a message: Being a homosexual was so terrible that the merest suggestion could damage someone's life and career. This was blood in the water for Outfit sharks, and countless gay men found themselves victim of extortion and blackmail.

Homosexuality had been one of the many money-making perversions offered at Outfit brothels since the days of Big Jim Colosimo. Sodomy represented a sub-sector of prostitution, line-items on a buffet of sexual services, something else for degenerates to do when they weren't shooting heroin, smoking opium, or having sex with small animals. The fact that homosexuality was technically illegal put it naturally in the Outfit's domain. If there was a way to make money off something illegal, the Outfit would find it, which was exactly what happened when they started converting money-losing strip joints into money-making gay bars in the 1960s.

That's how an act like The Criss Cross Revue got booked at Orlando's Hideaway. Money. Dad said the drag show was the most profitable act during the entire time he owned the place. That they could be raided by the police at any minute made the show irresistible. Chicagoans hadn't had that kind of fun since Prohibition. "Say, honey, let's go out for dinner, drinks, and a raid. *Gunsmoke's* a rerun." It was *illegal* but not *dangerous*, safe for mom and dad, but best to leave the kids at home. Homosexuals were freaks to be gawked at, men who dressed up like women, and were only tolerated as long as the cash register kept singing. That was the prevailing attitude, particularly in the nightclub business. They didn't care what you did backstage – the show (profits) must go on.

Mike Gentile had the same attitude about homosexuality as many of his era. It wasn't malice; it was misinformation. Saying "that's how it was at the time" always rings hollow. But that's how it was at the time. He had a homosexual cousin on his father's side. A florist, no less, and by all accounts a very nice man. The cousin and his "companion" never attended family gatherings and were whispered about, complete with snickering and gasps. It was a family scandal, something that ran on Dad's side, like hemophilia or male-pattern baldness. Dad couldn't help his attitude.

My father was born the day the world changed and rode a wave of change for the next sixty-five years. Born in a time of ruin and reared under a cloud of war, his world had rigid roles and codes for men, women, and children. The Great Fiction about love, sex, and marriage formed the foundation of post-war society in the 1950s. But by the 1960s, a new war raged. Teenagers revolted violently. Women left their kitchen, burned their bras, got jobs, and demanded equal pay. Then the women who brought home the bacon and cooked it up in a pan realized they didn't need the man and started getting divorced in the 1970s. By the 1980s, those who became adults in the time of the Great Fiction faced a world they barely recognized. Dad had a headful of absolutes on a broad range of topics. Good luck getting him to change his mind. The idea that homosexuality was shameful put Dad and me on opposite sides of an immovable line.

In the dark ages of the 1970s, homosexuals were called fags, fruits, fairies, and other degrading names. After all, it had barely been a decade since the Liberace jury essentially affirmed that being a homosexual was terrible. I went through the motions in high school, as people did back then. But I hadn't fit in my skin from the time I was thirteen-years old and got my first crush on a boy. The boy was unaware of my infatuation because I refused to look in his direction. Something deep inside told me those feelings were wrong – and shameful. So, I buried those feelings, hated myself, sometimes wanted to die, and tried to live the boy/girl fiction.

Away from Chicago, I made the life I wanted to live, just like Aunt Doris. I also confronted a diligently avoided reality: I was gay. My clumsy, passionless, fumbling sex with women (exactly seven) had been rationalized as bisexuality.

But having sex with a woman while thinking about a man doesn't make you bisexual; it makes you a closet case, and a cad, and it makes the woman a victim of your denial. Not cool. You might even get one of the girls pregnant.

Over the years, Mom was unrelenting: Have you met any nice girls? When are you going to get married? Do you still hear from that nice Diane? Mom wanted the matter settled. She mined relentlessly for details about my personal life and complained about the lack of transparency. Michael and Lisa shared every passing thought, action, and deed, sometimes to their regret. I chose differently. "Everything with you is a secret," Mom griped.

I'd insist on a right to privacy, but Italian mothers recognize no such right. While the AIDS epidemic decimated the gay population in the 1980s, I lived safely removed from the carnage through the simple good luck of a long-term monogamous relationship. Jon Vandersteeg and I met in the Student Center at Southern Illinois University during the last semester of my last year of college. We dated, broke up, and got back together. Eventually, he moved from Houston to Redondo Beach, and we settled into domesticity. A broad circle of friends became our extended family. With someone in my life to stay, I couldn't avoid telling my parents the truth.

The first thing Dad said was he loved me, "no matter what." He told me to remember that. Mom echoed his sentiments. No matter what. She said she'd had suspicions, but there was a comfortable difference between suspicion and confirmation. Then Mom delivered the stipulation that went along with their unconditional love: I could continue to attend all family events and celebrations. But a male partner would not be welcome at any gathering. I didn't see my family much over the next ten-years, except for a few tense days here and there. Mom and I maintained a weekly telephone fiction that everything was perfectly normal, with Dad popping on for a few words at the end.

The question came annually: Did I plan on coming home for Thanksgiving and Christmas? No, I did not. One year, Mom badgered me relentlessly. She said it wasn't fair they didn't get to spend the holidays with me. Couldn't I come this year?

I said, "If I lived with a girl, you wouldn't expect me to leave her at home alone for Christmas."

"That's completely different."

"No, Mom, it isn't."

Christmas was Dad's favorite holiday, and Mom said he was disappointed every year when I wouldn't come home. I stopped arguing for fairness and built a life away from a family that wasn't ready to accept me. That Jon's family welcomed me warmly served as salt on an open wound.

Then rather dramatically, I was diagnosed with a brain tumor in 1991. All else got pushed aside, and my parents practically hopped on the next plane. The operation was relatively simple – the doctor made a five-inch incision under my upper lip, peeled back my face, dismantled my nose, and used the existing pathway to reach my pituitary gland. Doctor Donald Sage (Really, that was his name) then cut out the tumor in pieces and removed as much as possible. He couldn't take all of it without damaging the pituitary gland. Then he put my nose back together, stuffed it with gauze packing, and sewed up the incision. Simple, right? I was blessed with a full and speedy recovery.

When I was released from the hospital less than a week later, Mom and Dad came to my apartment. Once he saw my perfectly ordinary home and my perfectly ordinary life, he eased up. After they went back to Chicago, Dad started asking oblique questions about how things were "at home," and I would say fine, thanks for asking. He did the best he could. But a plus-one invitation still wasn't offered for the next family holiday.

My brother lived on a cycle of marriages, separations, divorces, arrests, and legal and fiscal catastrophes; I had a steady job, a stable home, and a constant companion. His "lifestyle" got a giant pass from my parents; mine did not. Apart from my preferred sexual activities, my life was as normal as my heterosexual counterparts. It seemed so normal that sometimes I forgot it wasn't. When that happened, life reminded me.

The neighbor kid came sailing around the corner into the courtyard. Dressed in shorts and a T-shirt and barefoot on a skateboard, thirteen-year old Ryan was a classic California beach kid. I lived next door to his divorced mother, Jean. I'd met both sisters, but this was my first encounter with the youngest sibling. Ryan was a good kid trapped between feuding parents. Here's what sealed our friendship: Early one Saturday morning, there was a knock on the door. It was Ryan carrying a cereal bowl like a waif out of Dickens. He asked, "Do you have any milk?" That did it. I dragged him inside and made pancakes. We were pals after that.

Jean was a nurse who worked the night shift. That left Ryan alone a lot, and he gravitated toward a place he felt safe and welcome. It happened to be our apartment. He knew from the start Jon and I were gay, but it never bothered him. Ryan was comfortable in our home, popping in and out freely, and eating constantly. We talked about life, girls, family, and school. I would listen, encourage and be supportive without having actual responsibility. I was having the time of my life playing Auntie Mame!

I asked if he'd like to go to a matinee of the new James Bond movie. Ryan said it sounded like fun and went to ask his mother. Jean gave her permission and issued a warning: "If he tries anything, run." Ryan was mortified. He tried making light of it, but he was bothered. I could tell. As I drove to the theater, my face was hot with shame and rage. I sat in the dark as James Bond saved the world and wondered how Jean could think such a thing. I thought I was a family friend, something of a surrogate parent, babysitter, tutor, mentor, or big brother. Instead I was reminded I was a faggot and, therefore, automatically, inevitably, and absolutely suspect. I was indeed part of the family: I was the funny uncle with grabby hands. "If he tries anything, run."

Jean and I were good friends. That's what made it so unexpected. We swapped recipes. We talked about her job, her dates, her children, her shattered marriage. We spent holidays together. One Christmas when my presents didn't arrive from Chicago, she bought me a gift so I had something to open. Jean attended my parties and met my friends. But when it came to getting into a car with a homosexual, she felt compelled to warn her son. There had been countless nights when Ryan fell asleep on the floor of our apartment while watching old movies (and getting an education in film classics). Nothing ever happened, nor would it. I'd go upstairs to bed. When Ryan woke up, he'd turn everything off, lock the door, and walk to his mother's apartment. I couldn't tell you how many times it happened.

I used to work with a bi-racial woman raised by her white mother in a white environment. Every now and then, one of her white friends would get mad. "Then they'd call me a you-know-what," she said. It was automatic, inevitable, and absolute. There was a line that separates. On one side, Polite Society says you are This. But right across the line is Something Else. Something Ugly. I'd never seen the line before, so I hadn't known it existed. But there it was.

I had a relatively easy time "coming out." I was never gay-bashed, fired, evicted, or felt discriminated against (other than by my own family). The idea that someone considered me dangerous was devastating. But I forgave Jean, and our friendship continued. Her reaction was instinctive, like the parent who's driving and stops suddenly – her right arm came out to stop her son from going through the figurative windshield.

The years separated us, and Ryan became the stuff of memories and photo albums. Many years later, I walked into a store. Ryan looked up, did a double-take, and ran toward me. "No way!" he shouted. "No way!" He hugged me and demanded, "Where have you been?" The missing decade tumbled out in a rush. He was married now. "I sent an invitation, but it came back." Updates on family followed. Ryan made it clear that losing track of each other again was unacceptable. "You were an important part of my life, and I want you to be an important part of my child's life." Rewards don't come sweeter. We're still friends today.

Jon and I separated after sixteen years, and I spent a rocky decade bouncing from job to job and trying to get my life back on track. I had the bad luck to get laid off from five consecutive high-tech companies, but the good luck to receive a nice severance package each time they showed me the door. I also had the good luck to catch the California real estate wave at the right time and found myself sitting on a nice nest egg as the Bush economy shot its last wad.

Along the way to realigning my life, I met someone new. Jeffrey Jordan moved to California from Arkansas. We met in 2006 and quickly discovered mutual interests in movies, theater, music, art, cooking, travel, and sarcasm. I introduced him to New York, Las Vegas, and Chicago. He introduced me to fried green tomatoes, pimento cheese, butter drop biscuits, and the fine art of using "y'all." In June 2013, the United States Supreme Court finally read a tattered copy of the Constitution and realized bans on same sex marriage violated the equal protection statutes and were, therefore, unconstitutional. Bigots and religious fanatics still prefer the idea that some people are entitled to more civil rights than others. Fuck them. With the last legal obstacle removed, Jeffrey and I decided to get married.

There would be no table of mobsters in the back of a hall and no fat envelopes from honorary uncles. First, those days were the stuff of history. Second, none of the traditional wedding practices fit. We opted for a private ceremony at Beverly Hills City Hall conducted by Judge Nancy Clairborne. We told no one. Instead, we brought a box of stamped wedding announcements. After the ceremony, we dropped the envelopes at the Beverly Hills Post Office and wondered who would call first. (Michael's daughter Kristyn.) A couple of days later, we left on a road trip honeymoon up the California coast. A gift basket arrived at our hotel from my daughter Erin.

I'd never expected to be a father, but things happen when you're careless and twenty-two. Over the years, I'd been called many things – some deserved, some not. I've been a son, grandson, nephew, brother, cousin, uncle, friend, lover, writer, traveler, husband, and father. I've missed nothing. But what I most looked forward to being called was "grandpa" when Erin had a daughter in 2015. Both girls are unexpected blessings and gifts. Erin and Jeffrey became fast friends, too. I may not have followed the traditional path, but I ended up in the right place.

30 CELEBRITY ADJACENT

In my youth, I liked to believe my brother and I were nothing alike. Beyond a superficial physical resemblance, we shared exactly zero common interests. He the extrovert, me the introvert, and seldom the twain met. But it turned out we were more alike than either realized. While Michael was fascinated by organized crime and sports, I was fascinated by movies and television. Thanks to Mom, I grew up movie crazy. And thanks to Dad, Michael became a walking encyclopedia of mob history. We each embraced a glamourous otherworld.

Michael never aspired to mobdom; likewise, I never aspired to stardom. Maybe I had fleeting Lana Turner thoughts about being discovered. (Even Lana had a gangster.) But once I moved to Los Angeles and met actual working actors, I knew it wasn't for me. The long, dull grind of movie-making held absolutely no appeal. The only part of "celebrity" that seemed like fun was the red-carpet stuff, which is arguably the least consequential part of the process. Also, I didn't have the bottomless wellspring of ego and ambition that seemed so necessary.

Not long after moving to Los Angeles, I met a man named Richard. Fast forward a few dates. Richard mentioned a brunch at the home of legendary film director George Cukor. Would I like to go? Was he insane? George Cukor had been among the top directors of Hollywood's golden era. Everyone from Joan Crawford to Greta Garbo attended Cukor's parties. Katherine Hepburn lived in his pool house during her Spencer Tracy years. Vivien Leigh went for secret acting sessions after Cukor was fired from *Gone With the Wind*. Yes, I wanted to go! Then Richard said something odd: "George loves your type."

Cukor's homosexuality had been an open secret in Hollywood for decades, and Richard explained how one must be on his best and most discreet behavior. Nothing overt, no physical displays of affection, and no "camping." At best, Richard said, phone numbers might be exchanged. He added that the pool house (where Tracy and Hepburn shacked up) was sometimes used for "meetings" during the afternoon festivities. Richard advised, "If George invites you to the pool house, you should go."

He saw the confusion in my eyes and talked down to me as if I were brain deficient. "If you want to get anywhere in this town, you're going to need a patron." Then he mentioned a big star who started out as a pool boy for a television producer. I'm not repeating his name. I called Richard the following Saturday and cancelled brunch. He'd already given my name to Cukor's houseman, and it involved some embarrassment to call in a replacement plus-one. Richard was through with me after that, and the feeling was mutual. George Cukor died a year later. I never regretted skipping his brunch. A year later I saw Richard driving a car in the Hollywood Christmas Parade. He'd gone from panderer to chauffeur, so he clearly hadn't found his patron.

Wolfgang Puck began his assault on Hollywood nightlife when he opened Spago in 1982. The hilltop location had a spectacular view of the Los Angeles basin, and his restaurant quickly became the In Place. The Spago era also augured a changing of the guards. For decades, super-agent Irving "Swifty" Lazar practically owned Oscar-night entertaining. The annual party Swifty hosted became the pinnacle of Hollywood's social scene. When Swifty decided not to host his annual fete at home, he looked to Beverly Hills-adjacent West Hollywood.

Around that same time, my best gal pal Ruth lived in a quirky, kooky apartment building on Horn Avenue, above Tower Records, across from Shoreham Towers, and up the street from Spago. We'd occasionally go down for a drink at the bar. Good luck getting a dinner reservation, even if we could have afforded it back then, which we couldn't. When it was announced that Swifty would be moving his Oscar party to Spago, Ruth and I decided to walk down and watch the celebrities arrive. By 1985, I'd settled into a lucrative career in the high-tech industry. But that didn't mean I stopped loving movies and movie stars.

In today's security-focused world, it's hard to believe that "more stars than there are in heaven" walked within arm's reach that night. No guards. No velvet ropes. Just cars stopping on a side street off the Sunset Strip and letting out their famous passengers. The revelers included news giants Walter Kronkite and Mike Wallace. Shirly MacLaine arrived with her golden guy fresh off her Oscar win for *Terms of Endearment*. It went on for hours – Olivia Newton-John, Sissy Spacek, Raquel Welch, Candace Bergen, Laurence Olivier, Jack Lemon, Cary Grant, Gene Kelly, Roger Moore, Steve Martin, Angie Dickenson, George Segal, Andy Warhol, Farrah Fawcett, Ryan O'Neal, Jackie Collins, Diana Ross, Faye Dunaway, and others.

I have never asked a celebrity for an autograph or a photo. I let them go about their business, and they let me go about mine. It seems like a fair social contract. Celebrity places – whether Hollywood or Underworld variety – can be fun. The best food. The best booze. The best entertainment. The best ass. While Michael worked his way through Chicago's mob adjacent bars and nightclubs, I was doing roughly the same thing two-thousand-miles away, people-watching over a $15 martini at whichever place had the liveliest celebrity scene at the moment. It might be Spago, Nicky Blair's, Le Dome, or stalwart classics like the Polo Lounge, Chasen's, or the Beverly Hills-adjacent Hamburger Hamlet.

In the early 1980s Sonny Bono turned from show business to celebrity restauranteur as so many had, have, and will. Bono's sat on a small triangle of land on Melrose Place near La Cienega. For a few years, it held that In Place crown that rotated among Hollywood-adjacent restaurants. Sonny was there when I arrived, alongside his wife of the moment – a stunning fashion model named Susie Coehlo. A few people asked for his autograph, and he seemed pleased by the attention. But come on, without Cher, who gives a shit about Sonny Bono?

Joan Collins was dining with her family at Bono's that night. She'd burst like a second-act super nova in Aaron Spelling's *Dynasty* in 1981. Like millions of fans, I couldn't get enough of the show. And I couldn't help myself. Between courses, Miss Collins fixed her lipstick. I took advantage of the lull and walked to her table. The season-ending cliff hanger found "Alexis" trapped in a raging fire. Over the summer hiatus, Miss Collins chopped off her long, dark mane of hair for a shorter style.

"Excuse me, Miss Collins. I really love *Dynasty*, and I love you on it. And your hair looks great."

She smiled, patted the back of her head, and joked, "It got burned off in the fire."

"I'm glad you made it out."

She asked, "You don't want me to die in the fire? Many do."

"No. You're the best thing on the show."

She laughed brightly. "Aren't you a sweet boy?" Then she kissed my left cheek. I saw the waiter approaching and said goodnight. She went back to her evening, and I went back to mine.

Joan Collins caught a lucky break when Sophia Loren turned down the role of Alexis. Throughout her career, Collins gamely wore the mantle of "second-rate Elizabeth Taylor." And when it looked as if Taylor might die during production of *Cleopatra*, the studio tapped Collins to step into Taylor's shoes before the corpse cooled. But history had other plans for all of us.

In April 1992, I turned from the cosmetics counter at I. Magnin's on Wilshire Boulevard after buying a birthday present for Mom and nearly collided with Elizabeth Taylor. Our encounter lasted a millisecond. I turned from the counter and started to walk; she looked up as I moved forward. Our eyes met. I stopped. She stopped. We smiled. Elizabeth Taylor said, "Pardon me." I said something pithy and memorable: "No. Me," and moved aside.

When she looked at me with Those Eyes, I knew why Eddie dumped Debbie, why Richard dumped Sybil. And why Richard married her twice. My mother would demand details, and I needed to be prepared. So, I turned and looked over my shoulder: Elizabeth Taylor was small and busty with great cascades of dark hair. Heart-shaped face. Gold and diamond hoop earrings. Two-piece suit, dark. Patent leather heels. Black. Quilted handbag on a gold chain. Black. The diamond ring.

Later, I thought of a thousand things I wanted to say. Wisely, I upheld the unwritten, unspoken rules of celebrity adjacent behavior and said nothing. That's not to say I'm immune to titillation. I've driven past the house where Lucy and Desi lived on Camden and where Benny Siegel shacked up with Virginia Hill on Linden, past the house where Lana lived and Johnny died, and where Judy lived with Vincente Minelli. I even spent a couple of days with Liza.

Living in Los Angeles, my social circle occasionally put me celebrity adjacent. It began with lasagna in 1996. I'd made a pan for Christmas dinner at Sean's condo off Sunset. Among his guests was Laura, who'd just started a new job as Liza Minelli's assistant. Miss Minelli had recently relocated from New York to Los Angeles and launched a production company called Bandwagon (named after her favorite musical) to kick-start her film career. But first she was recuperating from hip replacement surgery before she could kick anything. Over dinner, Laura and I talked about computers and office technology, about as far from Hollywood-talk as it could get.

As the evening ended, I filled a container with lasagna and meatballs and sent it with Laura for Liza. Someone named Minnelli would surely appreciate homemade Italian comfort food, especially when recuperating from surgery. A few days later, Laura called. She was setting up an office in Liza's rented bungalow in the Hollywood Hills. There was equipment to be hooked up – computer, fax, printer, etc. She was at a complete loss. Would I be a darling and help?

When I arrived at the house on Miller Place the next day, Laura hustled me into the bedroom suite that would become the office. We needed to be quiet; Liza was in a meeting about a movie. Concurrently, Miss Minnelli was planning a stage show. The house was a hurricane of activity, with Liza the center of calm. A rehearsal pianist played a baby grand that had been a gift from Marvin Hamlisch (Laura said) while half a dozen chorus boys worked through a dance routine. Tuesday at Liza's.

The day disappeared in tedious office work – even if the office happened to be in the home of an Oscar, Tony, Grammy, and Emmy winner. The thing to remember is that Liza Minnelli is from Planet Celebrity, and the rules are different. Even Michael Jackson and Elizabeth Taylor had a few years before they became famous. But the first person to visit newborn Liza May Minnelli was Frank Sinatra. He was (so to speak) her opening act.

Suddenly, a head appeared outside the window and another assistant called to Laura in a panic. Minelli liked tall, thick, beeswax candles. At the time, she was entertaining on Saturday nights, and the candles were a staple of the decor. Several people were currently scouring every candle shop in the city for the elusive beeswax candles. No one could find them, and no one wanted to tell Liza. It seemed stupid – paying several people to run around looking for candles. But Minelli had the financial wherewithal to fund the expedition, and the hunt continued.

I'd seen the candles they described many times: Pure beeswax, twelve- and sixteen-inches tall, round, solid, thick as two fists, natural color. "Have you looked in the phone book for a church supply store?" This may seem like a quaint anachronism, but in 1996 telephone books were still a thing.

Laura ran for the Yellow Pages and flipped pages frantically. Then she dialed a number and discovered the fount from which beeswax candles flowed. She thanked the person on the other end with a level of gratitude on par with a kidney donation, scribbled an address on a piece of paper, and thrust it out the window. "Go," she said. "Get a case."

"I'm on it," the young man said and disappeared.

Laura turned to me and said, "You saved the day. I'm putting you on the guest list for the next party."

I didn't expect an invitation to appear (and indeed it didn't), but I took satisfaction in being the only person with enough sense to: A) suggest looking in the phone book, and B) recognize church candles.

Later, I was under the desk plugging cables into a surge protector when I heard a man's voice. A British man. A pair of legs walked in front of me. Tan gabardine slacks. Tan skin. No socks. Tan loafers that looked so soft I wanted to pet them. I crawled out and found myself at crotch-level with Roddy McDowell. We were both surprised. He looked down at the head near his zipper and said, "Hel-lo," that silky voice drawing out each syllable. I stood and introduced myself. Almost seventy at the time, McDowell remained Hollywood Handsome and camera-ready. After he left, Laura explained McDowell's second career as a photographer. He'd taken head shots of Liza and came to deliver the photos in person. He died a year later, with Elizabeth Taylor at his bedside. That's how an Old School Hollywood Star goes out, with Cleopatra as a handmaiden.

Toward the end of the day, Liza breezed into the office. Laura introduced us, and Liza thanked me for the lasagna. While I connected the new fax machine, they talked about the upcoming party: Jerry Herman wouldn't be able to make it. Faye Dunaway said yes. Michael Douglas thought he could, but wasn't sure. Streisand hadn't responded – again. Liza popped in and out all day. Everybody was part of the cast, and there were no small parts. But before I could complete my role, I discovered a critical cable was missing and offered to come back tomorrow with the missing component.

The front door was open when I arrived the next morning, and the carpet cleaner was just leaving. (Liza's dog had a habit of leaving little treasures everywhere.) I called out a few times, but no one answered. Great security system. I walked right in. A stack of steamer trunks and Vuitton luggage stood in the entry way. The Andy Warhol painting of Liza hung over the fireplace, beside one of her father. I could have committed a major art heist without breaking a sweat.

Laura arrived in a fury. Liza had done a fashion shoot recently, and the stylist told her she could keep the clothes. That morning someone from the designer's office called. They wanted the clothes back. Laura growled. "We're not talking a hand-beaded evening gown. It was a black miniskirt and a chiffon blouse. Cheapskates. Liza's going to be pissed."

On cue, the star entered. Liza was just out of bed. No makeup, pillow hair, wearing a black T-shirt and white panties. She was 53 and looked 35, despite the slight limp from surgery. She sat on the couch beside me and reviewed contact sheets. When I ran into difficulties with the computer, Liza asked what was wrong. I told her the operating system wouldn't launch. She looked lost, so I put it in more familiar terms: "It's crapping out halfway through the overture." Her big brown eyes lit up. Liza said, "Ah," and grimaced. I reinstalled Windows and crossed my fingers. She started autographing photos – the prints Roddy McDowell brought the day before. I didn't ask for one. It seemed so tacky. Not long after, Liza moved back to New York, but I kept track of the ups and downs of her tumultuous life. There were more surgeries, dependency issues, a wacky fourth marriage, and a near fatal attack of encephalitis. But she keeps on swinging. Our paths haven't crossed again. But I enjoyed the show while it lasted.

Even chance encounters can be fraught with entertainment. Around the turn of the century, I had a standing Sunday brunch date at Hamburger Hamlet. The restaurant straddled the line that divided West Hollywood from Beverly Hills. My brunch companion knew the hostess – the former wife of a jazz great – so we always got the best table. A large group of women sat on the other side of the enclosed patio behind me. Suddenly, their table erupted in loud laughter. I glanced over and saw one of the women with her face buried in her hands, shoulders shaking.

From the head of their table, comedienne Joanne Worley looked at me and asked, "Did you hear what Esther just said? That was the filthiest joke I have ever heard."

The woman looked up, and I stared into the face of MGM's great aquatic star Esther Williams. I hadn't heard the joke. "No," I said. "Tell it again."

Esther Williams blushed vividly and looked down. The filthiest joke remained a mystery.

Celebrity is a matter of opinion and fame a matter of perspective. I learned during my celebrity adjacent encounters that famous people sometimes have acne, bad table manners, camel toes and pee stains; they pickup dry cleaning, have prescriptions filled, shop for groceries, buy gasoline, and fart. None occupied pedestals, and none was backlit. Except Diana Ross.

After an hour or so watching celebrities outside of Spago on Oscar night, I'd had enough and walked Ruth back to her apartment. We said goodnight, and I drove down the steep incline on Horn Avenue. A limousine coming up from the other direction stopped in front of Spago, the rear door opened, and Diana Ross stepped out wearing an enormous, white ball gown. And where did she stop? Right in front of my car. My headlights backlit Diana Ross as she greeted a tumultuous crowd of fans, well-wishers, and photographers. She looked magnificent, like an ebony princess, smiling, turning, and blowing kisses. During this love fest, I sat idling in my car, wanting Diana Ross to get the hell out of the way. I still had a forty-five-minute drive home to Redondo Beach, and this broad's taking another bow. It's the price of living Hollywood adjacent. Celebrity encounters are to be expected. I learned that from Aunt Doris.

More than thirty-years after moving to Los Angeles, it still surprises me when a celebrity steps into my orbit. I'm still that kid from Bellwood, and I don't expect to bump into movie stars. But it still happens. The last time it was Shirly MacLaine and Sally Field. They were appearing before a special screening of *Steel Magnolias*. The two stars addressed the crowd before the movie started.

As MacLaine shared an anecdote about her past work with director Herb Ross, she blanked and asked, "What was the name of that dancing movie?"

From the front row, I barked, *The Turning Point*.

Shirley MacLaine pointed at me and said, "That's it" and continued with her story.

Michael had been celebrity adjacent at restaurants and nightclubs across Chicago for years. His celebrities worked in a different – but frequently adjacent – industry. I remember him talking about seeing a rare trifecta. "The Three Doms" were Prohibition-era legends: Dominick DiBella, Dominick Nuccio, and Dominic Brancato. Bootleggers, extortionists, murderers, and thieves, the Three Doms were perhaps the tightest gang in Outfit history, at one time even sharing a cold-water flat. Michael saw them having dinner together in the mid-1970s. He recounted each detail of the sighting like a sacred mantra. Then there was the time at Tom's Steak House he saw Jackie Cerone. I thought my brother would swoon when he told me how people approached their table, how Jackie shook hands, and how Clara fingered her water glass. I thought it was silly, but didn't I memorize every detail when I saw Elizabeth Taylor? I suppose that makes us deeply shallow people. But we all have our little hobbies.

31 LIFE ADJACENT

Despite all the years of expensive Catholic school and all the mandatory Masses, Holy Days of Obligation, and Stations of the Cross, the dogma never stuck. Sure, *Our Father*, *Hail Mary*, and the *Act of Contrition* still roll off my tongue almost involuntarily, and I have a passing familiarity with the Bible; but I never became one of those fall-on-your-knees, never-miss-church Christians. When you grow up surrounded by contradictions, it becomes impossible to accept anything on faith; even faith. That's because criminals and their accomplices populated our lives as dearest members of the family. The man who robbed the bakery was as valued and respected as the man who baked the bread.

Saying one thing and doing another was normal growing up mob adjacent. People may say they worked for a beer distributor, or they were in the trash collection business, or they were a union organizer. But they were gangsters, meaning they made money through methods that were currently – but not always – illegal. Everybody knew it, nobody can really prove it, so nothing happens. Some worshipped at the altar of Father, Son, and Holy Ghost. We grew up with a different trinity: Hear nothing; See nothing; Say nothing. God and I are comfortable with an arrangement where I accept a belief in Him without getting bogged down in the technicalities of religion. But I never wanted to believe in God and the hereafter more than when I stood in front of my mother's coffin.

On September 29, 2007, I spoke to my mother on my birthday. She said, "I love you" at the end of the call. A two-week nightmare started the next day. For the previous few months, she'd been having leg pain. Always terrified of doctors (they might give bad news), she preferred to rely on a quack who allowed her to self-diagnose and prescribed medications based on her self-diagnosis (a treatment plan I vigorously opposed). She lived in constant, undiagnosed pain, for which she increasingly relied on the vicious and highly addictive Vicodin. Michael finally had had enough by mid-September and insisted on taking her to the hospital (a plan she vigorously opposed). He told Mom he was coming to get her, and she was going, whether she liked it or not. Qualified doctors at Elmhurst Hospital quickly diagnosed multiple illnesses, including a kidney infection, dehydration, and vasculitis.

A quick medical lesson: Vasculitis afflicts the blood vessels. It causes painful inflammation that damages the walls of blood vessels and may lead to tissue and organ damage. It was a sneaky disease that could lay hidden and do terrible damage before being discovered. End of medical lesson.

Doctors believed a relatively simple surgery could correct the problem. I was kept apprised long distance, and the surgery was a success. I stayed away for a simple reason: My doctor-phobic mother would think the worst if I showed up. The fact that I didn't fly immediately to Chicago suggested to her that it wasn't serious. Otherwise, she knew I'd be there. My absence calmed her. Post-surgery and on the mend, I made plans to visit. She seemed like herself when I arrived, but her hair was a mess.

"Mom, what's with the head?" I pointed at the nest of tangled hair.

She laughed and said she hadn't thought about it. I grabbed a brush and created order. Once she looked presentable, I asked a nurse to bring a wheel chair. It was a beautiful fall day, and I wanted to take her for a spin around the block. As I pushed the chair, we talked about everything and nothing. Mom reached over her shoulder and patted my hand. "No one but you would think of doing this," she said. It wasn't the first time Mom used that phrase. On her fiftieth wedding anniversary in 2004, I called and asked what she had been doing exactly fifty years ago at that exact time. She and her new husband were having pictures taken at the photographer's studio. Then she sniffled a little and said, "No one but you would think to ask something like that."

By the time I left to return to Los Angeles, she was eating take-out food and looking, sounding, and feeling better than she had in months. Doctors said she could go home in a few days, and Mom was high on excitement. Nothing she feared came to fruition – no cancer, nothing fatal, a simple incision in her right leg allowed her surgeon to vanquish the vasculitis.

The day after my birthday, Michael called around seven in the morning.

"Ma's in ICU. They think she had a heart attack."

I was on a plane later that afternoon. This couldn't be. She was fine when I left. It was too much to ponder, so instead I thought about the past.

Before I knew what sexual intercourse was, I knew Elizabeth Taylor was having it with someone other than her husband, and this situation constituted a very bad thing, though I didn't know why. Over the decades, no subject would dominate more conversations in our home. More than God, the Pope, or Frank Sinatra, my mother talked about Elizabeth Taylor. Mom always knew if Elizabeth Taylor was fat or thin; to whom she was married, engaged, or having an illicit affair; where she was living; what projects occupied her time; and which illness presently plagued the great star. Because Mom knew, I knew.

Movies and movie stars had been the first interest we shared. Mom and I would stay up late watching old movies on TV. She'd talk about how she and her mother went to the theater around the corner from their home three times a week when she was a girl, every time the program changed – a newsreel, cartoon, and feature for twenty-five cents. She'd tell me about the old-time stars and the old-time scandals – Lana Turner, Mary Astor, Errol Flynn, Frances Farmer, and – of course – Elizabeth Taylor, Richard Burton, and "le scandale" as it came to be known.

They were born a year apart -- Elizabeth Taylor on February 27, 1932; Mom on May 1, 1933. Mom watched Elizabeth Taylor grow up in the movies. But while Mom was graduating high school on the south side of Chicago, Elizabeth Taylor was marrying Nicky Hilton in Beverly Hills. Decades later, I took her to the very church. I didn't tell Mom ahead of time. As we sat during the service, I told her Frank Sinatra had his invitation-only funeral mass here at the Church of the Good Shepard. I told her they used to call it Our Lady of the Cadillacs because it was the preferred church for Catholic movie stars like Rosalind Russell, Irene Dunne, Loretta Young, and Jane Wyman. Then I told her Elizabeth Taylor married Nicky Hilton here, and she perked up. She craned her head and looked around, probably trying to visualize an eighteen-year old Elizabeth Taylor in her Helen Rose wedding dress.

Mom leaned over and whispered, "That bastard beat her, you know."

Yes, Mom. I know. I know.

By age 25, Elizabeth Taylor was married to her third husband, Michael Todd. Fourteen months later, she was a widow, the mother of three, and the most famous woman in the world. The scandals began in 1958 when Taylor started an affair with her late husband's best friend, Eddie Fisher. He was married to Taylor's best friend, Debbie Reynolds. Then the scandal blasted into hyperdrive when Taylor pitched Eddie Fisher and picked-up with an also-married Richard Burton. The lurid details played out in the magazines on our coffee table, and it was The Topic in our neighborhood in the early 1960s.

Among the stay-at-home moms, you were a "Debbie" or a "Liz." You believed in family and fidelity, or you believed in free love and sexual liberty. Mom claimed to be a Debbie, but I think she always wanted to be a Liz. Why? Because I never heard Mom go on about Debbie Reynolds the way she did about Elizabeth Taylor. Debbie was the good one, but Elizabeth was the interesting one. Over the decades, Mom followed Elizabeth Taylor's every move. She would repeat a trashy tabloid story, and I'd ask, "Where did you read that?" Mom would become indignant and insist, "That's not important." Remembering the funny stuff helped.

When I got to Elmhurst Hospital it was nearly midnight. Michael was waiting in the Emergency Room. My first words: "How's Mom?"

"She's going to die." He explained what happened. Her kidneys stopped working, and her lungs filled with fluid. He said her blood pressure and oxygen levels were too low for dialysis, but the doctors planned to try "ultra-cleansing," basically dialysis lite, in the morning. She was in danger of a heart attack and on a respirator. The pulmonary specialist – Doctor Cozzi – didn't expect her to survive. All this happened in the time it took a plane to fly from Los Angeles to Chicago.

I followed Michael to room six. On the wall above the bed a monitor showed four rows of data: Pulse rate, blood pressure, oxygen level, respiration. A small, wild-haired woman lay in bed, with a tube down her throat. She looked up, surprised to see me, and tried to touch my face. But her wrists were restrained to keep her from tugging at the respirator, so I leaned over and let her caress my cheek. A little while later, a nurse came in and gave Mom something to help her sleep.

Doctors initially suspected a bad drug reaction, but the truth was worse. The vasculitis had destroyed her kidneys. Unable to cleanse her body and eliminate fluids, her lungs filled. It was Dad's nightmare all over again. Neither of us wanted to talk about what would happen when Mom died. There didn't seem to be an *if*.

By Monday morning, her blood pressure and oxygen level were rising, and she was stable enough for dialysis. A small East Indian woman wheeled a machine as big as a refrigerator into the room and placed a shunt in Mom's groin. One tube drew blood from her body, and then whirled it through spinners and filters before putting the clean blood back in. I stood in the doorway and watched what I called the "wash and rinse cycle." The machine removed more than two liters of fluid.

On Tuesday, the plan was to test her breathing capacity as a prelude for removing the breathing tube. I was first to arrive. They stopped the sedative drip and Mom began to wake. I tried explaining the plan, but she became agitated and started shaking her head and thrashing in bed.

"Calm down, Mom. Look at me and know I'm telling the truth. There was too much fluid in your lungs. That's why they had to put in the tube. They're going to run a test today. If your blood oxygen level is high enough, they can take it out." She calmed down after that and let the machine breathe for her. A moment later a nurse came in and filled a vial with blood. Mom's arm looked like a junkie's – swollen, red, yellow, purple, and green. Then we waited. And waited. A rare moment of humor presented itself: The longer it took for a verdict, the more impatient Mom became. Calm, but impatient. Finally, she made that timeless Italian gesture – she turned her palm upward, clasped her fingertips together, and shook her hand gently. The gesture said, "What the fuck is taking so long?"

The test failed. Mom sighed and shrugged and took it like a champ. It was the last time she was ever truly herself. Dr. Cozzi said the best course was to let her recuperate. She spent the next three days under the spell of Propofol, the same drug that killed Michael Jackson.

My brother never dreams about Dad, while my sister has a recurring dream where Dad is talking but she can't hear what he's saying. But Dad appeared in my dreams with a comforting frequency. Whenever I had a Dad Dream, I told Mom. They always cheered her. One of my favorites took place in an all-white Art Deco bar. Goombah Johnny stood at one end talking to Michael, but it was Goombah Johnny as he looked in the 1960s. Dad was at the other end, looking as he did when he died. He didn't recognize me when I approached.

I asked, "Dad, are you ever coming back?"

"No. I like it here."

I thought about that dream as I watched Mom sleep. The stuff they taught us in Catholic school had to be true. I needed it to be true. Her parents, siblings, and friends would be waiting on the other side. Dad, too. They'd have a couple of drinks – scotch and water for him; scotch and soda for her – then they'd go out for dinner at the hottest spot in the Hereafter. They would run into old friends, and the party would grow. Waiters would bring extra chairs. The ladies would freshen their makeup while Dad and his pals argued about who bought the next round. After dinner, they'd climb a cloud and go to a nightclub. They would be young, healthy, and eternally happy, with all the problems and grudges left behind in a place that no longer mattered.

Michael, Lisa and I went through the motions. Each took a turn at Mom's bedside. Beneath our false optimism, we didn't expect her to survive. We hoped. We prayed. Michael even bargained with God. But as the days wore on and the bad news piled up, it became clear she would never leave that hospital under her own steam.

The following Monday, her vitals were good, and Dr. Cozzi removed the respirator. Only two small plastic tubes blew oxygen into her nose. Mom was breathing on her own, and her kidneys were putting out urine, helped by "enough diuretics to make a dead man piss," according to my brother. She was also in "medication dementia" because her kidneys weren't flushing her system fully. I was in the hospital room late that night when Mom's eyes opened suddenly, despite the heavy sedation. Not only opened, they spun in circles, twirling like loose marbles. I shouted for the nurse. A team came rushing in, and they whisked Mom away for a CAT scan. The first setback came early Friday morning with a visit from the neurosurgeon. Dr. Cozzi called up the CAT scan on the computer. The small gray area was evidence of a stroke. The good news was that Mom was responsive. She spoke to the doctors and nurses and followed their orders – squeeze my hand, move your feet.

Mom had already spoken to Michael by the time I arrived. And what did she say? "Where's your brother?" Mom spoke to Lisa, too. But she never spoke to me. Worse, she didn't seem to recognize me as her son. Had the stroke destroyed the part of her brain that held memories of me? Did she wonder who this stranger was who kept brushing her hair? It broke my heart.

When they came to give Mom dialysis again, the shunt wouldn't go in. The technician suspected the line might be blocked inside her body. The doctor said the only option was surgically implanting a permanent shunt near her shoulder. The procedure would be done Saturday morning. The paperwork was signed and plans finalized.

Lisa stayed late that night. When she left, she said, "See you in the morning, Mom."

Mom said the one word that came out easily and clearly. She said, "No."

I arrived on Saturday at 8:45 AM, expecting to find Mom's room empty. Instead I found her in bed, thrashing from side to side and moaning. The nurse said Mom's vital signs kept falling, and she'd been agitated all morning. I looked at my mother and saw the anger and pleading in her eyes as she rocked from side to side and gripped the steel guardrails. She turned away and I rubbed her back gently. The nurse said that Mom's oxygen level had dropped again, and the only way to get her to surgery was to reinsert the breathing tube. I said, "No."

The surgical team was waiting in the operating room, and the nurse sent for the anesthesiologist. The minutes ticked by. Finally, I shouted, "Where the fuck is the anesthesiologist?" All the while, I held Mom's hand and tried to calm her. Nothing worked. I begged, "Breathe nice, Mom." But she moaned and flailed. "I'm not going to let them hurt you anymore." I heard myself repeating that sentence over and over.

The anesthesiologist showed up and several things became clear: To get her to the operating room and through the surgery, she required the breathing tube. But she was so weak that it was questionable whether she could survive surgery. While we were talking, the kidney specialist arrived. Mom's reduced kidney function meant she would need dialysis for the rest of her life, probably two or three times a week. She would be chronically susceptible to kidney infections. Eventually her kidneys might fail entirely. He, too, worried about the strain of general anesthesia on a body so weakened. I told the doctor it was time to stop "torturing" my mother and let her go. He said, "I don't agree with your assessment." I didn't care. I would not let my mother die in a cold operating room surrounded by strangers.

When Michael got to the hospital, we met quickly with Dr. Cozzi. Michael asked a simple question: What would you do if it were your mother? He would let her go. That's what we decided to do. What would happen next? Dr. Cozzi said it could take as little as an hour. In some cases, patients lingered for days. Some even rallied.

Please, I prayed, let it be quick.

We gathered around the bed – Michael, Lisa and Jerry and their children, Ashley and Jeremiah, and me. I held Mom's left hand. Michael stood over me with his hand on my shoulder. Lisa held Mom's right hand and stroked it gently. Already Mom's skin felt papery and cool. Her eyes were open, and the plastic breathing tube sent a hissing stream of air up her nose. Then her respiration stopped. The monitor line went flat and Mom's chest stopped moving. In that moment, I saw the thin curtain part between life and death.

Her heart kept beating as I watched the number on the monitor dropping, dropping. And then the line went flat. It read 11:30 AM, October 13, 2007. I let go of her hand and closed her eyes. I like to believe the last thing she saw was my face smiling through the tears. I leaned over and kissed her. "Goodbye, Mom," I whispered. "You were my best girl."

I barely remember the wake and funeral, even though I gave the eulogy. I hadn't slept more than an hour or two in thirteen-days. Mom's eulogy began with a simple truth: "My mother was a character in every sense of the word. Most recently, I compared her to Doris Roberts' character on *Everybody Loves Raymond*, the opinionated and sometimes meddlesome woman who always knew best. My mother failed to see the similarities. When my brother's children were little, I used to tell them Grandma had a disease – if she didn't say what was on her mind, the top of her head would blow off. Mom didn't disagree." The mourners laughed. When I finished, I walked off the altar and kissed her coffin.

Mom and Dad were in a good place when he died. There was a playfulness in their interactions, or maybe they were punch-drunk and didn't want to argue anymore. They made love a couple of nights before he died. (I didn't need to know, and I didn't want to know. But I do, and I shouldn't have to carry that burden alone.) They were happy and in love when he died. That's the part I use to comfort myself when I wake up screaming because I know about my parents' lovemaking.

It's been a decade since she passed, and I think of her often. Occasionally, I'll get a whiff of her favorite perfume – Estee Lauder Youth Dew – and I'll know she's close. Dad, too. I'll stand in a grocery store and see heirloom tomatoes for $4 a pound and swear I hear him laughing: "What kind of jag-off pays $4 a pound for tomatoes?"

32. MOB ADJACENT

Here's the thing: It wasn't that Dad was morally opposed to crime; he didn't want to work for *any* boss in *any* business. Period. But he had the quality essential to a successful Outfit guy – he kept his mouth shut. By keeping his mouth shut, showing respect, and going about his business, Dad made friends with men who made other men tremble in fear and piss their pants. The fact that he could get the leader of the most powerful criminal organization in the world on the telephone – and call the mob boss by his first name – didn't mean squat to us. Jackie Cerone was just another one of Dad's friends. Dad had lots of friends. Many came from Little Italy like us; some worked for the Outfit, and others found high-wage patronage jobs falling from the sky as often as high-end merchandise fell off the back of a truck.

It was all a ringy-ding-ding of a time. As clueless kids, Michael, Lisa, and I enjoyed the bounty and privilege that came from being mob adjacent. Later, we watched sadly as time, death, and the law took its toll. Old friends and honorary uncles went to prison or graves as the century neared its end. Whenever we siblings get together, inevitably something triggers a memory.

A peach pie memory still causes my family to convulse with laughter. Mom bought an alleged peach pie for a family dinner during one of my visits. She served it for Coffee And. And then she promptly announced in her most ladylike tone, "It tastes like shit." Each person at the table then took a bite of the horrible pie and agreed it was horrible, though no one could agree on the filling, except that it wasn't peach. Some thought apple or even pineapple based on the color. The entire family kept eating bites of this truly horrible pie.

Crazy things happened when we were growing up, and we learned these truly wrong lessons:

When you get stopped by a cop, hand him your driver's license with a $20 bill under it. The cop will hand your license back, and you'll drive away without a ticket. Caveat: This only worked in Cook County. In the 1970s.

Or: If you flunk your first driver's test (like I did), when you go back, put a $20 bill in with your paperwork. You'll get the signed paperwork back and leave with a driver's license. Was my driving better the second time? Did I nail that three-point turn? I hit the curb the first time – automatic fail in Illinois back then. Or, did a little gratuitous gratuity earn a little gratitude in return? When I shared this father/son life lesson with my beloved spouse, I was told the $20 explained my terrifying driving.

"I knew you shouldn't be on the road. I always wondered what kind of crazy DMV gives a driver's license to you!" Said with a southern accent, no less.

[For the record, I have had three minor fender-benders and two traffic tickets in as many decades.]

Because of the company my family kept, we became accustomed to luxury at an early age, not because we lived luxuriously. We had a modest suburban house and nice things, but not crazy nice. Despite these modest circumstances, the parade of luxury items that passed through our home would have made a Pharaoh jealous. It was always the same: A friend showed up, and next thing you're staring at about a dozen five-carat diamonds in different shapes sparkling on the kitchen table. Or there's a truck with racks of fur coats idling in the alley. Jewels and furs were the least of it.

There were the cars. Every other day it was like the auto show driving up the block. We'd see a car coming north on 47th Avenue and know it belonged to a friend of Dad, gleaming parade floats of steel, rubber, glass, and chrome. Uncle Anthony was the first person I knew with an exotic Mercedes Benz. It was chocolate brown, with tan leather interior, and a diesel engine. Dad said he was crazy for buying a diesel. For the record, my father also thought another friend was crazy for "buying" a condominium in the brand-new John Hancock Tower with a view of Lake Michigan for $26,000 in 1976. "All you own is the air between the walls. You don't even own the walls," Dad scoffed. That condominium is worth about $5,000,000 today. So, there's that on Dad's told-you-so tally.

Uncle Anthony wasn't the only guy driving prime wheels. Guys showed up in cars that hadn't hit the showroom yet, and they got rid of them when the ashtrays got full. Goombah Johnny was famous for fancy cars. He had a phone in one and a television in another. I remember standing at the curb outside our house, mouth agape, staring dreamily at a television screen in the middle of the dashboard. I could watch *Superman*. In the car! He had a blue Cadillac with fins taller than me. A white Lincoln Continental, too. It was the length of a ballpark, at least that's how it seemed. Uncle Tony drove a rainbow of luxury cars, too. He never seemed to turn up in the same one twice. He'd toss you the keys in the middle of winter and say, "Go start the engine for me and turn on the heat." Then he'd laugh and point a finger. "And don't go joy-riding." I was twelve. I didn't.

Those guys had all the best stuff, but they didn't take it seriously. Uncle Tony would literally give you the ring off his finger if you admired it. One time, Dad had to explain to his eager friend that just because little Jeffrey liked Uncle Tony's diamond pinky ring doesn't mean little Jeffrey should have it. But it was just a trinket to Uncle Tony and the other light fingers. That's what Mom called professional thieves: light fingers. Their job was to lift things from people and sell those things to other people. Tomorrow, there'll be another truck with more stuff. The stuff goes here, and the stuff goes there.

Being mob adjacent, I learned art appreciation in the home: One of Dad's light finger pals had a taste for artwork that belonged to other people. He arrived one day with a cardboard tube tucked under his arm. His name was Clifford. That's all I remember. He grew up around Grand and Ogden and worked with Dad at McCormick Place. Clifford was tight with Joe Glimco, the Outfit-friendly union organizer; Glimco was friendly with Ben Stein, the king of union janitors at McCormick Place, and Stein was friendly with Dad. Trace any Chicago relationship back far enough, and you'll find a link to a crooked union. Clifford did union HVAC work. A wiry little guy, he also had the ability to shimmy through heating and ventilation ducts and remove things from otherwise locked rooms. It turned out to be a skill more lucrative than duct work.

While Uncle Tony preferred the flash and sparkle of jewelry as a mainstay of his thievery, Clifford leaned more toward artwork. Paintings. Small statuary. He'd unzip a battered canvas duffle bag and pull out something he "came across" in a museum or a gallery or someone's home. On this particular visit, Clifford unrolled a canvas on the kitchen table. Dad stared at it while Mom made Coffee And. The painting showed squiggly black lines in varying thicknesses defining bold, irregular shapes in primary colors. I'd never seen anything like it. Mom curled her nose at the absurdity. Dad didn't know squat about art, modern or otherwise, but figured it had to be worth a lot of money and nodded approvingly. Good for Clifford. Bad for the insurance company.

Clifford looked at me staring at it and said, "It's a Joan Miró."

242

Me: "I like how she paints."

Clifford: "He."

Me: "I like how he paints."

Teach a kid, and he will learn. A couple of years later, I chuckled on a high school field trip to the Art Institute as I stood in front of a Miró and thought, "I saw one of your stolen paintings in our kitchen." I've always wondered where it ended up.

Today, I'll see something, or something will happen, and I'll wonder: Is my response normal, or is my perspective warped by the fact that I grew up surrounded by criminals? Is it normal to hope the bank robbers get away and to cheer for the bad guys? Probably not. Growing-up mob adjacent taught lessons that shade my life. The first and most obvious lesson was that things appear and disappear, and there's always a mechanism for making one or the other happen. If you want something, it arrives. I'd seen countless examples of things appearing – furniture, appliances, electronics, luggage, furs, jewels. Even an airplane appeared once, because I needed an airplane.

But it wasn't all fun and games and free merchandise. People disappeared, too. Some died, the lucky ones by natural causes like Jackie, Jimmy, and Skip. Others like Manny Skar got shot to death, while Lou Bombacino and Willie Bioff got blown to smithereens in Arizona. Ned Bakes got strangled and shot – because one or the other wasn't dead enough. Richard Cain got his head practically blown off. And nobody knows what happened to the man who called himself Sol Elegant. There was one lucky break: Goombah Johnny disappeared. Fortunately, he reappeared.

Sol Elegant's disappearance from his suite at the Air Host Motel in 1965 prompted questions. On the Outfit's side, Elegant took off with cash that did not belong to him, and the Outfit wanted it back. They also wanted to know what Sol Elegant knew, and who he might be talking to. Meanwhile, the Feds wanted to know about crooked unions and mob infiltration of restaurants and nightclubs, and the cops wanted to know about illegal gambling and prostitution. Dad found himself stuck in the middle. When the trail for Elegant went cold, Richard Cain aimed his anger at Dad. Deputies showed up and padlocked Orlando's Hideaway because of its "lewd" drag show. Then Cain added a soap opera plot twist and ran off to Mexico with Sam Giancana. I was barely ten-years old.

I learned from those events that the law is something to be respected – in public. One must play its game, or the law will seek ruthless vengeance.

Beyond Richard Cain's perversion of the law, the law also jailed Sam Giancana when he declined to answer grand jury questions. One way or another, the law planned on locking up Sam Giancana. So, they did. And once in jail, Giancana's stay was made more comfortable by luxuries and indulgences provided by mob-friendly guards. Amount of justice served: zero. The law seemed largely disreputable beneath its righteous veneer, and you could do what you want in private. The lessons learned at the intersection of Hoodlum and Gangster have influenced my perspective, actions, opinions, or all three.

Consider an ambitious senator from Tennessee named Estes Kefauver. He came to Chicago one night in 1950 to get the goods on mobsters. Sam Giancana exploited Kefauver's passion for call girls and derailed the investigation by morning, thanks to well-placed cameras. Phony investigation.

Consider Richard Nixon in 1960. He lost Illinois in the presidential election despite carrying ninety-three of 102 counties, losing the state by 8,858 votes, and securing Illinois' twenty-seven electoral votes for John F. Kennedy, thanks to ballot-fixing orchestrated by Sam Giancana. Phony election.

Consider how street crews had barely cleaned up after JFK's inauguration parade when Attorney Robert F. Kennedy started using the Justice Department to prosecute the very people who helped rig the election that put JFK in the White House. In old Joe Kennedy's calculations, prison sentences erased handshake deals made in smoke-filled rooms. Phony justice.

Consider Joe Accardo's annual Fourth of July barbeque. His Elmwood Park mansion attracted mobsters, judges, lawyers, politicians, cops, celebrities, and clergymen. The man considered the world's most powerful criminal threw a yard party for the cream of Chicago society, and the cream churned itself to butter lapping up a mob boss' hospitality. Phony morals.

I grew up hearing people rail against the hypocrisy used by the law to justify itself and excuse the damage caused by its laws. "They're no better than the crooks" was a popular refrain. While not a conspiracy theorist, I'm not surprised when people lie or reputations fail. Politicians on the take; reverends with strippers; and homophobic preachers with call boys. Clay feet everywhere. But I still believe in the Golden Rule and simple, human kindness.

Nevertheless, I'll see a couple of cops having coffee at a diner and wonder if the tall cop would take fifty to let me off a speeding ticket. Or if the short cop shakes down hookers for free blowjobs. Or I'll wonder if I commit a bank robbery and offered to split the money with the cops, would they let me go? I don't commit the crime. But I wonder. Idle speculation to pass time while I wait for my soup or salad. Is that normal? I can never tell. These are the fruits of my misspent youth.

We thought our days of being mob adjacent ended informally when Dad died, and officially when Jimmy and Jackie Cerone passed about a year later. We'd lived under the protective wing of successive mob bosses for more than six decades. Then when Aunt Jeanette died in 2010, we lost the last connection to limitless luxury goods at low, low, negotiable prices. It would be retail thereafter, and she would never rest in peace. They're all gone now, and it's all over. Or is it?

Small things demonstrated that the mob wasn't quite finished with Michael and me. After years bouncing between jobs, my brother settled lucratively into a career as a buyer at a wholesale produce house. Occasionally, he runs into the Old Lion at the South Water Market. They meet casually a few times a year for lunch or dinner. Mostly, it's nice for Michael to talk about the old neighborhood and the old ways.

My brother's got a whole network of Old Guys from the Old Neighborhood. But make no mistake – those Old Guys have seen everything, know everything, and they're saying nothing. Michael started talking about our project and the stories we hope to tell. It turned into a game of telephone – except with hoodlums. A says talk to B; B says talk to C; C says talk to D. And so on. Then Michael jumped generations and talked to the sons and grandsons of Outfit guys. One contact led to another.

That's how he ended up talking to the most decorated cop in the history of the Chicago Police Department, a man whose post-PD career as a criminal mastermind eventually earned him a long stay behind bars. Captain William Hanhardt was out of prison for his role in a string of spectacular robberies across the country. A stocky, white-haired, ruddy-faced man in glasses, he had the harmless look of a corporate executive. What led a dedicated, thirty-three-year, law-and-order man to a second career in crime is a story for another book.

Like everyone else Michael told about *Mob Adjacent*, Captain Hanhardt found the idea amusing – "incongruous" was the word he used – that our father grew up surrounded by hardened criminals and remained above the fray – and out of prison – his entire life, while maintaining long friendships with people of dubious reputations. He knew that neighborhood and its people. Hanhardt had worked as a technical advisor on a couple of mob-related films. Dennis Farina's character on NBC's *Law and Order* was said to be based in part on the captain. According to Hanhardt, the "incongruous" nature of *Mob Adjacent* made it ripe for a motion picture adaptation.

People who knew Hanhardt remarked that he spent his entire life helping people. Some of those people happened to be criminals. The captain wanted to help us, too. He and Michael talked about getting the eventual manuscript into the hands of his producer/director/writer friend. Alas, death interceded, and

William Hanhardt died of heart failure at age eighty-eight on December 30, 2016.

One of Michael's pals said, "You should talk to Ronnie." [That's not his real name. First, he's entitled to his privacy. Second, he's in prison and has an appeal working through the court system. Third, it's none of your fucking business.] Ronnie was sentenced to sixty-months in 1999 for conspiracy to commit a felony – a Hobbs Act violation. I later learned he'd lived a spectacular life of crime. It was said – though the government couldn't prove shit – that he led a violent Chicago street crew in the 1990s. Later, Ronnie led a daring daylight diamond heist in London that landed him in Her Majesty's prison for nearly a decade.

Actions have consequences, Ronnie says. So, he's very sanguine about the whole business of being in prison. It's like high blood pressure for stock brokers; it comes with the territory. He uses his time as a guest of the law enforcement industrial complex to teach screenwriting to fellow inmates, collect recipes, invent kitchen tools, innovate cook books, and write scripts and stories while reading extensively on a range of topics. You'd be hard-pressed to find a more productive member of society, except for the whole prisoner-of-the-federal-government thing.

I knew none of Ronnie's backstory, had no idea who he was, and never heard the man's name before Michael said, "Write him a letter."

"What am I supposed to say?"

"I don't know. Introduce yourself and our project."

That's what I did. I introduced myself, Michael, our project, and the people we knew. I talked about the old neighborhood back in the day and places we remembered. A week or so later, a letter arrived with Ronnie's prisoner ID in the return address. Jail mail. Eventually, I signed up for email access through the Correctional Link app. Now we communicate almost daily.

It turned out Ronnie and Dad knew many of the same people at the same time. But since Dad was a decade older, they moved in different circles. Ronnie was Grand Avenue, just like us. Whatever his crimes or alleged crimes, the man is a writer, intellectual, world traveler, gourmand, gardener, and interesting as hell. Funny, too. Letters, emails, and magazine clippings followed. Ronnie started sharing insights on how to tell our story. He also advised us on running a retail business (he had an apparel business), how to cook some classic Italian dishes (he collects recipes), and how to dig a proper English garden (he's a member of the royal horticultural society). He told me Italy has the best food, and the Netherlands have the best prisons. In case anyone wondered.

Ronnie asked for nothing – and I offered. Did he need books, magazines, stamps? Nothing. When he mentioned fading typewriter ribbons, I offered to send replacements. He declined. Ronnie wanted nothing except maybe someone to talk to, someone connected to his old life in the old neighborhood. It's been going on for over a year, and Michael will ask, "Have you heard from Ronnie lately?"

"Yeah, we're exchanging recipes."

"You guys! If there was ever an odd couple, it's the two of you."

It's been educational. He told me a story about a stolen diamond. The good news was that the diamond was eleven-carats; the bad news was that it was dirty, flawed, and cut in an undesirable pear-shape. Ronnie explained how the stone was recut into a flawless, six-carat, round diamond that was more valuable than its larger predecessor stone by a factor of three. It also turned a hot stone into a cold one. He appreciated the artistry involved in properly cutting a diamond, and I learned size isn't everything, even in diamonds. On the other side, I've been told nothing smells worse than a rotting human body, not even skunk. So, there's that.

We've talked about Machiavelli and the importance of luck and skill, and Sun Tzu and the art of war. Philosophy and religion, too. Minus Internet access, sometimes Ronnie asks me to do a little research (How to they make grappa? Is Madmen Muntz the car guy?) I complete his projects like a dutiful research assistant and send the results to prison. He offers reading recommendation (Stuart Dybeck, Daniel Woodrell, Stanley Elkin). I mentioned a favorite heist movie (*The Anderson Tapes*). Turned out he knew the guy the book was based on. When I mentioned having a cold in one email, he asked if I was feeling better in the next. That's how it goes. He's slated for release next year. Ronnie wrote that he's got a million ideas for what he wants to do next. He's looking forward to meeting up with old friends and new friends. And where does that put Michael and me? Mob adjacent. Still.

EPILOGUE

In 2013, I was writing the "About the author" text for my novel, *Love and Bullets*, a comedy about a Chicago drag queen and his gangster lover. I wrote that I was born "mob adjacent near the intersection of Hoodlum and Gangster." I thought it was a good line. At the time, I was trying to convince a New York literary agent to represent me on another novel. We were talking in his office on Broadway, and I mentioned being born mob adjacent and so forth. He laughed and said, "I'd buy that book." Trouble was, I didn't have that book. I had stories. Michael had stories. Lisa had stories, too. Amazingly, I didn't sit down and immediately begin writing a book about growing up mob adjacent. I had other projects and other priorities.

But Michael latched on to the phrase "mob adjacent" to describe our childhood. He'd call and say, "I was telling mob adjacent stories last night, and people were enamored." This happened repeatedly until it grew into a fever. He wanted to make YouTube videos telling our stories. He wanted these videos – according to my technology-challenged brother – to go "virus" so he could tell mob adjacent stories from "Jimmy Kimmel's couch." Blatant self-promotion is a noble goal, and I fully supported his theory that mob adjacent stories are very entertaining. But the videos seemed like half an effort. I wanted the videos to serve as Mob Adjacent 101, introducing people to our mob adjacent world – as a teaser for a book, before it all receded into the pages of disputed history.

It's all different today. Thanks to RICO laws, legalized dope, state lotteries, off-track-betting, river boat and Indian casinos, and Internet gaming, the Outfit became a shell of its former self. Hell, you can hire prostitutes over the Internet these days. Today's Outfit heir likely runs a hedge fund or a private equity firm, stealing legally via the U.S. Tax Code, or maybe running a charity that skims eighty percent for "overhead." There hasn't been a major Outfit bust in nearly a decade.

When we decided to write a book, I searched my files and collected hundreds of pages of short stories, novellas, journal entries, and letters to and from family members. (For example, Mom wrote me a letter when I was in college describing the night she met Dad; the chapter in this book contains large sections of her verbatim descriptions of people and events.) Then I sent everything to Michael as a starting point. A marathon series of telephone calls between Lisle, Illinois, and Pasadena, California, probably burned up several telecommunications satellites over the next year.

Once we started putting things on paper, Michael got more excited and started sharing some of our initial stories with friends in the Cerone family. He outlined the project to Uncle Anthony and Aunt Sis' daughter, Rosa. She later said it was as if she "stepped back in time." Rosa added, "It brought out so many emotions of the times our families were around the table laughing and joking around. This may sound funny, but I had to go to the cemetery and talk to my parents about it!"

When Michael mentioned the video concept to Rosa, she referred him to her son, Jason Nitti (Jason is related to Frank Nitti, Al Capone's #2, because being mob adjacent IS a thing). It turned out Jason knew people at a marketing company with full video production capabilities. Michael met with director Steve Clarke on the logistics, and I kept working on my portion of the project – the wordsmithing.

Having been the occasional son and brother from age seventeen, I missed a lot of the mob adjacent action. Michael and I would be talking on the phone, and he'd ask casually, "Did I ever tell you about the time I pushed a guy's face through the top of a juke box?" Uh, no. "Well, here's what happened," he'd say. I'd go into stenographer mode and try to capture the details while he talked a mile a minute. Or he'd say, "Did you know Aunt Jeanette was at Rose's Sandwich Shop right before Richard Cain got whacked?" No.

We quickly realized that sometimes each of us knew only part of a story. One would reach the end of an anecdote, and the other would pick up the narrative and complete the tale. An example: I remembered when Dad "allowed" Mom to get a driver's license, but I didn't know Skip gave Dad that black Oldsmobile 98 – the one with the power windows that Michael used to nearly amputate my fingers. Naturally, he didn't remember that part.

Lisa helped from the sidelines. The seven-year age difference between us meant she missed the heaviest and headiest days of "mob adjacency," as Michael and I started calling it. Lisa was an infant during the heyday of Orlando's Hideaway and a toddler when Dad's Outfit friends filtered in and out of our lives on a regular basis. She remembers waking up on Christmas morning to find the living room filled with every new little girl toy. It was purely coincidental that those toys debuted at the McCormick Place trade show for toy manufacturers. Her recollections of the people and events in our lives helped fill out the story from all perspectives.

Mob Adjacent launched on YouTube on November 7, 2016, our parents' 62nd wedding anniversary. Thousands of people have watched our ten-webisode documentary so far. Our efforts to capture a vanished era have been equal parts love letter and thank you note to the overburdened parents who stood strong against waves that sunk lesser ships so their children could have better lives. We're all standing on our own, and that's because of the hard work of a humble fruit peddler and his wife – several generations of fruit peddlers and their wives, in fact – and a few mob guys here and there.

Today, Michael lives in a sprawling ranch house on nearly an acre of property adjacent to a golf course. He's married to Lou Ann and they are great grandparents. Lisa is still married to Jerry, and they have two self-sufficient adult children. She *still* hasn't used all the merchandise she got at those bridal showers more than thirty-years ago. I'm a husband, father, and grandfather. I live in a 100-year old house in a historic section of Pasadena. The Rose Parade passes just down the street. I pick oranges off the tree in my backyard, and my brother is my best friend.

The end

ACKNOWLEDGMENTS

Special thanks to Stacy Woldt for her invaluable assistance.
To Lauren Taylor Shute for helping us tell a better story.

To Rosa Cerone and Jason Nitti.
Thank you for helping us bring back our shared past.

To KB, JS, MS, and WH for your insight and generosity.

Finally, we acknowledge every dumb, stupid, rude, reckless, ridiculous, annoying, illegal, ignorant, irresponsible, unreasonable, self-defeating, and depraved thing we did. We like to believe each contributed to making us the reasonably sane and rationally grounded people we are today. More or less.

ABOUT THE AUTHORS

Jeffrey Gentile and Michael Gentile, Jr. were born in Chicago, Illinois.

Michael is a buyer for a produce wholesaler at the South Water Market. He lives with his wife Lou Ann in Lisle, Illinois. They have five children, twelve grandchildren, and one great grandchild (at this count)

Jeffrey is a marketing copywriter for a global firm, and the author of *Love and Bullets: A Comedy with a Body Count*. He has a daughter and a granddaughter and lives with his husband Jeffrey Jordan in Pasadena, California.

Jeffrey Gentile

Michael Gentile, Jr.

Made in the USA
Lexington, KY
11 December 2017